THE COMPETITIVE ADVANTAGE OF NATIONS: THE CASE OF TURKEY

To Peter

The Competitive Advantage of Nations: The Case of Turkey

Assessing Porter's framework for national advantage

ÖZLEM ÖZ
Middle East Technical University, Ankara, Turkey

Routledge
Taylor & Francis Group

LONDON AND NEW YORK

First published 1999 by Ashgate Publishing

Reissued 2018 by Routledge
2 Park Square, Milton Park, Abingdon, Oxon, OX14 4RN
52 Vanderbilt Avenue, New York, NY 10017

Routledge is an imprint of the Taylor & Francis Group, an informa business

Copyright © Özlem Öz 1999

Publisher's Note
The publisher has gone to great lengths to ensure the quality of this reprint but points out that some imperfections in the original copies may be apparent.

Disclaimer
The publisher has made every effort to trace copyright holders and welcomes correspondence from those they have been unable to contact.

A Library of Congress record exists under LC control number: 98073853

ISBN 13: 978-1-138-34356-6 (hbk)
ISBN 13: 978-1-138-34357-3 (pbk)
ISBN 13: 978-0-429-43908-7 (ebk)

Contents

List of Figures		vi
List of Tables		vii
Preface		viii
Acknowledgments		xi
List of Abbreviations		xii
1	The Competitive Advantage of Nations	1
2	The Competitive Advantage of Turkey	28
3	The Turkish Glass Industry	59
4	The Turkish Construction Industry	77
5	The Turkish Leather Clothes Industry	98
6	The Turkish Automobile Industry	117
7	The Turkish Flat Steel Industry	139
8	Conclusion	160
Appendices		173
Bibliography		194
Index		212

List of Figures

Figure 1.1   The Diamond Framework   5
Figure 2.1   Percentage Increase in Real GDP of Turkey (1979-1995) 31
Figure 2.2   Methodological Process in *The Competitive*
              Advantage of Nations   39
Figure 3.1   Internationally Successful Turkish Industries
              Related to the Glass Industry   68
Figure 5.1   Internationally Successful Turkish Industries
              Related to the Leather Clothes Industry   108
Figure 6.1   Automobile Sales in Turkey (1971-1996)   120
Figure 6.2   Market Shares in the Turkish Automobile Industry   128
              (1971-1996)

List of Tables

Table 2.1   Top Fifty Turkish Industries in Terms of World
             Export Share, 1992   43
Table 2.2   Clusters of Internationally Competitive Turkish
             Industries, 1992   45
Table 2.3   Percentage of Turkish Exports by Cluster and
             Vertical Stage (1978-1985)   53
Table 8.1   Sources of Advantage/Disadvantage in the Turkish
             Glass Industry   160
Table 8.2   Sources of Advantage/Disadvantage in the Turkish
             Construction Industry   161
Table 8.3   Sources of Advantage/Disadvantage in the Turkish
             Leather Clothes Industry   161
Table 8.4   Sources of Advantage/Disadvantage in the Turkish
             Automobile Industry   162
Table 8.5   Sources of Advantage/Disadvantage in the Turkish
             Flat Steel Industry   162
Table 8.6   Sources of Advantage and Key Findings That do Not
             Comply With the Diamond in the Selected Turkish
             Industries   163
Table A1.1   Clusters of Internationally Competitive Turkish
             Industries, 1985   173
Table A1.2   Clusters of Internationally Competitive Turkish
             Industries, 1978   181
Table A1.3   Clusters of Internationally Competitive Turkish
             Industries, 1971   186
Table A2.1   Percentage of Turkish Exports by Cluster and Vertical
             Stage (1985-1992)   191
Table A2.2   Percentage of Turkish Exports by Cluster and Vertical
             Stage (1971-1978)   192
Table A2.3   Percentage of Turkish Exports by Cluster and Vertical
             Stage (1971)   193

Preface

The issue of identifying the sources of international competitive advantage has attracted considerable attention from various disciplines and has been the subject of numerous studies, the first major contributions dating back to the 18th century. Although these studies have generated interesting approaches improving our understanding of the issue, we still lack a holistic model that explains the sources of international competitive advantage in full. A recent contribution to the area, Prof. Michael Porter's diamond framework (1990a: 10), which tries to explain 'why firms based in a nation are able to compete successfully against foreign rivals in particular segments and industries', attempts to provide a coherent and comprehensive explanation concerning the role of a nation in influencing the international competitiveness of an industry.

Porter's (1990a) approach views the international competitiveness of industries as essentially driven by the home economic environment. The major motive for innovation and upgrading of competitive advantage is seen as deriving from influences that force firms to improve quality and find less expensive methods of production. Porter argues that the diamond captures the most important influences on the competitive process and some of the most important ways they interact. According to him, these influences are evident in many of the large number and diversity of industries and countries included in his book *The Competitive Advantage of Nations* (Solvell et al., 1993).

Porter's diamond framework, however, needs further investigation, especially in application to developing countries, since he has constructed the model mainly deriving from the case studies of the industries in the selected developed nations. Moreover, the framework has been the subject of much criticism (see Chapter 1), pointing to yet another motive for its further investigation. A study of Turkey, a middle income developing country, which has recently opened up its economy to the international market, presents a good opportunity to achieve this undertaking.

This study applies Porter's diamond framework to Turkey. The major objective of the book is to contribute towards an improvement of this framework, and thus towards a better understanding of the sources of competitive advantage. The study also aims to shed some light on the competitive structure of Turkish industry. In fact, the book provides a new perspective to evaluate the competitiveness of the Turkish economy as well as a comprehensive analysis of the sources of competitive advantage in several key Turkish industries. Given that alternative studies of competitiveness treat it as a phenomenon determined by factors like exchange rates, and the cost of labour and raw materials, I believe this book will introduce a contrasting viewpoint.

Since the emphasis is on the determinants of competitive advantage, the main contribution of this research is based upon industry case studies. In addition to showing whether or not the framework can be successfully applied to a developing country, the selected Turkish industries reveal how well the diamond can explain the sources of advantage in the particular cases in question. One specific contribution afforded by this study is to see how the diamond can be used to understand the sources of advantage/disadvantage in an uncompetitive industry. This issue is of particular interest, given that the original Porter study has been criticised widely because it does not include unsuccessful cases.

Although its focus is on the Turkish economy, I expect the book to be appealing to a wider audience. In general, it is undeniable that Prof. Michael Porter is one of the most influential scholars in the management field. In particular, it is also unquestionable that Porter's diamond framework, which touches upon an extensive range of disciplines including international trade, competitive strategy, industrial economics, economic development, economic geography, political science and industrial sociology, has attracted considerable attention. In addition to the ten nations included in the original work, others (e.g. Canada and New Zealand) have also been studied by the project teams headed by Porter himself, and other researchers have replicated it for several other countries such as Austria, Ireland, Finland, Mexico, and the Netherlands. Some of these (e.g. the Sweden and New Zealand studies) have been published in a book format. Most of them have been conducted by project teams headed by Porter himself, and they have been largely validating. They, in other words, take the value of the framework for granted. This study, on the other hand, tries to contribute to an improvement in the diamond framework.

The book, therefore, mainly addresses an academic audience. Given that international competitive advantage is high on their agendas, however, it is also likely to attract the attention of strategic planners in firms and policy makers in the government. Moreover, it may be of interest to both undergraduate and post-graduate students since Porter's diamond is under taught in international business courses.

The structure of the book is as follows: In Chapter 1, I explain the analytical framework and give a summary of Porter's *The Competitive Advantage of Nations*. I also provide an evaluation of it linked to a review of the academic debate in the literature on this highly influential work. Chapter 2 then proceeds with the analysis of trade data identifying the patterns of advantage in Turkey, after giving an overview of the Turkish economy. In Chapters 3 to 7, I examine in detail the five Turkish industry case studies - namely; glass, construction, leather clothes, automobiles and flat steel industries. Since the material derived from the case studies constitutes the core of the study, they are given the most attention in the book. Chapter 8, conclusions, presents a summary of the key findings and the implications of the study.

Acknowledgments

For his constructive feedback and encouragement throughout the study, I would like to thank Prof. Peter Abell from the LSE, to whom this book is dedicated. I am also grateful to numerous managers, state officials, union representatives and academics who spared their time for the interviews. I should particularly mention the generous helps of Devrim Yaman from the Turkish Eximbank, Aziz Çelik from the Kristal-İş Union and Yusuf Işık from the State Planning Organisation.

I am indebted to Selçuk and Nilgün Erol, whose support during the field work in particular was extremely helpful. Special thanks go to Viki Eliot and Michelle Fawcett for doing the proof-reading. I also owe much to Ioannis Konsolas for his useful comments and critiques. Lastly, I would like to thank Kaya Özkaracalar whose ideas and invaluable moral support made this study possible and enjoyable.

List of Abbreviations

AID	: Agency for International Development (USA)
ASO	: Ankara Chamber of Industry
BOT	: Build-Operate-Transfer
CIM	: Capacity Improvement and Modernisation
C.I.S.	: Commonwealth of Independent States
CU	: Customs Union
DIE	: State Institute of Statistics
DPT	: State Planning Organisation
ECSC	: European Coal and Steel Community
ENR	: Engineering News Record
FDI	: Foreign Direct Investment
GM	: General Motors
HDTM	: Undersecretariat of Treasury and Foreign Trade
IMD	: International Institute for Management Development
İMKB	: İstanbul Stock Exchange
İSO	: İstanbul Chamber of Industry
İTO	: İstanbul Chamber of Commerce
İTU	: İstanbul Technical University
METU	: Middle East Technical University
MITI	: Ministry of International Trade and Industry (Japan)
MNE	: Multinational enterprise
OSD	: Automotive Manufacturers' Association
SEE	: State Economic Enterprise
SITC	: Standard International Trade Classification
TCA	: Turkish Contractors' Association
TDÇİ	: General Directorate of Turkish Iron and Steel
TİSK	: Turkish Confederation of Employers Associations
TÜBİTAK	: Turkish Scientific and Technical Research Association
TÜSES	: Turkish Social and Political Research Foundation
TÜSİAD	: Turkish Industrialists' and Businessmen's Association
UIC	: Union of International Contractors
UNCTAD	: United Nations Conference on Trade and Development
UNIDO	: United Nations Industrial Development Organisation
VRA	: Voluntary Restraint Agreement

1 The Competitive Advantage of Nations

A Summary of Porter's *The Competitive Advantage of Nations*

Porter (1990a) argues that there is a need for a new paradigm in order to understand in full why a nation succeeds in particular industries but not in others. In order to derive this new analytical framework, which he calls the 'diamond', Porter conducts a study of ten nations, purposefully chosen to vary widely with regard to different attributes like size, location and government policy toward industry. The nations studied are mostly developed countries: Denmark, Germany, Italy, Japan, Sweden, Switzerland, United Kingdom and the United States, with the exception of South Korea and Singapore, which are accepted as newly industrialised countries. The next section summarises the diamond framework which aims to capture the major determinants of competitive advantage as well as their interaction with each other and has been constructed in the light of information from over one-hundred case studies selected from these countries.

The Diamond Framework

According to Porter (1990a), the home base plays a critical role in that firms tend to build up competitive advantage in industries for which the local environment is the most dynamic and challenging. He finds out that four attributes of the home environment -namely; factor conditions, demand conditions, related and supporting industries, and firm strategy, structure and rivalry- play a major role in shaping the context which allows domestic firms to gain and sustain competitive advantage. He also includes the roles played by the 'government' and 'chance' as factors influencing the functioning of these four major determinants. For a better understanding of this framework, it is essential to know how Porter explains each determinant as well as the functioning of the diamond as a system, each of which will be summarised in the pages that follow.

Factor Conditions Porter (1990a) defines two basic distinctions for factors of production. In accordance with the first one, they are grouped into two: basic and advanced factors. The basic factors include natural resources, climate, location, unskilled and semi-skilled labour, and debt capital, while the advance factors include 'modern digital data communications infrastructure, highly educated personnel such as graduate engineers and computer scientists and university research institutes in sophisticated disciplines' (Porter, 1990a: 77). The second distinction he defines is built on 'specificity'. There are 'generalised factors' including 'the highway system, a supply of debt capital, or a pool of well-motivated employees with college educations' and 'specialised factors' including 'narrowly skilled personnel, infrastructure with specific properties, knowledge basis in particular fields, and other factors with relevance to a limited range or even to just a single industry' (Porter, 1990a: 78). Porter believes that basic and generalised factors are either inherited or easy to create and the advantage stemming from them is not that difficult to replicate, hence not sustainable. Advance and specialised factors, on the other hand, are viewed as being more decisive and sustainable basis for competitive advantage. Another interesting argument that he puts forward is that selective factor disadvantages may sometimes turn into bases for competitive advantage, provided that other determinants are favourable.

Demand Conditions Porter (1990a) believes that home demand has a considerable influence on competitive advantage, and he presents the composition, the size and pattern of growth, and the internationalisation of home demand as three broad attributes of it. Porter (1990a) thinks that the role home demand plays in shaping the competitive advantage is more important than that played by foreign demand because proximity makes it easier and faster to observe and understand immediate buyer needs and preferences. The composition of home demand relates to its qualitative features. Porter, for instance, argues that the more sophisticated and demanding the buyers, the more likely the firms in this industry are to create and sustain competitive advantage since such buyers put pressure on firms to upgrade and meet high standards in product quality, features and service. Similarly, the size and pattern of growth of home demand can reinforce competitive advantage in an industry, since, according to him, 'the presence of a number of independent buyers in a nation creates a better environment for innovation than is the case where one or two customers dominate the home market for a product or service' (Porter, 1990a: 94), and a rapidly growing home market provides a dynamic advantage to local firms, mainly because it fosters investment. The third way in which home demand conditions contribute to the competitive advantage of an industry is 'through mechanisms by which a nation's domestic demand internationalises and pulls a nation's products and services abroad' (Porter, 1990a: 97). This may happen, for instance, when the buyers of a product or service are mobile, or when they are multinational companies.

Related and Supporting Industries The existence of internationally competitive related and supporting industries in a nation, according to Porter (1990a), is an important determinant of creation and sustainability of competitive advantage. The competitive related industries that 'share common technologies, inputs, distribution channels, skills, customers or activities, or provide products that are complementary' (Crocombe et al., 1991: 30) may be beneficial for several reasons. Their similarities may, for instance, foster technological spillovers and interchange as well as joint research projects. The process of innovation is facilitated by a free and open information flow in a geographically and culturally proximate environment. Furthermore, a wider dissemination of business information may allow firms to perceive new business opportunities and facilitate the spin-offs. Know-how may spread amongst firms 'as they draw upon the same pools of educated people and research institutions, and as managers and technical engineers move between firms or start up new spin-off firms' (Solvell et al., 1991: 37). Lastly, firms from the related competitive industries may pose threats of new entry putting the necessary pressure on the existing firms to upgrade and advance their competitive advantage. Another reason for the importance of the presence of related competitive industries is that firms can enjoy externalities and share activities such as technological development, manufacturing, distribution and marketing. Apart from externalities, there are 'pull through' effects which occur when international success in one industry creates demand for complementary products or services as well. All these, according to Porter, make it quite likely for a nation to be competitive in groups of linked industries.

Firm Strategy, Structure and Rivalry Porter (1990a) defines the fourth broad determinant as including the strategies and structures of firms as well as the nature of domestic rivalry. According to him, although it is unrealistic to expect uniformity across all firms, there are noticeable distinct national patterns of goals, typical strategies and ways of organising firms. The resulting argument is that there should be a good fit between an industry's sources of competitive advantage as well as its structure, and the strategies, structures and practices favoured by the national environment. The existence of intense domestic rivalry, on the other hand, is of special importance since it encourages firms in the industry to break the dependency on basic factor advantages. Moreover, domestic rivals compete not only for market share but for human resources and technological breakthroughs as well.

Government and Chance Porter (1990a) sees the role of government in the competitive development of an industry as an important but indirect one, mainly through influencing the four major determinants of competitive advantage. The proper role for the government, according to Porter, should be reinforcing the underlying determinants of national advantage rather than trying to create the advantage itself. It is necessary to note that Porter anticipates a more direct but still partial role for the government in the early stages of development of a country since 'the tools at its disposal, such as capital, subsidies and temporary protection are most powerful at these stages in a nation's competitive development' (Porter, 1990a: 671). The second 'outsider' to the diamond is the role of chance. Porter defines the chance events as the ones that have little to do with circumstances in a nation and are often largely outside the control of firms. Examples include inventions, oil shocks, and wars. Chance events may create forces that reshape the industry structure altering the way the diamond operates and, thus, may allow shifts in competitive position.

The complete framework Porter (1990a) offers to capture the sources of competitive advantage in an industry can be seen in Figure 1.1. According to him, each determinant is influenced by the others, turning the system into a dynamic one in which all elements interact and reinforce each other. Actually, it is this systemic nature that makes it difficult to replicate the exact structure of the industry in another country. It is, therefore, essential that the advantage is based on the entire system rather than only one determinant. In fact, Porter (1990a: 145) believes that 'where a nation has a disadvantage in one determinant, national success normally reflects unusual advantage in others and some way of compensating for the disadvantages'.

The dynamic character of the diamond is mostly magnified by the effects of domestic rivalry and geographic industry concentration. Domestic rivalry promotes improvements in all other determinants whereas locational proximity amplifies the interaction between the sources of competitive advantage. Pressure and challenge are of special importance in the emergence and sustainability of competitive advantage, and both are driven by intense domestic rivalry and felt more heavily in the case of physical proximity.

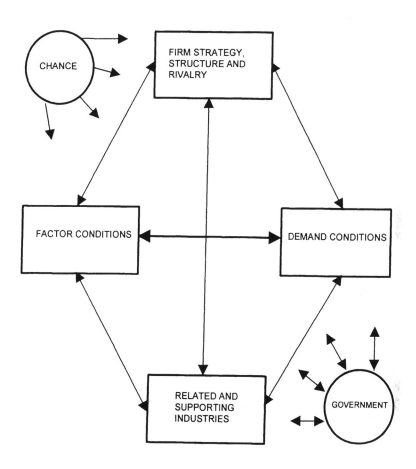

Figure 1.1   The Diamond Framework
Source: Porter, *The Competitive Advantage of Nations,* 1990, p. 127

Stages of Economic Development

After analysing the competitive industries and clusters of them for each of the ten nations, Porter (1990a: 543) extends his theory to the national economy as a whole and tries to 'provide some ways of thinking about how entire national economies progress in competitive terms'. Although he accepts the uniqueness of the case of each country, he thinks that it is possible to classify the economic development process into four broad stages -the factor-driven, investment-driven, innovation-driven and wealth-driven stages-, which are identified according to the prevailing sources of advantage in the nation.

In the factor-driven stage, the major advantage for almost all internationally successful industries stems from basic and generalised factors of production such as abundant natural resources and low cost labour, limiting the range of industries in which the nation can be internationally competitive. This factor-driven advantage is often vulnerable to changes in costs and availability of factors. Firms usually compete on the basis of price, and technology is imported from other nations. The role played by the government is usually more direct. According to Porter (1990a: 548), nearly all developing countries are at this stage. Furthermore, at the expense of being the subject of severe criticism, he argues that Canada and Australia are also at this stage.

In the investment-driven stage, on the other hand, willingness and ability to invest, as the name implies, is the key for competitive advantage. The related investments concentrate not only on new production facilities but also on factor creation mechanisms. Unlike the factor-driven stage, technology is not only adopted but also improved upon. Firms, however, still usually compete in the relatively price-sensitive segments. At this stage, advantages are no longer entirely dependent on factor conditions. Although to a limited extent, home demand (not its sophistication but its size and growth) as well as firm strategy, structure and rivalry also play a role, whereas the related and supporting industries are still largely undeveloped. Industries are usually mature and typically produce end products, basic components and/or undifferentiated materials. Increases in the overall employment rate as well as in wages and factor costs are frequently observed. According to him, very few developing nations ever make the jump to this stage. Among the few, he includes South Korea, which is definitely at this stage, and Taiwan, Singapore, Hong Kong, Spain and to a lesser extent Brazil, which constitute the other likely candidates.

In the most ideal stage, that is the innovation-driven one, the full diamond is in place in a wide range of industries (Porter, 1990a: 552). Competitive advantage no longer stems from factor endowments, since success in many industries results in increases in factor costs and value of currency. If a nation's firms are competing on the basis of cost, the related advantage usually stems from relatively higher productivity rates rather than low factor costs. Clusters of competitive industries deepen both vertically and horizontally, reducing dependence on any one sector. The economy becomes less vulnerable to external shocks. The increasing importance of services in the competitiveness of the nation is also typical in the innovation-driven stage. This stage necessitates an indirect role for the government such as encouraging the creation of more advanced factors and the establishment of new businesses. Japan, Germany and Italy are the leading innovation-driven economies of the 1980s, according to Porter (1990a).

In contrast to aforementioned stages, the wealth-driven stage signals a decline. Since the economy is mainly driven by past success and wealth, innovation and sustaining competitive advantage lose their importance. Firms start to lose competitive advantage for several reasons including fading rivalry, the decreasing role of entrepreneurs but increasing role of administrators and lack of motivation. Mergers and acquisitions are widespread reflecting the desire to reduce rivalry. Government is typically busy with redistribution of wealth rather than its creation. Due to customer loyalties and established market positions, symptoms may be slow to appear. According to Porter (1990a: 573), 'the momentum created when a nation enters the wealth-driven stage takes decades or longer to halt or reverse'. He considers Britain as a country at the wealth-driven stage, adding, however, that recent improvements, which are evident from the productivity growth, are encouraging.

The Debate on Porter's *The Competitive Advantage of Nations*

It is undeniable that Porter's *The Competitive Advantage of Nations* has attracted considerable attention from a wide range of disciplines. In addition to the ten nations included in the original work, others, including Canada and New Zealand, have also been studied by the project teams headed by Porter himself, and other researchers have replicated it for several other countries such as Austria, Ireland, Finland, Mexico, and the Netherlands. Some scholars have come up with interesting improvement proposals that distort the nice shape of the 'diamond'. In fact, even a summary of the criticisms about the diamond model has been provided recently (see Penttinen, 1994).

In this section, the debate spawned by the publication of Porter's (1990a) study and findings will be analysed. Before proceeding with the resulting summary, I should state that it has become inevitable to mention a few points, which have created some dispute in the literature throughout the book. To avoid repetition, here the reader is referred to the relevant sections when necessary.

General Criticisms About the Study

Formal Modelling One of the most important criticisms of the study is the lack of formal analytic modelling. Gray (1991: 510), for instance, points to the problems of a less formal approach by stating that this 'allows Porter to introduce superficially certain phenomena not identified as integral parts of the diamond, so that the treatment of some phenomena becomes an obiter dictum rather than a closely reasoned deduction'. Similarly, Stopford and Strange (1991: 8) state that the 'diamond' is just an explanatory framework rather than a deterministic theory. Another criticism concerning the lack of formal modelling comes from Greenaway (1993: 146) who believes that 'many economists will be irritated by the constant reference to a 'theory' of competitive advantage which is never formally presented, nor formally tested'. Although these criticisms are mainly true, it should be stated that by preferring to use such a qualitative framework, Porter introduces several interesting points like the advanced and specific factor creation mechanisms and sophistication of demand conditions, which would have been very difficult, if not impossible, to capture if he had just focused on quantitative methods and formal modelling.

Originality Another frequently mentioned criticism of Porter's work is its 'lack of originality'. Many (for instance, Bellak and Weiss, 1993; Rugman and D'Cruz, 1993; Dunning, 1992; Grant, 1991; Rugman, 1991) argue that none of the determinants offered by Porter is neither new nor unexpected. Coté (1991: 312), for instance, draws our attention to the point made by several economists who argue that Porter's work is basically a 'rehash'of the theory of comparative advantage. Similarly, Gray (1991: 506) argues that hard work, a high rate of investment, an intelligent strategy and good factor conditions (Gray calls these the 'Puritan ethic') would cover a great deal of the diamond at first glance. He goes on by stating that it is possible to reduce what Porter says to the fact that international trade in certain categories, mainly advanced goods, requires a consideration of a wide range of industry-specific variables and such trade will understandably change over time. According to him, these facts have already been recognised by the theory of intra-industry trade. Magaziner (1990: 189) argues that the points put forward by Porter are not new to business strategists, but it is important to raise them to the agenda of the policy makers. According to Thurow (1990: 96), there is nothing particularly new in Porter's conclusions: 'We all know that we should consume less and invest more in education, research and development, plants and equipment, and infrastructure'.

In sharp contrast to the arguments mentioned above, Smith (1993: 399) makes the following evaluation about Porter's work: 'It is the first serious attempt to develop a really original grand theory of national economic development process since the early years of Post-war development economics, and represents one of the most original ways of thinking about development policy in years'. In fact, it is true that each element in the diamond model has been the subject of many studies, and therefore it is hard to describe the framework as 'original'. As Penttinen (1994) writes, the cluster concept is nothing new, the role attributed to factor conditions parallels the theory of comparative advantage, the idea of demand side effects dates back to Vernon (1966), and lastly, most of the issues that are related to the 'firm strategy, structure and rivalry' determinant have been covered under industrial economics. Porter's contribution, however, is to combine all of these thoughts and, by linking them to his own earlier work in competitive strategy, form a coherent framework as a result of field research that can help us understand the possible sources of competitive advantage. By so doing, he makes a contribution both to the theory of international trade by offering a framework that may be a good complement to more quantitative studies of competitive advantage and to the theory of strategic management, since it is, in a sense, an attempt to understand a relatively premature area in this discipline: the national environment in which a firm operates.

Suitableness for Every Country To some researchers, Porter's framework cannot be used to model every country. Rugman (1991: 61), for instance, believes that 'while most of Porter's analysis would work for managers based in the US, the European Community or Japan, much of it is superficial and plain wrong when applied in a Canadian situation'. The most important reason for that, according to Rugman, is the lack of a serious effort in

Porter's study to incorporate the true significance of multinational activity. He argues that 'this weakness in Porter's model would not only apply to Canadian-based firms but to multinationals from all small open economies, that is, 90 per cent of the world's nations potentially cannot be modelled by the Porter diamond'. Similarly, in Hodgetts's (1993: 44) view, 'since most countries of the world do not have the same economic strength or affluence as those studied by Porter, it is highly unlikely that his model can be applied to them without modification'. Porter's overemphasis on home markets and national firms, according to Bellak and Weiss (1993: 117), may be justified for large countries but is of little relevance for small nations. Narula (1993: 85) and Yetton et al. (1992) make a similar point by arguing that since it is based on and applied to them, the diamond is most relevant to mature and manufacturing-based economies and cannot be applied to explain the international competitiveness of developing countries or development. These criticisms may or may not be true, but there is no way to learn this without applying the model to other countries, especially to the small and/or developing ones. By so doing, we may have a better idea, based on more reliable grounds, about whether the framework is suitable just for large developed countries or can give some insights regarding the competitive advantages of the other countries as well.

The Role of Macroeconomic Policy   Porter (1990a) is heavily criticised about his treatment of macroeconomic policy. Both Daly (1993: 130) and Jasinowski (1990: 196) think that Porter underestimates price competitiveness and plays down macroeconomic policies that affect the relative costs of producing similar manufactured products in different countries. Gray (1991: 154) similarly argues that both profits and the influence of exchange rates on profits are not confronted in Porter's study. Porter (1990b: 192) replies by stating that although, according to him, macroeconomic factors like the value of currency and interest rates play a role by affecting the export performance in the short-run, 'they are not the causal, the sufficient, nor the most important influence on competitiveness'. He gives Japan and Germany as examples for countries, which succeeded because of many other reasons and despite overvalued currencies. There is, however, no reason to leave this point as an unresolved issue. There are many studies trying to capture the relationship between export success and exchange rate adjustments, and it can be said that the literature suggests a positive relationship between exchange rate devaluation and export performance. The point Porter makes, however, is that there are indeed countries that succeed despite overvalued exchange rates, and those that continuously use devaluation as a strategy to increase exports, by so doing, indirectly encourage more price sensitive segments which are, according to him, not preferable and sustainable sources of competitive advantage in the long-run. This, in fact, brings us to a more meaningful basis for discussion: Is Porter right by giving more emphasis to 'advanced goods' and by seeing them as more sustainable sources of competitive advantage? This point is also vital for Porter's model of national economic development, and I find it more meaningful to have further discussion of the topic in that section.

The Role of National Culture   A quite interesting point, that is the impact of national culture on the competitive advantage of a country, is raised by van den Bosch and van Prooijen (1992) who believe that Porter (1990a) pays very little attention to this issue. By using the four dimensions developed by Hofstede (1980), which are namely individualism versus collectivism, large or small power distance, strong or weak uncertainty avoidance, and masculinity versus femininity, they try to show the influence of national culture on competitive advantage. Although they insist on the argument that national culture is the base on which the national diamond rests, and it should be given the importance it deserves while explaining the differences in international competitive advantage, they admit that national culture works through determinants, and therefore it is not necessary to add it as a fifth determinant to the diamond framework. Porter (1992: 178) replies by stating that national and even regional culture are important elements in the analysis of competitive advantage and that they have been given the necessary importance in the study. He, then, summarises some findings of his study related to the national culture. First, cultural factors are more sustainable bases for competitive advantage since they are difficult to duplicate, and cultural changes occur very slowly. Second, the influence of culture on competitive advantage is an indirect one since it acts through the determinants, rather than on its own. Moreover, according to him, culture does not have to be exogenous to firms, it can be changed by them, and it is a national, regional, or even local phenomenon. He concludes that 'advantage grows out of national and even local circumstances in the diamond, one of which is culture. The importance of cultural factors only reinforces the notion that a firm's home base remains crucial even in global competition' (Porter, 1992: 178). In short, there is little disagreement concerning the importance as well as the appropriate role of national culture in the determination of the competitive advantage of a country.

Criticisms About the Methodology

The methodology Porter employed has also been the subject of much criticism (see Chapter 2 for a summary of the methodology as well as a discussion of a few additional points). Greenaway (1993: 146) mentions one of the general problems of the case study method which is used for the analysis of the competitive industries in Porter's study: 'When used well, as here, the case study approach is capable of yielding insights which escape more formal methods. The great weakness of the approach, however, is that many of the insights which are yielded are inevitably case-specific'. According to Bellak and Weiss (1993: 116), who also draw our attention to the limited generalisability of the case study material, the subjective component resulting from using the case study method makes it almost impossible to compare countries with each other. It is of course hard to talk about the generalisability of the evidence obtained from case studies in a statistical sense. Yin (1994), however, argues that by using multiple case designs, it is possible to make analytic generalisations (see Chapter 8, Conclusion, for a further discussion of this issue). In short, if its limitations are kept in mind, the case study method may be quite informative, especially when the researcher has little control over events and seeks to answer 'how' and 'why' types of questions.

There are some technical concerns pointed out by several scholars. Many (Bellak and Weiss, 1993; Cartwright, 1993; Eilon, 1992; Grant, 1991; Rugman and D'Cruz, 1993), for instance, criticise the heavy dependence on world export shares as a measure of international competitiveness but they fail to offer a better, internationally comparable measure as an alternative (see Chapter 2 for a discussion). Another concern has been introduced by Rugman and D'Cruz (1993: 22) who note that smaller nations will understandably have weaker elements in their home diamonds; one likely candidate is the demand conditions. It is, then, unfair to condemn their clusters to a second rate status. They also criticise the tables prepared by Porter showing the number of industries lost or gained between two points in time. They rightly think that given that the industries in terms of world and country export share are not of equal importance, these tables are misleading. Another point they question is the fact that Porter does not consider an industry as competitive when its trade is almost exclusively with neighbouring nations. Porter justifies this point by stating that if trade is exclusively with the neighbouring nations, this is an indication that the nation's competitive advantage in this particular industry solely reflects geographic proximity rather than true international success. Although this criticism should be seriously considered when analysing such countries as Canada for instance, for the case of Turkey this does not pose a big problem since it is hard to specify a particular neighbouring country dominating trade in all areas, like the United States does for Canada. In fact, Porter, in a way, takes this into consideration in the Canada study by including such industries in the detailed case studies (Porter and The Monitor Company, 1991).

According to Jacobs and Jong (1992: 236-7), who also raise some technical issues related to the methodology employed by Porter, there is a danger of a bias towards the 'primary goods' category. Having prepared the world cluster chart, I have also observed that there is a bias towards this category, and even towards some clusters since there are, for instance, very few items that the 'defence' cluster can potentially include as opposed to many that the 'food/beverages' cluster can. This is, in fact, a direct result of the SITC system and Porter's classification, and there is not much that can be done about that apart from keeping this in mind while interpreting the charts. We should also note that, supporting Rugman and D'Cruz's (1993) related criticism stated above, it becomes apparent that world export shares are much more meaningful indicators of the competitive position of a country as compared to the number of industries in a particular cluster.

Related to the inadequate treatment of the relatively less competitive industries, Harris and Watson (1991: 248) criticise Porter by focusing mainly on the successful industries and state that 'if failing industries were treated in essentially the same way as industries that did eventually succeed, this would be a very useful lesson'. Yetton et al. (1992) also argue that Porter only studies the success of successful industries, whereas unsuccessful and/or non-exporting ones have not been paid enough attention. Porter's preference for examining the relatively more competitive industries together with his lack of attention for the relatively less competitive ones is indeed a drawback of his research (see Chapter 2 for a discussion of this issue). In this study, I include one uncompetitive sector, the Turkish automobile industry, and one non-exporting sector, the Turkish flat steel industry, which may shed some light to the ongoing disputes on that issue.

Another point of criticism made about the work of Porter (1990a) is related to the predictive power of the 'diamond'. According to Grant (1991: 542), for instance, 'the key weakness of the theory is in its predictive power. Ambiguity over the signs of relationships, the complexity of interactions, and dual causation render the model unproductive in generating clear predictions'. Although there are indeed ambiguities about the relationships

Porter envisages among the variables he defines, it is still possible to derive some general conclusions that can also form the necessary bases for generating predictions. Just to give an example, it is quite obvious that Porter favours a very strong positive relationship between the international competitiveness and the intensity of domestic rivalry in an industry.

A very interesting point, which is a source of debate in the literature, is about the relevant geographical unit of analysis. Porter (1990a: 157) himself reveals his suspicion on this issue by stating that, according to his findings, the geographic concentration of competitive industries is so important that this raises questions about whether the nation is a relevant unit of analysis since competitive advantage seems to be often localised within a nation. In the final analysis, however, he believes that nations are still important, and 'many of the determinants of advantage are more similar within a nation than across nations'. This approach has been widely criticised. Dunning (1993: 12), for instance, emphasises the importance of globalisation and integration in several parts of the world. Regarding the EU, he argues that national diamonds will have to be replaced by 'supranational diamonds' to be able to capture the true competitive advantages of the Community. Jacobs and Jong (1992: 239-46), on the other hand, argue that there is a type of dialectic relationship between divergence and convergence, and appreciate Porter's idea that globalisation paradoxically leads to more emphasis on local conditions and consequently creates an opportunity for firms to take advantage of them. Yet others (e.g. Hodgetts, 1993; Rugman and D'Cruz, 1993; Rugman and Verbeke, 1993; Rugman, 1991) share the idea that double and/or multiple-linked diamonds may reflect the sources of competitive advantage better than Porter's single diamond framework for the smaller nations that are highly interdependent with one or more of the triad blocks (i.e. Europe, North America, Japan). It is, of course, difficult to come up with a clear conclusion from these discussions since the issue is very complex reflecting the broader debates on globalisation in general.

Porter's treatment of multinationals and foreign direct investment is also widely criticised. According to Rugman (1991: 63), the narrow understanding of foreign direct investment is the major conceptual problem of Porter's model. Dunning (1993: 13), on the other hand, states that he can appreciate some of Porter's concerns about inward FDI. This point does not pose a serious problem for the ten countries included in the original study since Porter (1990a: 740) states that few industries have been excluded for this reason. What is to be done in the process of deciding whether or not to exclude a competitive industry due to substantial inward FDI, however, continues to be a question that requires an answer given the above criticisms even though Porter's attitude is clear: he doesn't find it healthy at all. In the specific case of locating the source of competitive advantage, I favour Porter's method that requires determining whether the firms in the industry operate as branches of a multinational company or they can be associated with the host nation without any difficulty. Expectedly, in the former case the industry is excluded, while it remains in the list of competitive industries in the latter case.

In fact, Dunning's (1993) emphasis is on the treatment of multinationals in Porter's study, rather than locating the source of competitive advantage. According to him, 'there is ample evidence to suggest that MNEs are influenced in their competitiveness by the configuration of the diamond in other than their home countries, and that is, in turn may impinge upon the competitiveness of home countries'. He then, introduces the transnational activity as the third outsider to the diamond and tries to explain its relation with each of the determinants of competitive advantage specified by Porter. Although Rugman and D'Cruz (1993: 25) agree with Dunning in the sense that multinational activity is missing from Porter and that it should be a part of the diamond framework, they first offer a different place for it, in the determinant called 'firm strategies, structure and rivalry'; and, after discussing whether it may create a confusion to assume that the same rivalry determinant can include multinational and domestic industries at the same time, they conclude that 'it is questionable that multinational activity can actually be added into any, or all, of the four determinants, nor included as a third exogenous variable'. Relatedly, Rugman and Verbeke (1993: 72) challenge 'Porter's allegation that the core competencies of large MNEs and the innovative processes occurring within these firms necessarily need to depend upon the characteristics of a single home base'. They argue that especially multinationals from small nations may rely on a host nation in a way that it becomes rather difficult to make a distinction between the home base and the host nation or nations. In short, many critics are of the opinion that, for the MNE, determinants of the diamond are sourced all over the world, whereas, according to Porter, they are created within a nation, which constitutes the home base for that particular MNE. Porter further states that such criticisms mainly stem from an unnecessary confusion: the geographic scope of competition and geographic locus of competitive advantage are two different things. In his view, competition can be global but sources of advantage are local (Porter and Amstrong, 1992). In fact, since the diamond by definition rests on the assumption that sources of advantage are local, proposing to add the transnational business activity as a third exogenous variable contradicts the basic rationale of the framework. The importance of the role foreign multinationals play differs from country to country, and for the case of Turkey we can safely say that in general domestic firms dominate many internationally competitive sectors. I, nevertheless, study in detail one uncompetitive sector, the Turkish automobile industry, which at the same time exhibits multinational involvement. We, therefore, expect this study to make a contribution to clarify the above stated disputes about the role of multinational activity in shaping the competitive advantage of a country (see Chapter 6 and Chapter 8).

Criticisms About the Diamond Framework

Firm Strategy, Structure and Rivalry   The diamond framework itself has also been the subject of many criticisms. In particular, 'firm strategy, structure and rivalry' is found to be 'an awkward catch-all' category (Grant, 1991: 542). It is questionable whether these variables can form a coherent group or if they are just a 'rest of' category. The roles attributed to structure and strategy are not that clear, and it is not so easy to justify why domestic rivalry, a well-explained industry level variable, stands together with strategy and structure in the framework. The intensity of criticisms increases sharply when the issue at hand is the relationship between domestic rivalry and international competitiveness. Dobson (1992: 254), for instance, argues that 'many will disagree with his [Porter's] conclusion that unregulated competition is the way forward, even dismissing the need for co-operation in research and strategic alliances'. Deriving from the Japanese case, Heinz (1990: 192-3) also has some concerns about Porter's emphasis on competition and argues that Porter's antipathy to co-operation and relaxation of antitrust rules should be reconsidered. In his reply to this criticism, Porter (1990b: 191) argues that the case of Japan is widely misunderstood since suspending antitrust is not what has happened in most successful Japanese industries. On the contrary, there are numerous and fiercely competitive local rivalries. It seems rather difficult to come up with a clear conclusion from these discussions. Apparently, the relationship between international competitiveness and intensity of domestic rivalry is a complex one and requires further investigation.

As for the 'firm strategy and structure' part of this category, criticisms are usually about the inadequate treatment of these variables. Harris and Watson (1991: 246) argue that 'although the firm is the crucial agent in Porter's story in fact very little is said about it'. Dobson (1992: 255) also states that the study is not so satisfactory as far as the implications for management are concerned. We should however keep in mind that the unit of analysis in Porter's study is industry, rather than the firm. Nevertheless, it has important implications for firms, which are clearly identified and discussed at the end of Porter's (1990a) book.

Demand Conditions According to Porter (1990a), domestic demand conditions of an industry are amongst the important determinants of the international competitiveness of this industry. The relationship between international competitiveness and the size of home demand, however, is one of the issues that is open to dispute since there are two conflicting but perfectly justifiable arguments concerning this relationship. According to the first argument, if home demand is large, firms may feel secure to invest in industries where there are economies of scale, and given that there is intensive domestic rivalry and local buyers parallel foreign demand, this may encourage international competitiveness. According to the second one, however, if home market is large enough, firms may not bother trying to export and may prefer to concentrate solely on the home market. If, on the other hand, the home market is small, they have little chance but they have to be more active in the international markets. Although he recognises that home market size plays a complex role in national advantage, Porter (1990a: 92) seems to favour the former line of thinking: 'Provided that its composition is sophisticated and anticipates international and not just domestic needs, the size and pattern of growth of home demand can reinforce national advantage in an industry'. He, however, notes that other variables, especially intensity of domestic rivalry, determine whether a large home market is a strength or a weakness. Furthermore, according to him, other attributes of home demand, like its sophistication, are more important than its size.

Related and Supporting Industries There are also criticisms about the concept of clustering, which is probably the most important contribution of Porter's (1990a) study. Yla-Anttila (1994: 10) argues that competitive success is not necessarily created in national clusters and that it is possible to detect many winners also outside clusters. On the contrary, according to Jacobs and Jong (1992: 237), who have applied the method to the Netherlands, Porter's technique of cluster analysis indeed provides a new tool for capturing the stronger and weaker points of an economy. O'Donnellan (1994: 221), on the other hand, examines the extent to which industrial clustering, as defined by Porter, exists in Ireland, and its association with industrial performance. He concludes that 'linkages between manufacturing sectors are not substantial and spatial concentrations in two urban centres are more an effect of general urban economies than of sectoral linkages'. It will be interesting to find out the extent to which the clustering process works in the Turkish manufacturing and service sectors in terms of existence and intensity of horizontal and vertical relationships amongst the internationally competitive industries as well as the geographic concentration of them.

Chance Narula (1993: 88) thinks that the role attributed to chance events is too great. Similarly, Bellak and Weiss (1993: 112) argue that other elements, which are probably included in the 'chance' category in Porter's classification, may be quite important. The idea, however, is not that chance events are not important, rather that they are largely uncontrollable and unexpected. Relatedly, Porter draws our attention to the point that giving a role to chance does not mean that industry success is unpredictable. On the contrary, according to his findings, the determinants play a major role even 'in locating where invention and entrepreneurship are most likely to occur in a particular industry' (Porter, 1990a: 126).

Government The indirect role Porter (1990a) attributes to government in the diamond framework is one of the most criticised areas of his study. Harris and Watson (1991: 250-1) criticise one of the roles Porter envisages for government, that is, supporting potentially competitive clusters, which, according to them, can be termed as 'picking clusters', 'a more advanced, probably more dangerous, and certainly more expensive, complicated, and difficult variant of picking winners'. Interestingly, there is a disagreement between the two colleagues (i.e. Harris and Watson) about what Porter means by supporting cluster development. Harris believes that Porter recommends 'picking clusters', whereas to Watson this is a likely candidate for a common misinterpretation of Porter. A closer examination of Porter's approach to government's effect on cluster development shows that Porter does not recommend picking clusters. He believes that 'clusters often emerge and begin to grow naturally' (Porter, 1990a: 655) and defines the role of government in cluster formation in the following way: 'Once a cluster begins to form [...] government at all levels can play a role in reinforcing it. Perhaps the most beneficial way is through investments to create specialised factors such as university technical institutes, training centres, data banks, and specialised infrastructure' (Porter, 1990a: 655).

According to Stopford and Strange (1991: 8-9), in order to be able to adopt Porter's analysis to the developing countries, a more explicit treatment of government is necessary since 'small, poor countries cannot afford the luxury of letting market forces determine outcomes'. According to them, government should be added as a fifth determinant to the framework, instead of being an outsider, since it plays a more active and direct role than the one attributed in the diamond. Van den Bosch and de Man (1994) also discuss whether or not government can be considered as a fifth determinant. They argue that Porter's analysis is at the macro-level with respect to the government and that 'the more new policies are created which are directed at the meso- and micro-levels and which have a more direct role in influencing the diamond, the less the government can be treated as an outside factor'. It is not true that Porter's analysis of the government is at the macro-level. In fact, the lack of enough attention to the macro-analysis of government behaviour, (the inadequate treatment of the effects of exchange rate fluctuations on the export success of a country, for instance) is one of the criticisms I have already mentioned previously. The conclusion they reach from this point, however, which is at the same time the proposal made by Stopford and Strange (1991: 8-9), is a more interesting issue to discuss: Whether it makes sense to add government as a fifth determinant to the diamond, or put it another way, is it more appropriate to assume a direct vs. indirect role for the government in the framework? In his reply to these criticisms, Porter repeats that, to him, the essential role of government is challenging and pressing industry and that too much help may undermine industry success (Porter, 1990b: 190). A detailed discussion of the 'ideal' level of government intervention, which is an unresolved issue, is beyond the scope of this study. I will however try to understand the role of government in shaping the sources of competitive advantage of Turkey, a developing country in which government plays a major role, which may in turn give some insights into the indirect role Porter attributes to it.

Criticisms About the Model of Economic Development

As has been already mentioned, in the second part of his study, Porter (1990a) tries to explain how entire nations develop in competitive terms by using the diamond framework. This can be considered as a type of economic development model from an 'outsider' (since Porter is widely known by his contributions to the management discipline) and has been the subject of many criticisms. According to Narula (1993: 85), for instance, Porter neglects the cumulative nature of technology in his attempt to explain the economic development process. He argues that technology should be regarded as an endogenous variable since 'it affects the endogenous variables as much as it is affected by them' and 'the exogenous variables influence accumulated technology only indirectly through the endogenous variables'. Narula, then, offers a 'dynamic' economic development model for which economic growth is also linked to the technology accumulation process.

According to Grant (1991: 547), the analysis of economic development at the national level is the least successful part of Porter's study. He argues that as Porter gets further away from the micro-foundations of his theory, he experiences more difficulty in explaining the relationships among the related variables. Thurow (1990: 96) also finds Porter's explanations for national economic development inadequate: 'Porter fails exactly where everyone else has failed. Why do some countries grow? Why do other countries decline?' Bellak and Weiss (1993: 115) draw our attention to the 'vague' nature of Porter's economic development model and criticise him for not being clear enough either in explaining the transition process from one stage to another or in setting the criteria for the classification of the countries amongst the stages. Similarly, Hodgetts (1993: 44) questions the fixation that countries move from one stage to another rather than spanning two or more of these stages. Furthermore, according to him, a country is likely to have industries or companies operating in each of these stages. Porter admits the fact that a nation may have a range of industries with widely different sources of competitive advantage. He thinks, however, it is still possible to identify a 'predominant pattern' in the nature of competitive advantage in a nation's firms at a particular time, which is reflected in the similarity of the diamonds across a range of industries in the nation (Porter, 1990a: 545).

Coté (1991: 311), on the other hand, questions the general trade-dependent approach Porter (1990a) follows in explaining the development process; that is, the reliance on the assumption that the expansion of an economy follows the expansion of its tradable sectors. A similar evaluation comes from Harris and Watson (1991: 247-9) who think that by using just two sets of evidence, that is trade and investment statistics and case studies, Porter tries 'to construct a grand generalisation about whether a national economy is factor-driven, investment-driven, innovation-driven or wealth-driven'. It is true that Porter's emphasis is on the traded sector. He argues that 'the ability to upgrade an economy depends heavily on the position of a nation's firms in that portion of the economy exposed to international competition' (Porter, 1990a: 545). He further justifies his point by stating that in an open economy, the nation does not need to produce all goods and services by itself and can increase the overall productivity level by specialising in industries where its firms are relatively more productive. The country's resources, then, are not wasted on products and services where its firms are less productive, and thus can be imported (Porter, 1990a). Similarly, foreign investment allows focusing on the production of the goods and services where the nation's firms are relatively more productive, whereas the low productivity sectors can be moved abroad (Van der Linde, 1991). Furthermore, the true test of success is in the international markets where firms from many nations compete. It is the place where one should concentrate to understand how the economic context in different nations provide their firms with advantages or disadvantages (Porter and The Monitor Company, 1991). The emphasis on the traded sector in an attempt to understand the sources of international competitiveness is, therefore, well justified.

What is less justified is whether or not the same logic can be applied to the overall economic development process. Krugman (1994a: 34), for instance, argues that 'even though world trade is larger than ever before, national living standards are overwhelmingly determined by domestic factors rather than by some competition of world markets'. He also challenges the argument that non-competing sectors (e.g. a large portion of the service sector) are less important than the competing ones (1994b: 277). According to him, which of these is more important for the growth of national economy depends on which one raises the overall productivity growth more, and in the case of the United States, for instance, it is the non-competing service sectors. As a result, while Porter's emphasis on the traded sector is well justified for investigating the sources of competitive advantage at the industry level, it is by no means guaranteed that the same concept can be applied to explain how national economies develop over time. This is mainly because the emphasis on the traded sector prevails in Porter's study although he tries to correct for that by adding some industries (e.g. some service sectors) based on in-country research.

Another point Harris and Watson (1991: 247-9) note is the argument that it may be difficult to place countries with large endowments of natural resources into Porter's taxonomy. In their view, it is not undesirable if countries have such resources and can obtain a high standard of living by exploiting them. Related to this point, Hodgetts (1993: 45) gives Canada as an example, whose firms, according to him, turned the country's comparative advantage in natural resources into firm specific advantages in resource processing. In fact, it is hard to say that Canadian scholars welcome Porter's classification of Canada as a 'factor-driven' economy. Rugman and D'Cruz (1993: 23-5) term this as a 'classic mistake' Porter makes several times in his Canada study. They claim that 'the views expressed by Porter on the role of natural resources is old-fashioned and misguided'. According to Rugman (1991: 62-3), for instance, there is substantial value added due to managerial and marketing skills in the natural resource dependent sectors of Canada, and these are sustainable sources of competitive advantage. This is an interesting issue raised by Porter's model of economic development and has been subject to heavy criticism, the majority of which comes from Canadian scholars since Canada is a typical example of countries known as 'developed' but which are still largely dependent on natural resources. With regard to this issue, Porter's attitude is quite clear. He states that although some nations enjoy high living standards, thanks to their remarkable natural resource endowments, in the long-run there may be a problem of depletion, new sources may emerge, or technological changes may reduce or eliminate resource needs. Possessing abundant natural resources may even make it more difficult to move towards higher stages, according to Porter (1990a: 564), since 'they provide a satisfactory or even high level of national income without the need to upgrade the diamond'. It is even possible for a nation to move directly from the factor-driven stage to the wealth-driven one if resource abundance is great enough. These views are obviously in conflict with the criticisms of the Canadian scholars stated above, who believe that it is not undesirable if a nation with abundant natural resources can achieve international competitiveness by exploiting them.

The issue of natural resource dependency is, in fact, closely related to another question which has already been mentioned previously: Is Porter right by giving more emphasis to 'advanced' goods and by seeing them as more sustainable sources of competitive advantage? It is quite clear that Porter favours being competitive in 'higher-order', 'more sophisticated' and 'advanced' industries. Furthermore, according to him, 'the upgrading process is loss of position in price-sensitive segments and in products involving less sophisticated skills and technology' (Porter, 1990a: 544). On several other occasions, however, he states that it is possible to have a good national position, despite a majority of the competitive clusters including so-called 'mature' or 'traditional' industries. Reviewing his discussion about the categorisations used to prioritise industries may be helpful for a better understanding of what Porter says exactly about this sensitive issue. According to him, 'there is a temptation to classify a nation's industrial base into categories such as high-tech and low-tech, sunrise and sunset, growing and mature, manufacturing and service, and labour- (or capital-) intensive and knowledge-intensive. The implication drawn from such distinctions is that some categories are better than others' (Porter, 1990a: 624). He does not approve of this line of thinking and gives Italy as an example of the countries that have achieved competitive advantage in the industries considered as 'mature' or 'traditional'. One explanation to this seemingly confusing situation can be the fact that it may still be possible to find some segments that require 'higher-order' and 'more sophisticated' sources of competitive advantage in these mature and traditional industries.

We are, then, left with the following question: What are these 'higher-order' and 'more sophisticated' sources of competitive advantage? One can deduce some hints concerning what Porter (1990a) means by these terms from his discussion of the innovation-driven economy. For instance, he states that 'firms in an innovation-driven economy compete internationally in more differentiated industry segments. They continue to compete on cost but where it depends not on factor costs but on productivity due to high skill levels and advanced technology' (Porter, 1990a: 554). From these sentences, we can understand that the competitive advantage stemming from high skill levels and advanced technology is possibly a 'higher order' competitive advantage. Similarly, from the following sentences it is possible to pick up what is meant by sophisticated services: 'Factor- and investment-driven nations are rarely successful in international service industries except those dependent on labour costs (for example, general cargo shipping and some segments of international construction). In an innovation-driven economy, more advanced firms develop increasingly sophisticated service needs, such as in marketing, engineering, and testing' (Porter, 1990a: 555). In addition, we can consider many segments in the industrial and supporting functions (the middle row of the cluster chart) as more advanced, since Porter argues that economies are first likely to begin upgrading on the top (upstream) or the bottom (final consumption goods and services) level of the cluster chart (Porter, 1990a: 563).

To summarise, Porter does not mean that cost advantage is not important. He, however, argues that it is preferable if it stems from relatively favourable productivity rates. An advantage that is largely dependent on the pure availability of natural resources, according to him, is vulnerable and not sustainable. It follows that it is not so desirable if the competitive structure of an economy is overwhelmingly based on those industries, which he thinks Canada's is.

The attempt to form a model that explains how and why national economies develop is apparently a very difficult, but still an important and interesting task. It is unavoidable that such a model will have some weaknesses as has been pointed by Rostow (1990a: 1): '[A]ny way of looking at things that pretends to bring within its orbit, let us say, significant aspects of late eighteenth-century Britain and Khrushchev's Russia; Meiji

Japan and Canada of the pre-1914 railway boom; Alexander Hamilton's United States and Mao's China; Bismark's Germany and Nasser's Egypt- any such scheme is bound, to put it mildly, to have certain limitations'. Although Porter's stages are defined to explain the national competitive development process for the post-World War II period, it is perfectly possible to raise similar arguments concerning the difficulty of placing all nations into four broad categories. This challenging task is the subject of a vast literature of economic growth including the contributions of very influential theorists from David Hume to Karl Marx (Rostow, 1990b). It is obviously beyond the scope of this study to conduct a detailed analysis and discussion of the economic development process. In light of the preceding discussion, however, we can conclude that Porter's attempt to understand how entire nations develop over time with the help of the diamond framework is shadowed by doubts whether or not the same concepts that are used to explain the sources of international competitiveness at the industry level can also be used at the national level. In this book, I concentrate on understanding the sources of competitive advantage at the industry level, which is the main contribution of *The Competitive Advantage of Nations*. The second part of Porter's study, examining the economic development process, in other words, is of little relevance.

Empirical Tests and Improvement Proposals

Although Porter's study is replicated for many countries, there are few attempts to 'test' it, probably because it is rather difficult, if not impossible, to conduct a formal test for the model proposed. As mentioned previously, O'Donnellan (1994) tries to test one aspect of the study by examining whether the Porter type of industrial clustering exists in Irish manufacturing as well as its relation to industrial performance. He finds that there are few linkages between manufacturing sectors in Ireland. He also tries to test the geographical concentration hypothesis. He concludes that there is a general preference for the greater urban areas like Dublin and Cork, rather than a geographic concentration of the industrial clusters. His results also show that there is little association between sectoral clustering and various aspects of industrial performance for the case of Ireland.

The second test of Porter's study is conducted by Cartwright (1993: 55), and it is an attempt to test the whole model in light of the New Zealand experience. To conduct such a test, he develops a simple model based on interval scales. Maximum scale values are given according to Porter's apparent views about the relative impact of the determinants on the international competitiveness of an industry. He chooses ten industries, grouped into two, on the basis of international competitive performance, which is measured by their share of world trade and changes in overall industry profitability. By analysing the content of each case study, he judgmentally gives the impact scores on the scales specified previously. The test results show that the Porter-ideal model is more closely associated with the industries, which are characterised by moderate competitiveness and static/declining profitability rather than those which are characterised by strong competitiveness and increasing profitability. These results, however, at best put a question mark to one's mind, since there are obvious limitations of the testing method.

Apart from these tests, there are several proposals to improve the diamond framework. Since most of them have already been mentioned above, I will give here a brief summary of the most noteworthy. According to Stopford and Strange (1991: 8-9) and van den Bosch and de Man (1994), it is worth considering whether or not government can be added to the diamond framework as a fifth determinant. Dunning (1992, 1993) thinks that it is possible to treat the 'transnational business activity' as a third exogenous factor, along with 'chance' and 'government'. Van den Bosch and van Prooijen (1992), on the other hand, call for a more explicit treatment for the impact of national culture on the sources of competitive advantage. Narula (1993) argues that 'accumulated technology' should be added to the diamond framework as a fifth endogenous variable. Jacobs and Jong (1992) introduce the idea that the relevant geographical entity may change from cluster to cluster. They also make several technical proposals such as changing the label of the category 'primary goods' in the cluster chart to 'end products', changing the label 'specialty inputs' to 'intermediary inputs', and adding 'research and development specialisation' as a fifth vertical classification to each cluster. Several scholars (e.g. Hodgetts, 1993; Rugman and D'Cruz, 1993; Rugman and Verbeke, 1993; Rugman, 1991) share the idea that double and/or multiple-linked diamonds may reflect the sources of competitive advantage better than Porter's single diamond framework. The underlying thesis is that Porter's model can explain the sources of competitive advantage for the European Union countries, the USA and Japan, but cannot be applied to the other smaller nations that are highly interdependent with one or more of these triad blocks. In such situations, they argue that it may be more meaningful to relate the home country diamond to the diamond of the triad nation; that is, a double diamond framework may better explain the true sources of competitive advantage.

Other Strengths and Weaknesses

Porter is also criticised about some other issues. Both Magaziner (1990: 189) and Grant (1991: 548), for instance, find the model too ambitious. In fact, according to Grant, the ambitious scope of the study is one of the reasons for its shortcomings in theory, exposition and empirical analysis. Dunning (1992: 139) and Stopford and Strange (1991: 8) criticise Porter about the lack of a detailed consideration of entrepreneurship and investment. According to Sagasti (1990: 188), Porter's study gives an impression that acquiring and sustaining competitive advantage are not that difficult and are within the reach of any company or nation, whereas in reality, just the opposite is true. Porter (1990b: 190) replies by stating that 'companies and nations do have the power to seek and achieve competitive advantage if they have the conviction to do so'. He, however, adds that this is indeed an uncomfortable process and probably few will be able to do so.

Having summarised the major criticisms, tests and proposals for the improvement of Porter's diamond, we can finally state several credits for the study mentioned in the literature. Penttinen (1994: 67), for instance, states that the diamond model is indeed useful but requires modifications before being applied to a specific industry in a specific country. Maucher (1990: 188) believes that '*The Competitive Advantage of Nations* may become one of those articles that makes history, setting a new framework for an old problem'. Jelinek (1992) thinks that 'this research should have a profound and far-reaching impact on academic course work, managers' perceptions, and public policy as well'. Greenaway (1993: 146) states that it is an excellent complement to a more formal analysis of competitive and comparative advantage. Smith (1993: 404) believes that 'Porter's firm-oriented approach is an original contribution to the development theory. According to him, 'the alternative of simply applying an unalloyed paradigm of neo-classical analysis plus the assumption that government failure is always greater than market failure seems weak by comparison'. According to Gray (1991: 506), in addition to the valuable and rich material derived from the diamond framework, Porter's contribution is to stress the role of clusters and the dynamic and mutually reinforcing nature of the four determinants he defines. According to Dunning (1992: 137), Porter's 'extensive field research has advanced our knowledge of why corporations domiciled in some countries have been successful in penetrating foreign markets in some product areas but not in others, and also why some countries have been able to attract the participation of foreign owned firms in some value added activities but not in others'.

According to Grant (1991) 'the main contribution of *The Competitive Advantage of Nations* is in extending the theories of international trade and international direct investment to explain more effectively observed patterns of trade and investment between the developed countries' (Grant, 1991: 539). In terms of the contribution of the study to the theory of competitive strategy, Grant (1991: 543) believes that two points are noteworthy: 'First, Porter's integration of the theory of competitive strategy with the theory of international trade and comparative advantage extends the analysis of strategy formulation to an international environment. Second, Porter's emphasis upon innovation and 'upgrading' as central to the creation and sustaining of competitive advantage represents further steps towards the reformulation of the strategy model within a dynamic context'. One implication is that while determining the sources of competitive advantage and formulating strategy, it should be recognised that the resource base of a firm is not only determined by its own past investments but also by the conditions of resource supply and resource creation within its environment. Grant further states that shortcomings of the study are trivial when compared to its achievements: 'A single analytical framework provides a cogent explanation of competitive advantage within industries which range from chocolate to auctioneering, and among countries as different as Sweden and Singapore' (Grant, 1991: 548). Finally, he envisages that Porter's study encourages further research, both theoretical and empirical, about the role of national environments in determining international competitive advantage, and that process will probably result in 'a redefinition of the boundaries of strategic management and a lowering of the barriers which separate strategic management from economics' (Grant, 1991: 548).

2 The Competitive Advantage of Turkey

An Overview of the Setting

Historical Background

The period beginning from the foundation of the Republic in 1923 and ending in the early 1930s can be considered as relatively 'liberal' in Turkish economic history. The involvement of the state in economic activities was rather limited during these years, except for the establishment of certain state monopolies (Kepenek, 1987).

Like many countries in the world, Turkey was also seriously affected by the Great Depression, and began to emulate the relative success of the planned economies, which started a new period (1933-1945) in Turkish economic history called 'etatism', during which the government heavily intervened both in production and consumption of goods and services. In the post-World War II period, until 1960, some liberalisation attempts were made which were shaped by a new type of etatism where the government supported the private sector. It is, however, hard to say that these policies were successful, and the resulting disappointment, together with the parallel tendencies towards more intervention in the world, caused the military government of the early 1960s to introduce a development strategy favouring 'planning in a mixed economy', which would continue for the following two decades. During the planned period, there were impressive improvements both in the growth rate of overall output and in industrial production. However, the coincidence of an unfavourable economic environment in the world with an unstable political one in Turkey led the Turkish economy into a major crisis in the late 1970s, resulting in another military take-over in 1980 (Öniş, 1986).

In short, prior to the 1980s, Turkey mainly pursued an inward-oriented, protectionist, import-substituting development strategy, the origins of which can be traced back to the etatist period of the early 1930s. Starting from 1980, however, Turkey initiated a stabilisation programme under the auspices of IMF and the World Bank, known as the 'January 24 Resolutions' in Turkish economic history, introducing structural adjustment policies intended to shift the economy from an inward-looking to an outward-looking orientation, emphasising export-led growth (Kirkpatrick and Öniş, 1991). The Resolutions consisted of structural reforms in a number of key areas, one of which was trade policy with the introduction of extensive export promotion measures and gradual liberalisation of imports. The results were impressive in terms of exports in general and manufacturing exports in particular, despite the fact that the increase in exports was matched by a corresponding boom in imports. If we, for instance, compare the share of exports in GDP for the years 1978 and 1985, we see a considerable rise from 5.2 per cent to 20.6 per cent (Kumcu and Kumcu, 1991). Moreover, the composition of exports also changed with an apparent shift in favour of the manufactures. Total value of industrial exports grew at a rate of 20 per cent per year on average, marking a tenfold increase from 1980 to 1990. The proportion of industrial products in total exports reached 80 per cent by 1992 whereas it was as low as 30 per cent in 1980 (Pazarbaşıoğlu, 1995). The relative positions of Turkey's trade partners also changed in that Turkey was transformed, within a few years, from a country that exported agricultural products to Western Europe to a country that exported industrial products to the Middle East. Turkish exporters, as they gained experience, increased their industrial exports to the developed countries as well (Kumcu and Kumcu, 1991). Now, the most important markets for Turkish products are unquestionably the European Union countries, led by Germany which captures more than 20 per cent of total Turkish exports (The United Nations, 1995). We should, however, state that the performance as well as the impact of the programme, when areas other than exports are concerned, have been widely criticised by several scholars. Just to give a few examples, according to Öniş (1986), the results are not that satisfactory with respect to economic welfare indicators such as growth, employment and income distribution; the achieved growth rate is in fact lower than that of the planned period of the 1960s and 1970s, as emphasised by Boratav, Türel and Yeldan (1995); and the programme has slowed the industrialisation process in Turkey, according to Şenses (1993). Moreover, the existence of a military government ironically made easier the implementation of these otherwise politically difficult to confront policies.

The second half of the 1980s witnessed a considerable reduction in export subsidies. Meanwhile, tariffs and quotas, thus the level of import protection, were further reduced (Pazarbaşıoğlu, 1995). Finally, together with the unexpected but comprehensive financial liberalisation achieved by initiating the convertibility of the Turkish Lira in 1990, the main policies of the liberalisation process have been completed. The immediate result of these recent developments was the worsening trade deficit of Turkey in the late 1980s and 1990s, mainly stemming from the increase in imports rather than a decrease in exports which actually continued to increase gradually, Turkey's world export share remaining fairly stable. I would like to conclude this historical summary by mentioning the very recent phenomenon of a customs union between Turkey and the EU that has been in effect since January 1996, and is likely to bring both challenges and opportunities for Turkish industry. The long-run effects of the union, of course, are not yet clear[1].

Current Environment

Turkey is accepted as a lower-middle-income developing country in the World Bank classifications. Although it is not a member, it has close ties with the EU, the last example of which is the above mentioned customs union agreement. Turkey has a very advantageous geographical position, constituting a natural link between the West and East, and recently, it has started to make greater use of this, especially in trade and tourism.

The adult illiteracy rate in Turkey is around 18 per cent, lower than many other countries which are included amongst the lower-middle-income economies category, but only one fifth of the literate group in Turkey has a high school degree (The World Bank, 1996). Labour force participation rates in education, on the other hand, are quite high and compare well even to those of the other OECD countries. When we examine the university degrees by subject, we see that Turkey's position is relatively good in terms of engineering, architecture and human sciences, whereas it is rather weak in natural and physical sciences (OECD, 1995b). The relatively poor position of the research and development activity in Turkey, which has shown a slight revival in recent years, has definitely some relation with the latter (OECD, 1995c). The enrolment rates in education across all disciplines, however, have been increasing in recent years, as Turkey's population has become younger.

The overall annual growth rate of the population, on the other hand, though decreasing slightly during the 1990s, averages around 2 per cent, which is still very high as compared to the corresponding figure of 1.4 per cent for the lower-middle-income developing countries. This increase in population comes with the increasing rate of urbanisation. In fact, the urban population in Turkey grows at an annual rate of 4 per cent, amongst the highest attained by the lower-middle-income developing countries. As a result, almost 70 per cent out of Turkey's population of about 62 million now live in cities (The World Bank, 1996). Creating job opportunities for a

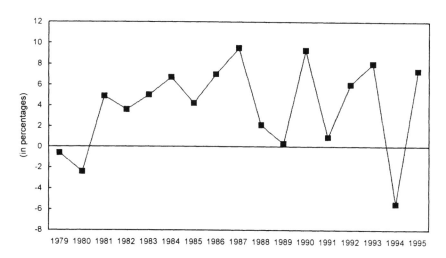

Figure 2.1 Percentage Increase in Real GDP of Turkey (1979-1995)
Source: *Economic Outlook*, OECD, 1996

population growing so rapidly is not so easy, and Turkey has had difficulty in doing so. In fact, given Turkey's economic situation, an average unemployment rate of 8.2 per cent for the period 1960-94 seems reasonable (OECD, 1996a). However, it should be observed that around 45 per cent of the labour force is employed in agriculture, and 40 per cent is in services, whereas the related figure for the industry is only 15 per cent (DIE, 1994a), and the high employment figure for the agricultural sector is quite likely to include considerable hidden unemployment (EIU, 1994).

Turkey's standard of living, as measured by GNP per capita, is typical for a lower-middle-income developing country, and has increased gradually with an annual growth rate of 1.4 per cent between 1985-94 to reach $2,670 in 1995 (The World Bank, 1996). The average annual growth rate of the Turkish economy, as measured by the rate of growth of real GDP, on the other hand, averaged of around 4 per cent in the post-liberalisation era (OECD, 1996a). This rate, though fluctuating widely (see Figure 2.1), is above the average attained by the middle-income countries (around 2-3 per cent) during the same period (The World Bank, 1996). Although both the overall domestic production and per capita income have been increasing at above average rates as compared to the other lower-middle-income developing countries, the inequalities in income distribution are significant and worsening both across the geographical regions, and between urban and rural areas.

Persistent high inflation rate, which accelerated in the late 1970s and became chronic after the liberalisation, is another characteristic of the Turkish economy. In fact, when we examine the post-liberalisation trend of the inflation rate in Turkey, we see a pattern such that it settles down around a plateau for a couple of years, and, then, jumps into a new plateau following an economic recession. Currently, the rate seems to have levelled off at around 80 per cent, rather high compared to many countries, which is evident from the fact that the OECD prefers to present an additional average for all OECD countries excluding Turkey, since it definitely constitutes an outlier as far as the inflation rate is concerned. Needless to say, it follows that interest rates are also high, blocking many of the otherwise quite likely investments.

I have mentioned the key developments in the foreign trade situation in the previous section. To avoid repetition, I prefer to focus here on another related issue; namely, on the trade and current account balances of Turkey, from an examination of which we infer that Turkey has a persistent trade deficit which has worsened in the 1990s, whereas the current account is more or less balanced. At a first glance, it is difficult to explain this situation, but it becomes more clear once Turkey's foreign exchange earnings from the highly competitive tourism sector and from workers' remittances which are amongst the highest of all middle-income countries (Turkey has around 2 million workers just in Germany) are considered, together with the Turkey's 'grey' economy which has been anticipated likely to reach 10-50 per cent of GDP.

The Republic of Turkey was established as an indebted country in that, according to the Lausanne Treatment, it had to pay about two thirds of the Ottoman debts. Now, external debts, which accelerated in the 1950s and increased even further later in the 1970s, amount to $74 billion, corresponding to almost half of GNP (The World Bank, 1997). What is even more worrying, however, is that the country services its debts by borrowing more, hence inducing a vicious circle, which led the economy into a number of severe crises, the last one being in 1994. In fact, this is often considered as one of the basic obstacles that prevents macroeconomic stability in Turkey. Relatedly, Turkey's record on tax collection is not particularly good, reducing tax revenues (The World Bank, 1996).

In short, the macro-economic situation in Turkey looks rather bleak. The above mentioned structural problems of the economy are further complicated by the continuous political uncertainty which has been worsened by the recent phenomenon of successive weak coalition governments. Such an environment obviously creates serious obstacles preventing firms from improving their international competitiveness further. Given this picture, it is also not surprising that Turkey has failed to attract much FDI, which as a result is not comparable to the level achieved in some other emerging markets like Mexico and China. FDI outflows by Turkey, on the other hand, are increasing, but still negligible (OECD, 1994; The United Nations, 1984).

The last issue I would like to address with regard to the context in which business activity takes place in Turkey concerns the nature of the state and business as well as their relations with each other[2]. The first thing that should be stated in this respect is, of course, the high degree of state involvement in business activity in Turkey, whether it is in the form of subsidised credits, input supply or output demand. Given such a high degree of government involvement in the economy, good connections in government circles contribute significantly to business success. The uncertainty and instability in government behaviour, arbitrary use of the legal system by the ruling politicians, incompetent public sector management and unexpected changes in key policies are further problems (Buğra, 1994).

An examination of the broad characteristics of the business environment in Turkey reveals a domination by the small and medium enterprises, whereas big businesses are rather a recent phenomenon. The family-dominated nature of the management, no matter how big or diversified the firms are, is another distinguishing feature of Turkish firms. Their other related characteristics include the lack of commitment to a particular industry and popularity of diversification to hedge the risks prevailing in the environment, a commercial rather than industrial outlook and rent-seeking behaviour which discourage investments, a rather hierarchical structure, and reliance on personal trust rather than professionalisation. However, we should also mention the fact that Turkish businessmen are, on average, a well-educated group that attributes high value to education, and their level of education is superior to that of most politicians and bureaucrats (Buğra, 1994).

Literature on Industry Competitiveness in Turkey

Before starting a review of literature on industry competitiveness in Turkey, we should state that since Porter's (1990a) diamond framework touches a wide range of disciplines, an attempt to provide a complete review of the relevant intellectual history is simply not realistic[3]. This section, therefore, should be considered as giving a broad picture of the relevant literature for Turkey, focusing on the major lines of thinking and the most outstanding results.

The first thing such a review for Turkey reveals is the fact that some studies treat the issue of competitiveness at the national level. Two typical examples are the World Competitiveness Report (IMD and The World Economic Forum, 1997) which includes Turkey as well, and the TISK study (1995) which is the application of the framework conducted by the UNICE (Union of Industrial and Employers' Confederations of Europe) for the case of Turkey. These two pieces of work are, in fact, very similar to each other in that they share a common approach which sees competitiveness of a nation as determined by a combination of national-level factors, but does not offer an explicit explanation to integrate them.

The World Competitiveness Report presents a ranking of national competitiveness of 46 countries according to their scores on a set of variables which are derived from a group of statistical indicators and the perceptions of business executives on the competitiveness of their countries drawn from an annual survey. The variables which the Report views as the determinants of competitiveness are domestic economic strength, availability and qualifications of human resources, scientific and technological capacity, attributes of management, existence and quality of country infrastructure, performance of capital markets, nature of government policies, and extent of internationalisation. The average values for the recent years (1993-1997) place Turkey as the 35th amongst the 46 countries included in the ranking. According to these averages, Turkey's position is relatively better with regard to finance, internationalisation, government and infrastructure; weaker in terms of domestic economy and management; and the weakest as far as science and technology, and human resources are concerned (IMD and The World Economic Forum, 1997).

The TISK study (1995) assesses the competitiveness of Turkey by utilising a similar list of attributes. The main categories included are productivity, cost of production, profitability, domestic market characteristics, public sector characteristics and macroeconomic policies. The major conclusions reached for Turkey are as follows. The cost of capital is high, and the cost of labour has been increasing since 1989. The overall productivity rate and technological level attained are both relatively low. The entrepreneurial variables are very favourable; in fact, with regard to them, the country has been ranked as fifth amongst 22 OECD countries.

The government variables are very negative in Turkey; the prevailing macroeconomic instability, which is further driven by the inconsistent monetary policies and huge public spending, being the most important drawback.

There have been, however, ongoing discussions in the academic literature concerning the highly diverse uses of the word 'competitiveness', especially concentrating on the question of whether it can be used at the national level[4]. It is, in fact, not at all clear what is meant by the 'competitiveness' of a nation. When applied to a national economy, it usually implies the relative standard of living achieved by that nation, which is related to the relative level of development and economic growth of a country, each being the subjects of a vast literature. Furthermore, since any nation is relatively more successful in some industries and relatively less successful in others, it is inappropriate to ask what an internationally competitive nation is. A good example may be the case of Japan, which is widely regarded as a 'competitive nation', but, in fact, not so placed in such industries as defence, food and beverages, consumer packaged goods, health care or many service industries (Porter, 1990a: 405-6). This reveals a common misinterpretation of Porter's work, who also believes that we must abandon the whole notion of a 'competitive nation' (Porter, 1990a: 6).

Other noteworthy relevant literature includes studies investigating the firm-level determinants of export performance[5]. These studies usually control the industry-specific variables, and concentrate on the firm-specific, usually marketing-related ones, that are believed to determine international competitiveness. Since the unit of analysis in this study is industry, however, the rest of this section will focus on the studies of industry competitiveness, which include, or are particularly conducted about, Turkey. To make the picture clear, I will follow the diamond elements, and try to relate the relevant literature to the framework. An examination of the literature, however, reveals that most of the work concentrates upon two determinants in the Turkish case; namely, factor conditions and the role of government, which, therefore, will be given more emphasis in this section.

Factor Conditions

Most of the studies addressing different aspects of the issue under the broad heading of 'international trade' can be associated with the factor conditions category of the diamond framework[6]. The findings of this literature, with regard to the competitive structure of Turkish industry, seem to converge on the fact that Turkey exports labour-intensive products, and imports capital-intensive ones, reflecting its relative factor endowments. The relative resource position of Turkey is strongest in semi and unskilled labour, weaker in highly-skilled labour, and the weakest in physical capital. As a result, we see a highly concentrated competitive structure in a handful of labour-intensive industries, particularly in food, and textiles and clothing.

As an example, we can take a closer look at the work of Leamer (1984), which among other nations includes Turkey as well and is considered to be one of the most influential empirical studies in this literature. By using one of the least aggregated factor definitions, he calculates resource abundance profiles for the countries included and compares their sources of comparative advantage for the years 1958 and 1975. Accordingly, reflecting its resource profile, Turkey, which was not very trade-dependent during these years, exported raw materials and agricultural products in 1958, and some labour-intensive manufactures in 1975.

For more recent studies revealing the Turkish competitiveness, we can take Togan's (1996) study as an example. To discriminate the competitive Turkish industries, he employs two indicators: domestic resource cost and revealed comparative advantage. Confirming the findings of previous literature, he concludes that Turkey has a comparative advantage in the production of the following sectors: agriculture, iron ore mining, vegetable and animal oils and fats, other food processing, clothing, leather and fur products, footwear, fertilisers, pharmaceutical products, other chemical products, petroleum refinery, iron and steel, non-ferrous metals, non-electrical machinery, and agricultural machinery.

The Role of Government

Another major line of thinking in the literature concerns the role of government and the effects of factors like exchange rates and subsidies on the competitive performance of Turkish industry. Comparing the competitive structure of the Turkish economy before and after the liberalisation process of the early 1980s has been a particularly prevalent focus of attention for many, which is, in fact, not surprising, given that this experience provides a unique experimental setting to conduct such investigations. One example is the study of Temel et al. (1995), who, amongst other things, examined the effects of exchange rates and subsidies post 1980 on the export boom in Turkey, and concluded that these effects are significant and positive. According to another study conducted by Temel (1990), the exchange rate advantage is more effective for the industries that are new in the export markets, like intermediate and investment goods, as compared to more traditional Turkish export sectors.

Kazgan, Tuncer and Kırmanoğlu (1990), on the other hand, who study the period 1980-88, find out that shifts in the exchange rate affect the leather, chemicals, food and beverages industries most, whereas the textiles/apparel, rubber and plastic, glass, paper, metal, electrical and other machinery, and automotive industries are most sensitive to tax rebates. Lastly, exports of stone and grave products derive outstanding benefits from the increase in capacity utilisation associated with the rise in exports.

Other studies reach distinct conclusions, depending on the time period, the variables included, and the type of model employed in the analysis. The general tendency is supportive of the hypothesis that government policy has been effective in the export boom experienced after liberalisation. What kind of support has been the most influential in increasing exports of specific industries is, however, rather unclear.

Other Studies

Studies linking the domestic demand conditions and international competitiveness are relatively rare for Turkey. One related recent example that includes six countries one of which is Turkey is the work of Gagnon and Rose (1995) who try to quantify the overall importance of product cycle phenomena in international trade. They conclude that, for a majority of the goods, the trade data show a striking absence of the dynamics, as product life cycle theory predicts on trade flows. The Turkish data also support this result in that most of the goods that were net exports (imports) in the early 1960s were still net exports (imports) in the late 1980s.

The literature regarding the clustering of industries in general, and geographic concentration in particular in Turkey usually concentrates on urban economics and local economic development in certain provinces, or on the general spatial distribution of economic activity[7]. The findings of the studies investigating geographical concentration of industries point to the existence of the clustering of industrial activity. Üser (1984), for instance, by using several different indices of geographic concentration, finds evidence for significant agglomeration of the majority of the Turkish industries. Specifically, many key sectors of the Turkish economy like iron and steel, textiles and clothing, non-ferrous metals, paper and publishing, and chemicals have been found to be highly concentrated geographically.

One popular area that can be associated with the determinant 'firm strategy, structure and rivalry' has been the relationship between market structure and international trade in the structure-conduct-performance tradition. Tests have been made of the imports-as-market-discipline hypothesis. Levinsohn (1993), for instance, finds support for the hypothesis deriving from a study of 11 industries in the greater İstanbul region. Katırcıoğlu, Engin, and Akçay (1995) conduct a very similar study to that of Levinsohn's, and try to understand the impact of increased import penetration on industries with higher than average concentration ratios. Their results are also supportive of the imports-as-market-discipline hypothesis, as are those of Foroutan (1991) and Gökçekuş (1995). Erlat (1993), on the other hand, seeks a relationship between industrial concentration and exports, and finds out that there is evidence indicating a positive relation. Another contribution that can be considered under this determinant comes from Oral (1986), who develops a model measuring industrial competitiveness by incorporating the potential, current and comparative positions of the individual firms in an industry. In a later field study, Oral and Özkan (1986) apply the model to the Turkish food, textiles and glass industries, and conclude that the competitive positions of the Turkish firms in these industries are quite satisfactory.

Apart from the studies that can be related to the individual diamond elements as summarised above, there are other relevant areas of interest that should be included in this review. Some, for instance, consider the international competitiveness of individual industries[8]. Some are, on the other hand, interested in the competitive position of Turkey in relation to specific trade partners such as the EU[9].

The above summary of the relevant literature reveals that although the area has been the subject of numerous studies, they usually focus on the factor conditions and the role of government as the major determinants of competitive advantage. There is, in other words, an obvious need for more attention to new approaches like that of Porter (1990a). This study, therefore, in addition to contributing towards the improvement of the diamond framework, will serve to fill this gap.

The Competitive Structure of Turkish Industry

Methodology

Figure 2.2, which is an improved version of the schema prepared by Cartwright (1993: 57) deriving from Porter's New Zealand study, depicts the main steps used in Porter's methodology. Accordingly, statistical data,

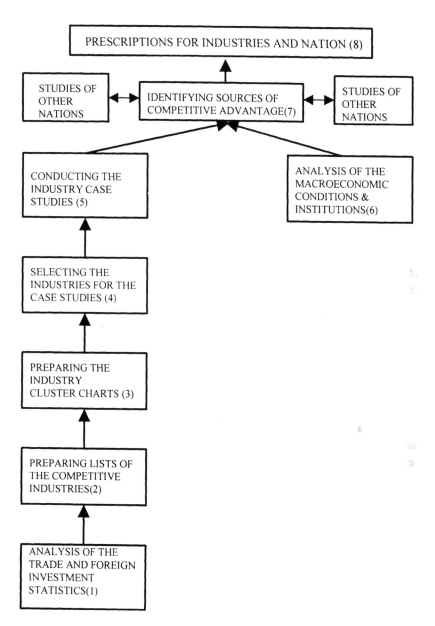

Figure 2.2 Methodological Process in *The Competitive Advantage of Nations*

Source: Cartwright, *Management International Review*, 1993

mainly the United Nations international trade statistics, are used to identify the internationally competitive industries of each nation. The basic measure of international competitiveness employed is the world export shares of the industries, which is defined as a country's exports in an industry divided by the total world exports in that particular industry at a given year. As a second step, all 3-digit, 4-digit and 5-digit industries defined in the Standard International Trade Classification (SITC), at the lowest possible level of disaggregation, are sorted by world export share. Then, the cut-off rate is calculated by dividing the total exports of a country by the total world exports. The industries that have world export shares above the cut-off rate constitute the initial list of the relatively more competitive industries of the nation. Next, the ones that have a world export share between the cut-off rate and twice its value, are checked to exclude the industries with a negative trade balance. In the following step, industries are sorted by country export share, which is defined as the share of an industry in the country's total exports. The industries that are among the top fifty in terms of their country export share but below the cut-off rate in terms of theirworld export share are included in the relatively more competitive industries list, provided that they have a positive trade balance. If the nation's firms have considerable foreign direct investment in an industry, this industry is also included in the list, while the industries dominated by foreign firms are excluded. Finally, with the addition of the internationally competitive service sectors, the preparation of the list of the relatively more competitive industries is completed for that particular year and country.

After preparing the lists of the internationally competitive industries as described above for the years 1971, 1978 and 1985, Porter uses a cluster chart to figure out the connections and interrelationships amongst the nation's competitive industries. The chart has three broad groupings each of which themselves include different clusters. The first group in the chart is called 'Upstream Industries' and its primary products are inputs to products of many other industries. The clusters included in this category are semiconductors/computers, materials/metals, petroleum/chemicals and forest products. 'Industrial and Supporting Functions', the second group, on the other hand, consists of the clusters of multiple business, transportation, power generation and distribution, office, telecommunications, and defence. The final category includes sectors related mostly to 'Final Consumption Goods and Services', and contains the food/beverage, textiles/apparel, housing/household, health care, personal, and entertainment/leisure clusters. The industries in each cluster are further classified into four groups, revealing the vertical relationships among industries as well as the depth of national clusters. These four groups are: the 'primary goods' themselves, the 'machinery' used to produce them, the 'specialty inputs' required, and the related 'service industries'. Porter uses this clustering of industries to prepare charts for all the nations studied showing the pattern of changes in world export share and country export share by cluster and vertical stage. The latter presents further information about how deep a country's clusters are as well as how changes have occurred over time among these vertical stages (see, for instance, Table 2.3 in the next section).

Having identified the successful industries, connections amongst them and changes in the pattern of competitiveness, he tries to find out the sources of advantage by examining over one-hundred industry cases. While conducting the industry case studies, he looks at the main characteristics and history of the industry 'to understand how and why the industry began in the nation, how it grew, when and why firms from the nation developed international competitive advantage, and the processes by which competitive advantage had either been sustained or lost' (Porter, 1990a: 28). The methods used to perform this analysis include the examination of secondary data, and field interviews with executives, government officials and the other industry experts. From each nation five-to-ten industries are selected for detailed case study, and each of which is chosen to be representative of the most important clusters in the economy. He mentions that he tried to avoid industries that were highly dependent on natural resources since capacity to compete in such industries can be mostly explained by classical theory. Overwhelmingly, he studied competitive industries. In other words, the analysis excludes the relatively less competitive industries. Porter justifies his focus on the successful cases by stating that the large sample of industries studied globally in the original ten nation study also exposed many of each nation's failures since recent developments in the world -thus failures as well as successes- have been given considerable attention in each industry study (Porter and The Monitor Company, 1991). Another possible explanation relates to Porter's broad purpose of trying to capture the competitive structure of a country. Having defined the objective like this, one may probably concentrate on the successful ones since these constitute the basis of the industrial structure in an open economy. Following this rationale, it is not surprising that, to achieve maximum coverage, he deliberately includes some failures in the Canadian study (Porter and The Monitor Company, 1991). Since my emphasis is on trying to understand if the diamond framework is successful in explaining the sources of advantage and disadvantage, the following analysis will include one relatively less competitive sector study, the Turkish automobile industry (further discussion of this issue and other weaknesses of the methodology can be found in Chapter 1).

Although it is undeniable that there are some methodological weaknesses, Porter's study stands up to most of the criticisms. The scholars who criticise Porter's heavy dependence on world export shares as a measure of international competitiveness fail to offer a better alternative measure. One likely measure, profitability, is not so easily comparable among industries in different nations due to various reasons such as diverse accounting practices. Moreover, using profitability as a measure of competitiveness can be misleading since an industry may be protected from foreign competition. Outward foreign direct investment is another frequently stated possibility. However, it does not necessarily reflect the competitiveness of the industry. It may be motivated, for instance, by foreign import restrictions. Furthermore, comparable data on foreign direct investment at a reasonably disaggregated level, at which the real competition takes place, is not available for many countries. In short, compared to such alternatives, Porter's measure is a better indicator of competitive advantage, and the detailed comparable statistics are usually available; although the possibility of overestimation due to subsidies remains. We should repeat here that subjective criteria can, according to Porter (1990a), also be used, allowing the inclusion of competitive industries for which regular trade data are not available, as it is the case for services. I have done this for the Turkish construction industry (for the reasons see Chapter 4). The Turkish flat steel industry which has a negative trade balance mainly due to high domestic demand has also been considered a competitive industry (for the reasons see Chapter 7).

The following pages will present the application of Porter's methodology to Turkey. In addition to the years Porter studies (1971, 1978 and 1985), I include 1992, the latest date the UN data was available at the required detail. The competitive Turkish industries have been identified according to the criteria defined above, and the resulting analysis will be presented in the next section. The chapter will end with a discussion of the criteria used to choose the five industry studies.

Industrial Clusters in Turkey

Table 2.1 shows Turkey's fifty leading industries in terms of their world export shares. They predominate in industries from two major clusters of the Turkish economy, namely food/beverages and textiles/apparel. The

Table 2.1 Top Fifty Turkish Industries in Terms of World Export Share, 1992

INDUSTRY	SHARE OF TOTAL WORLD EXPORTS (%)
Grapes, dried	18,02
Tobacco, not stripped	17,11
Carpets, of other textile materials	14,52
Iron, other steel bars	14,23
Edible nuts, fresh or dried	10,82
Chromium ores & concentrates	10,65
Sunflower seed oil	9,05
Iron, simple steel blooms	8,79
Leguminous vegetables, dry	8,75
Margarine and shortening	8,26
Carpets, carpeting, rugs etc.,other than tufted	8,23
Women's dresses, knitted	8,00
Leather clothes, accessories	7,45
Iron, simple steel hoop,	6,91
Under garments, of cotton, nonelastic	6,78
Other outer garments and clothing accessories	6,25
Lemons, grapefruit	6,24
Flour of wheat or of meslin	5,77
Cotton seed oil	5,13
Iron, simple steel wire rod	5,06
Discontinuous synthetic fibres, blend yarn	4,91
Carpets, of wool or fine hair	4,65
Articles of furskin	4,59
Other crude minerals, exc. clay	4,34
Cement	4,14
Groats, meal and pellets, of wheat	3,91
Potatoes, fresh, exc. sweet ones	3,66
Made-up articles, exc. linen	3,51
Linens	3,46
Clothing accessories, knitted	3,32
Jerseys, pull-overs	3,30
Suits, women's & infants', of textile fabrics	3,20
Sinks, wash basins, bidets	3,16
Cotton linters, waste & cotton, carded or combed	3,14
Guts, bladders etc., nonfish	3,11
Mandarins, clementines etc., fresh or dried	3,02
Glass surface-ground	2,92
Soap, cleansing & polishing prep., exc.washing prep.	2,77
Vegetables, prepared, preserved	2,65
Household and hotel glass	2,64
Synthetic fibres, other than carded or combed	2,63
Refined sugar	2,62
Spices	2,62
Men's shirts, of cotton	2,51
Liquid dielectric transformers	2,39
Iron, steel cable, rope etc.	2,38
Man-made pile etc. fabric	2,34
Fruit, preserved and fruit prep., exc. fruit juices	2,23
Other wheat and meslin, unmilled	2,21
Yarn, of continuous polyamide fibres, nontextured	2,12
SHARE OF TOTAL TURKISH EXPORTS	

Source: UN International Trade Statistics Yearbook, 1993.

remaining industries are either in the materials/metals or housing/household categories, the other two relatively strong Turkish clusters. Turkey's top fifty industries accounted for 54.4 per cent of total Turkish exports in 1992, which is rather high. In fact, when we compare the related 1985 figure for Turkey, which is 56.4 per cent, with the corresponding values for the other nations studied in the original Porter study for the same year, we see that it is higher than any, and nearest to that of South Korea (52 per cent), the only developing country presented in the book. Furthermore, compared to other nations, the range of top fifty Turkish industries is relatively narrow.

At a first glance, the 1992 cluster chart presented in Table 2.2 shows that Turkish competitiveness is linked to four major clusters: textiles/apparel, food/beverages, materials/metals, and housing/household. Another striking feature is the negligible presence in the machinery category of many clusters. Instead, Turkish advantage seems to be concentrated in the 'primary goods' category and to a lesser degree in specialty inputs. The chart also reveals that Turkey has virtually no position in five clusters, namely, semiconductors/computers, health care, office, telecommunications, and defence.

If we take a closer look at the leading clusters, we see that Turkey's position is especially strong in textiles/apparel. Its market share in 1992 in that cluster is 1.5 per cent, almost four times more than the average Turkish world export share of 0.41 per cent. The cluster accounts for almost 40 per cent of the total

Turkish exports, most of which are concentrated in the primary goods category, with a world cluster share of 2 per cent. Turkish positions in outergarments and leather clothes are particularly strong; for instance, Turkey captures 8 per cent of the total world exports in knitted dresses and skirts, and 7.45 per cent in leather clothes and accessories. If we put the machinery industries related to textiles aside, the breadth and depth of the Turkish textiles/apparel cluster is impressive. Turkey exports a great variety of items in almost all categories included in this cluster, which are almost exclusively products of competitive industries. A few exceptions are found in the specialty inputs category, especially in segments like raw hides and skins, which are largely domestically consumed by the highly competitive Turkish leather clothes industry. Lastly, we should also mention that, although it has always been the most important cluster in the Turkish economy, in terms of world market share, the textiles/apparel cluster has improved remarkably after the liberalisation (see Appendix A1 for the cluster charts of 1971, 1978, and 1985).

Table 2.2 Clusters of Internationally Competitive Turkish Industries, 1992

Primary goods	**MATERIALS/METALS**
	IRON AND STEEL
	Iron, other steel bars
	Puddled bars and pillings, of iron or steel*
	Iron, simple steel blooms
	Iron, simple steel hoop, strip
	Iron, simple steel wire rod
	Angles, shapes and sections of iron and steel*
	Pig iron, spiegeleisen etc.
	Ferro-silicon and other ferro-alloys*
	Iron, simple steel coils
	Iron, simple steel wire
	Blooms, billets etc., of high carbon etc. steel*
	Flat-steel products#
	FABRICATED IRON AND STEEL
	Iron, steel cable, rope etc.
	Other iron, steel tubes or pipes
	METAL MANUFACTURES
	Nails, screws etc., of iron, steel or copper, exc. bolts and nuts*
	Steel storage tanks
	NONFERROUS METALS
	Chromium ores and concentrates
	Other crude minerals, exc. clay*
	Unrefined copper
	Copper bars, wire
	Stranded wire, cables etc., of copper or aluminium*
	Aluminium bars, wire etc.
	OTHER MATERIALS AND WASTE
	Natural abrasives
	Precious metal ores, waste
Machinery	
Specialty inputs	
Services	

Primary goods	**FOREST PRODUCTS**
Machinery	
Specialty inputs	
Services	

Table 2.2 (continued)

Primary goods	**PETROLEUM/CHEMICALS** PETROLEUM PRODUCTS *Fuel oils* INORGANIC *Other inorganic chemicals** POLYMERS Unhard rubber tubes Alkyds in primary forms
Machinery	
Specialty inputs	
Service	

Primary goods	**SEMICONDUCTORS/COMPUTERS**
Machinery	
Specialty inputs	
Services	

Primary goods	**MULTIPLE BUSINESS**
Machinery	
Specialty inputs	
Services	**Construction/Engineering#**

Primary goods	**TRANSPORTATION** *Buses* *Other cargo vessels*
Machinery	
Specialty inputs	*Tyres new for buses and lorries* Tyres new for motor cars
Services	**Shipping#**

Primary goods	**OFFICE**
Machinery	
Specialty inputs	
Services	

Table 2.2 (continued)

Primary goods	**POWER GENERATION AND DISTRIBUTION** **Liquid, dialectic transformers** *Insulated wire, cable, bars etc.*
Machinery	
Specialty inputs	
Services	

Primary goods	**TELECOMMUNICATIONS**
Machinery	
Specialty inputs	
Services	

Primary goods	**HOUSING/HOUSEHOLD** FURNISHINGS **Carpets etc., of other textile materials*** **Carpets, carpeting, rugs etc., other than tufted*** **Carpets, of wool or fine hair** **Floor coverings, exc. knotted carpets etc.*** GLASS, CERAMICS AND STONE PRODUCTS **Sinks, wash basins, bidets etc.*** **Household and hotel glass** *Glazed ceramic sets* *Building stone etc., worked* PACKAGED GOODS **Soap, cleansing and polishing preparations, exc. washing preparations*** HOUSEHOLD EQUIPMENT *Household equipment of base metal, exc. domestic type** *Domestic refrigerators* Domestic heating and cooking apparatus Central heating equipment Lighting fixtures, exc. lamps and lighting fittings*
Machinery	
Specialty inputs	**Cement** **Glass surface, ground** Lime, cement etc., exc. Portland cement*
Services	

Table 2.2 (continued)

| Primary goods | **FOOD/BEVERAGES**
BASIC FOODS
Edible nuts, fresh or dried
Guts, bladders etc., nonfish
Spices
Flour of wheat or meslin
Live animals for food
Mutton etc., fresh, chilled or frozen
Stone fruit, fresh
Malt, including flour
FRUITS AND VEGETABLES
Grapes, dried*
Leguminous vegetables, dry
Lemons, grapefruit etc.
Potatoes, fresh, exc. Sweet
Mandarins, clementines etc., fresh or dried*
Figs and other fruit, fresh or dried*
Other vegetables*
Apples, fresh
Tomatoes, fresh
Oranges, fresh or dried
PROCESSED FOOD
Fruit, preserved exc. fruit juices*
Refined sugar
Margarine and shortening
Vegetables, prepared, preserved
Pastry, cakes etc.
Fruit juices, exc. Orange juice*
Sugar candy, nonchoclate
Chocolate and products
Other edible products and preparations**
Shell fish, prepared, preserved
EDIBLE OILS
Sunflower seed oil
Other fixed vegetable oils, exc. coconut oil*
Cotton seed oil
Olive oil
Processed animal and vegetable oils and fats |
| Machinery | |

Table 2.2 (continued)

Specialty inputs	**Groats, meal and pellets of wheat*** **Other wheat and meslin, unmilled** **Barley, unmilled** *Seeds for other fixed oils* *Insecticides* *Glass bottles* Durum wheat, unmilled
Services	

Primary goods	**DEFENSE**
Machinery	
Specialty inputs	
Services	

Primary goods	**HEALTH CARE**
Machinery	
Specialty inputs	
Services	

Primary goods	**PERSONAL**
Machinery	
Specialty inputs	**Tobacco, not stripped** Essential oils, resinoids
Services	

Primary goods	**ENTERTAINMENT/LEISURE** *Colour TV receivers* Zoo animals, pets etc. Sound recording tape, discs**
Machinery	
Specialty inputs	
Services	**Tourism#**

Table 2.2 (continued)

Primary goods	**TEXTILES/APPAREL**
	FABRICS
	Made-up articles, exc. linens etc.*
	Linens, etc.
	Man-made pile etc. fabric
	Pile etc. cotton fabrics
	Grey woven cotton fabric
	Continuous regenerated weaves nonpile
	*Fabrics, woven, of wool or fine hair, combed**
	Knitted etc. fabrics
	*Special textile fabrics**
	*Cotton fabrics, woven, finished, exc. pile fabrics**
	*Fabrics, woven, of man-made fibres, discontinuous**
	Tulle, lace, ribbons etc.
	APPAREL
	Women's dresses etc., knitted
	Under garments, knitted, of cotton, nonelastic
	Other outer garments*
	Articles of furskin
	Jerseys, pull-overs etc., knitted
	Women's suits, of textile fabrics*
	Men's overcoats and other outer garments*
	Undergarments, of textile fabrics, exc. men's shirts*
	Women's blouses
	Men's shirts, of cotton
	Women's dresses, other than knitted
	Skirts
	Women's coats and jackets
	*Under garments, knitted, other than of cotton**
	Men's trousers
	Men's shirts, of synthetic fibres
	Men's suits
	Men's jackets, blazers etc.
	Women's outer garments of man-made fibres
	ACCESSORIES
	Leather clothes, accessories
	Clothing accessories knitted
	Clothing accessories of textile fabrics*
	LUGGAGE
	Handbags
	FOOTWEAR
	Footwear, rubber, plastic
	Footwear, of leather**
Machinery	

Table 2.2 (continued)

| Specialty Inputs | FIBRES AND YARNS
Discontinuous synthetic fibres, blend yarn
Cotton yarn
Cotton; linters, waste; carded or combed*
Synthetic fibres, other than carded or combed*
Yarn of continuous polyamide fibres, nontextured
Synthetic yarn*
Silk yarn, yarn of regenerated fibres etc.*
Yarn of continuous polyamide fibres, textured
Waste of textile fabrics
Raw cotton, exc. Linters
OTHER
Other dyes and tanning products |
| Services | |

KEY

TimesNR	0.41 per cent world export share or higher, but less than 0.82 per cent share
Italics	*0.82 per cent world export share or higher, but less than 1.64 per cent share*
Bold	**1.64 per cent world export share or above**
*	Calculated residuals
**	Added due to high country export share
#	Added based on in-country research

Exports in the food/beverages cluster capture 0.8 per cent of the world total, twice as much Turkey's average world export share, constituting almost 20 per cent of total Turkish exports. The structure of this cluster resembles that of the textiles/apparel cluster. There are no agriculture-related machinery segments in which Turkey is competitive. If we put the machine category aside, however, the cluster has considerable depth since it includes industries with strong positions in basic and processed food, oils and specialty inputs. Again almost all (99 per cent) of Turkey's exports in this cluster are in industries with above average world export shares. Exceptions are often either climate (like in the cases of coffee and cocoa), or demand (like in the case of pork) related.

These two major clusters are followed by the materials/metals cluster, which has a world cluster share of 0.5 per cent and represents around 12 per cent of total Turkish exports. Competitive industries in this cluster are exclusively concentrated in primary goods with virtually no presence in machinery and specialty inputs. Moreover, within the primary goods category, we see a further concentration on the simple 'long products' of iron and steel. The housing/household cluster has the same world cluster share as the materials/metals cluster (0.5 per cent), while its share of total Turkish exports is less at around 6 per cent. However, it exhibits a healthier structure as compared to the materials/metals cluster in that we see a greater variety of processed products as well as some, though few, positions in specialty inputs. In this cluster, Turkey's position in carpets, reflecting a well-established tradition and constituting around 15 per cent of world exports, is particularly spectacular. Important positions in glass and cement products are also noteworthy.

There are also some isolated successes in other clusters. The special cases of 'unmanufactured tobacco' and 'tourism' are worth mentioning in this respect. Although the personal cluster, in which 'unmanufactured tobacco' is placed, seems to have a considerable world cluster share, it would be wrong to consider it as one of the important clusters of the Turkish economy since this figure mainly results from one single item, unmanufactured tobacco, which had a world export share of 17.11 per cent in 1992. Although Turkey is undoubtedly among the major exporters of unmanufactured tobacco, this only important item in the cluster can be considered as highly dependant on natural resources. Given these two facts, I believe it gives the wrong impression to say that one of the biggest clusters of the Turkish economy is the personal cluster. It may be more appropriate to consider 'unmanufactured tobacco' as what Porter calls 'an isolated industry', meaning that it is competitive despite the fact that the nation has few or no positions in the world market as far as the other industries of the same cluster are concerned. The highly competitive Turkish tourism industry constitutes another isolated case. This service industry holds a rather lonely position in the entertainment/leisure cluster, only accompanied by a few industries. Turkey's strong position in tourism is unquestionable, although comparable services statistics are still limited (OECD, 1995a; GATT, 1986). The success of the Turkish tourism industry is apparently very much linked to the country's favourable geographic position, climate and historical attractions as well as to the competitive food/beverages cluster. Such locational advantages may also help us explain another internationally competitive but isolated Turkish industry: shipping. Lastly, the position of the highly competitive Turkish construction industry, one of the case studies presented in this study, in the rather empty multiple business cluster will be discussed in Chapter 4.

Having given a picture of the competitive structure of Turkish industry, we can proceed to study its evolution over time. Here, I prefer to compare 1978 and 1985, since this period enables us to see the effects of the trade

Table 2.3 Percentage of Turkish Exports by Cluster and Vertical Stage (1978-1985)

	MATERIALS/METALS				FOREST PRODUCTS				PETROLEUM/CHEMICALS				SEMICONDUCTORS/COMPUTERS				UPSTREAM IND	
	SC	CSC	SW	CSW	SC	CSC	SW	CSW	SC	CSC	SW	CSW	SC	CSC	SW	CSW	SC	SW
PRI. GOODS	19.2	+12.5	1.2	+1.0	1.5	+1.5	0.2	+0.2	4.4	+3.9	0.1	+0.1	0.0	0.0	0.0	0.0	25.1	0.3
MACHINERY	0.4	+0.4	0.2	+0.2	0.0	0.0	0.0	0.0	0.2	+0.2	0.9	+0.9	0.0	0.0	0.0	0.0	0.6	0.2
SPE. INPUTS	0.0	-0.2	0.0	0.0	0.0	0.0	0.0	0.0	0.0	0.0	0.0	0.0	0.0	0.0	0.0	0.0	0.0	0.0
TOTAL	19.6	+12.7	0.9	+0.8	1.5	+1.5	0.2	+0.2	4.6	+4.1	0.1	+0.1	0.0	0.0	0.0	0.0	25.7	0.3

	MULTIPLE BUSINESS				TRANSPORTATION				POWER GENERATION & DISTRIBUTION				OFFICE				TELECOMMUNIC.				DEFENSE				INDUS. & SUP. FUNCTIONS	
	SC	CSC	SW	CSW	SC	CSC	SW	CSW	SC	CSC	SW	CSW	SC	CSC	SW	CSW	SC	CSC	SW	CSW	SC	CSC	SW	CSW	SC	SW
PRI. GOODS	0.8	+0.8	0.2	0.0	0.6	+0.6	0.1	0.0	0.0	0.0	0.0	0.0	0.0	0.0	0.0	0.0	0.2	+0.2	0.1	+0.1	0.0	0.0	0.0	0.0	1.6	0.0
MACHINERY	0.3	+0.3	0.0	0.0	0.0	0.0	0.0	0.0	0.0	0.0	0.0	0.0	0.0	0.0	0.0	0.0	0.0	0.0	0.0	0.0	0.0	0.0	0.0	0.0	0.3	0.1
SPE. INPUTS	0.4	+0.4	1.3	+1.3	0.0	0.0	0.2	0.0	0.0	0.0	0.0	0.0	0.0	0.0	0.0	0.0	4.3	-5.7	6.2	+1.4	0.0	0.0	0.0	0.0	1.7	0.1
TOTAL	1.5	+1.5	1.5	+1.3	0.6	+0.6	0.1	+0.1	0.0	0.0	0.0	0.0	0.0	0.0	0.0	0.0	4.5	-5.4	1.0	0.0	0.0	0.0	0.0	0.0	3.6	0.1

	FOOD/BEVERAGE				TEXTILES/APPAREL				HOUSING & HOUSEHOLD				HEALTH CARE				PERSONAL				ENTERTAINMENT/ LEISURE				FINAL CONS GOODS & SER	
	SC	CSC	SW	CSW	SC	CSC	SW	CSW	SC	CSC	SW	CSW	SC	CSC	SW	CSW	SC	CSC	SW	CSW	SC	CSC	SW	CSW	SC	SW
PRI. GOODS	18.9	-16.4	0.6	-0.1	22.9	+17.1	2.1	+1.9	3.1	+0.6	0.5	+0.3	0.0	0.0	0.0	0.0	0.1	+0.2	0.1	+0.1	0.0	0.0	0.0	0.0	45.2	0.7
MACHINERY	0.9	+0.9	0.6	+0.6	1.1	+1.0	1.0	+1.0	0.0	0.0	0.0	0.0	0.0	0.0	0.0	0.0	0.0	0.0	0.0	0.0	0.0	0.0	0.0	0.0	2.0	0.8
SPE. INPUTS	1.6	-8.6	0.0	-0.5	9.3	-16.0	1.6	0.0	0.7	-1.4	0.5	-0.1	0.0	0.0	0.0	0.0	0.0	0.0	0.0	0.0	0.0	0.0	0.0	0.0	15.9	0.2
TOTAL	21.4	-24.2	0.5	-0.1	33.3	+2.1	1.9	+1.2	3.8	-0.8	0.5	+0.3	0.0	0.0	0.0	0.0	0.1	+0.1	0.1	0.0	0.0	0.0	0.0	0.0	63.1	0.8

KEY: SC Share of country's total exports 1985
CSC Change in share of country's exports 1978-1985
SW Share of world cluster exports 1985
CSW Change in share of world cluster exports 1978-1985

liberalisation policies of the early 1980s. The result of this comparison can be found in Table 2.3. Despite improvements after 1980, the Turkish economy continues to be dependent on relatively few clusters, the most noteworthy being textiles/apparel, food/beverages, materials/metals and housing/household. In 1978, the most important cluster of the Turkish economy was textiles/apparel with a world cluster share of 0.73 per cent, which was well above the country's 0.18 per cent overall share of total world exports. In terms of country export share, however, food/beverages captured the first place. We can observe a similar case for housing/household and materials/metals clusters, which interchanged third and fourth places according to their world cluster and country export shares respectively. As far as the other clusters are concerned, there is nearly a total absence in 1978 with the exception of a few competitive industries in the petroleum/chemicals cluster.

Although the largest clusters, as well as their relative importance continue to be more or less the same in 1985, the analysis shows an unquestionably improved picture for the Turkish economy compared to 1978 as can be seen from Table 2.3. In fact, Turkey's total export share in the world market increased twofold, jumping from 0.18 per cent to 0.41 per cent between 1978 and 1985. In all three levels of the cluster chart, we have plus signs for the changes in world cluster shares, meaning that Turkey increased its share of world exports in all of these combined groups. The highest increase can be seen in the top row, that is 'Upstream Industries', for which all clusters except semiconductors/computers improved considerably. The second highest increase in terms of world cluster share takes place in the bottom row, 'Final Consumption Goods and Services', mainly due to the increased contributions of both textiles/apparel and housing/household clusters. We also have some, though few, competitive industries in the middle row as compared to none in 1978. This, in fact, supports Porter's (1990a) hypothesis that in the earlier stages of development countries are more likely to be competitive in the bottom and/or top rows of the cluster chart; then, as they develop they start to gain positions in the middle row as well. As for the country export shares, we observe a shift from the bottom row to the others, especially to the top row. This is mainly because of the decreasing importance of the food/beverages cluster and increasing importance of the materials/metals cluster in the country's total exports.

A further examination of Table 2.3 relating changes in position by vertical stage, between the years 1978 and 1985, supports the findings of the previous analysis. As a general picture, the strength of the Turkish economy seems to be in the primary goods category for both years, although we observe a considerable improvement in machinery. To sum up, during this period, which includes the introduction of the trade liberalisation policies, Turkey not only increased its overall exports but also achieved a deepening in the existing clusters, though it failed to establish itself in other clusters.

Similar tables comparing 1971-78 and 1985-92 have also been prepared (see Appendix A2). The 1971-78 comparison does not reveal much in that both years show a very similar pattern. Whenever there is a change, it occurs in the leading clusters. Specifically, minor improvements are observed in the international positions of the food/beverages and materials/metals clusters, and shifts are observed in the relative importance of the four major clusters in Turkey's total exports; the food/beverages, materials/metals and housing/household clusters improving their shares, while the textiles/apparel cluster experiences a decline. A comparison of the results for 1985 and 1992 exhibits a similar pattern in that the noteworthy changes take place in the strongest clusters' country export shares. The salient change is the loss in the position of the materials/metals cluster, both in terms of its shares in the total Turkish exports and world cluster exports.

In summary, though improved to a considerable extent, the competitive structure of the Turkish economy still rests on four major clusters, namely, materials/metals, textiles/apparel, food/beverages and housing/household; the last three being covered by the heading 'Final Consumption Goods and Services'. The main strength of the Turkish economy is in primary goods and to a lesser extent in specialty inputs and services, whereas it is relatively weak in the machinery category. With this composition, the competitive structure of Turkey is most similar to those of South Korea and Italy (within the nations included in Porter's 1990 study). It resembles South Korea in terms of its narrow range of competitive clusters as well as their concentration on the primary goods and specialty inputs, while it resembles Italy in terms of its post-liberalisation dynamism and the types of clusters that are internationally competitive.

Towards an Exploration of the Reasons: Which Cases to Study?

According to Porter (1990a), to understand the sources of advantage experienced by the industries over time, we should turn to the 'diamond' and try to see how each determinant functions and interacts with the others in a particular sector by analysing its history. This is what I will attempt to do in the following five chapters. The industries chosen for the detailed case studies are the Turkish glass, construction, leather clothes, automobile and flat steel industries.

The Turkish glass industry served as a 'pilot case study' in that it is an industry I already knew relatively well, having worked there. Furthermore, apart from being an industry from an important cluster of the Turkish economy, the housing/household cluster, there is barely no domestic rivalry in this competitive industry, presenting an opportunity to think about the relevant strong hypothesis Porter puts forward. Although I have conducted a preliminary study of the highly competitive Turkish carpet industry from the same cluster, I have decided that tradition, hence probably historical accident, coupled with cheap labour, has played the key role in that industry. Therefore, the heart of the case was likely to repeat a point that had already been covered in the study of another tradition-oriented sector, the glass industry, which showed that even the very emergence of such historical accidents can be explained by the framework, not leaving much motivation to conduct another industry analysis replicating this aspect.

The second industry case study chosen is the Turkish construction industry, a very competitive, but 'isolated' sector, since it is best placed to the uncompetitive Turkish multiple business cluster. The main reason I have decided to include construction industry is to make use of the opportunity to study a service industry that Porter's framework provides, as opposed to quantitative studies of industry competitiveness. Other alternatives could be tourism or shipping; both are, I believe, less interesting than the case of construction, since the major source of success is a relatively easily detectable factor advantage in both cases: Turkey's favourable location.

It was a difficult decision to pick an industry for detailed study from the leading Turkish textiles/apparel cluster. An industry from the specialty inputs category would be too natural resource-dependent, an obvious advantage. Many other industries in the primary goods category probably would not be as interesting as the leather clothes industry, which imports a considerable amount of its raw material requirements and has experienced some losses in its international position recently.

As a fourth case I decided to study an uncompetitive industry to be able to see the power of the diamond in understanding the failures. Among the many candidates, the automobile industry was the most attractive one for many reasons. First of all, it is a giant industry by any standards. Second, major structural changes have been taking place in the industry, putting it amongst the top issues in the agendas of both the business community and the Turkish government as well as the researchers. Moreover, under intense pressure, the industry has started to increase its export performance, making it even more interesting. Lastly, it is an industry where foreign ownership and MNE involvement have been observed, providing yet another reason for considering it for detailed analysis, since this issue constitutes one of the major criticisms of Porter's study.

An overview of the materials/metals cluster to choose an industry for the final case study, revealed two main options; choosing one industry from the iron and steel sector or one from the non-ferrous metals sector. Many industries included in the latter are again dependent on the obvious advantage of natural resources. The iron and steel industry, on the other hand, apart from presenting an interesting case to discuss the indirect role Porter assumes for the government, imports a considerable part of its raw material requirements. Within the iron and steel industry, the flat-steel segment is even more interesting since there is no domestic rivalry. An examination of the flat steel industry, therefore, provides an ideal case for an intentional replication of the three previously detected question marks in the diamond framework: the importance of the factor conditions and the domestic rivalry as well as the indirect role of government. Furthermore, it is competitive although its trade balance is negative. This is a very special case providing an opportunity for contributing towards a better understanding of 'measuring' competitiveness.

The last issue I would like to mention concerning the identification of the industries for the detailed study is that I have not included any industries from one major cluster: food/beverages. Deriving from the fact that most of the items included in that cluster are unavoidably related to apparent natural resource advantages, thus making them less interesting to study in detail for an investigation of the effectiveness of the diamond framework in understanding the sources of advantage, given that Porter (1990a) himself states that such industries capture most of their advantage from factor conditions and can probably be explained by the classical theory to a great extent, I decided to study a failure case from that cluster. The most suitable candidate was the Turkish wine industry. After conducting some research and interviews, however, I concluded that the case study would not be interesting enough since the reasons for the relatively lagging position of the Turkish wine industry are as obvious as the natural resource advantage of the many competitive ones in that cluster. Specifically, demand conditions are relatively disadvantageous in a Muslim country, which can also be used to explain the relatively uncompetitive positions of other alcoholic beverages, and hence of their related and supporting industries. These are apparently too strong to let firms utilise their intrinsic advantages stemming from factor conditions, such as cheap labour and highly competitive grape supplies.

It would have been, of course, preferable to study more industries, but this had been simply blocked by time and resource constraints. I, nevertheless, believe that these five industries provide us with a quite interesting combination of issues that should be considered regarding the diamond framework and thus determinants of competitive advantage. The length of the cases is something I could not avoid since I believe it is essential that each study is exhaustive with regard to the key issues related to the competitiveness in that particular industry. Readers interested in a broader picture may refer to the summaries supplied at the end of each chapter and/or the overview conducted in the conclusion.

Notes

1   It will be interesting to see the effect of the customs union with the EU on the competitive structure of the Turkish economy. This, of course, requires the elapse of some time but our comparison with the Greek case suggests that we should not expect a substantial change (Öz and Konsolas, 1996).
2   A detailed examination of this crucial issue is beyond the scope of this study. Interested readers may refer to Buğra (1994) for a comprehensive investigation of the state and business relations in Turkey.
3   Some examples for the theory and evidence include the following: international trade, Jones and Kenen (1984), Leamer (1984), Helpman and Krugman (1985), Krugman and Obstfeld (1994); technology gap and product cycle theories, Vernon (1966), Wells (1972); studies of multinationals, Hood and Young (1979), Dunning (1981); studies about managerial and organisational differences, Yoshino (1968), Ouchi (1981), Lodge and Vogel (1987), Kogut (1989).
4   See, for instance, Krugman, 1994a and 1994b; and the responses to Krugman, 1994b by various authors in Prestowitz et al., 1994; and Krugman's responses to these responses in Krugman, 1994c.
5   A review of this literature can be found in Bilkey, 1978; Aaby and Slater, 1989; Chetty and Hamilton, 1993. For some examples of the Turkish studies see the works of Bodur and Çavuşgil, 1985; Kaynak and Gürol, 1987; Tuncer and Üner, 1993a and 1993b.
6   A short review of the traditional and new theories of trade as well as their implications for Turkey can be found in Fostner (1995).
7   Examples include Tekeli, 1981; Tekeli and Menteş, 1982; Ayata, 1982; Üser, 1984; Arslan, 1985; Eraydın, 1994; Özcan, 1995.
8   Examples include Baysan (1984) who investigates Turkey's comparative advantage in agriculture, and Kırım and Ateş (1989) who study the level of technological capability in the Turkish textile sector and relate these to the recent export success. Similar technology-related issues have been the subject of Ansal's (1993) work in the textile industry. As a last example, Duruiz and Yentürk (1992) consider the competitiveness of the Turkish automobile, steel and clothing industries.
9   Akder (1987), for instance, analyses the trade between Turkey and the EU (then EC) for the period 1981-1985, by using the constant-market-share-analysis technique.

3 The Turkish Glass Industry

The glass industry is amongst the important sectors of the Turkish economy since it is both internationally competitive and has high social and economic impact. In 1992, total glass production of Turkey reached 1.3 per cent of world glass production. The flat glass production of Turkey captures 7.1 per cent of world glass production, and this rate is 12 per cent for glassware (DPT, 1993e). The Turkish Glassworks, Inc. (Şişecam), which can be considered as a private monopoly in the Turkish glass industry, contributes 3.4 per cent to the Turkish GDP and constitutes 2 per cent of Turkish exports. The employment by this company alone reached approximately 12,300 (Şişecam, 1992).

The glass industry is one of the oldest and most important competitive industries of Turkey, and around 30 per cent of its production is exported. After 1980, which is the year that marks the beginning of trade liberalisation, Turkish glass exports accelerated considerably more than imports. The industry is very competitive especially in the segments of 'glass surface-ground' (SITC 6644) and 'household and hotel glass' (SITC 6652). Turkey has been within the top ten exporters in these segments since the beginning of the 1980s. In the table glassware segment, Turkey has second place after France in terms of its share of world production. Currently, the most important markets for exports are the EU, the Middle East, North Africa, the USA and Japan. Among the target markets are the former republics of the Soviet Union. The main competitors are from the EU and Eastern Europe.

Development of the Turkish Glass Industry

It is possible to trace the glassmaking tradition in Anatolia back to the ages of antiquity. Although I will not go into the details of these historical developments, it may be worth briefly mentioning the glassmaking tradition in the Ottoman Empire, which has had apparent effects in the development of the industry in the Republican era.

In the Ottoman Empire, the state always protected and promoted the production and sale of glass (Bayramoğlu, 1976: 31). The most commonly produced types of glass were ordinary, crystal and stained glass. İstanbul, which already had an important tradition of glassmaking during the

59

Byzantine Empire, was the centre of the Ottoman glass industry. Apart from being the capital and a trade centre, the region of İstanbul was also endowed with the necessary raw materials for the making of glass. The fine white sand, which was ideal for the making of glass and was exported to the other glassmaking centres, came from Kumboğazı, a district near İstanbul. Although the glass industry was well developed in the Ottoman Empire, glassware produced in accordance with Turkish tastes was imported from Europe as well, particularly from Venice and later from Bohemia. Bohemian glass manufacturers, who were producing the glassware known as 'Turkish Glass', had established warehouses in Smyrna, İstanbul, Beirut and Cairo. Later, Turks imported glass from England, Holland, Spain and Poland. We also know that, particularly in the eighteenth century, İstanbul was an export centre sending stained-glass for windows to Europe. Beykoz (a region of İstanbul) glassware used to be very popular in various regions of the Ottoman Empire, throughout neighbouring countries and other Moslem nations (Bayramoğlu, 1976).

In the nineteenth century, a glass factory was built on the Anatolian shore of İstanbul, near Beykoz, by Mehmed Dede. It was followed by the 'Glass and Crystal Factory' built by Mustafa Nuri Pasa at Çubuklu, which was later bought and enlarged by Sultan Abdulmejid. 'Çeşm-i bülbül', the famous glassware decorated with small coloured spots and the opalines were manufactured in this factory. The last development in the glass industry during the Ottoman period was the establishment of another glass factory, the 'Glass Factory of Modiano from İstanbul', in 1899 at Paşabahçe by an Italian Jew called Saul Modiano. These factories ceased to exist after the first World War, and together with the foundation of the Turkish Republic, a new era began for the Turkish glass industry (Bayramoğlu, 1976: 56).

After the foundation of the new republic, the first attempt came from a Turkish citizen, Y. Ziya Üçüncü, who built a factory to manufacture glassware in 1933 in the neighbourhood of the Tekfur Palace which used to be the centre of glassmaking in former times. This factory, however, bankrupted after a short while (Bayramoğlu, 1976: 83).

In accordance with the policies followed starting in the early 1930s (see Chapter 2 for details), which considered the state as the main driver of economic development, the subsequent attempts were triggered by the government. The First Five Year Plan, for instance, suggested the establishment of a glass industry since 'the factories that were built for this purpose were unable to continue production, either for political reasons, or because they did not adopt a modern technique and had not had enough capital. [...] There are technical and economic difficulties that do not permit the establishment of a glass and bottle factory that would manufacture goods on a large scale and satisfy all our needs' (Bayramoğlu, 1976: 84). The location of the suggested glass factory was also specified: 'The choice of a site should be determined not only by economic and technical considerations, but also by existing conditions pertaining to rapid sale and means of transport. These various considerations strongly favour the building of such a factory in İstanbul' (Bayramoğlu, 1976: 84).

In 1934, the government decided that one of the biggest banks in Turkey, İş Bank, should be responsible for the construction of a factory that would manufacture 'bottles and glassware', and then, of a second one that would manufacture 'window glass'. The first factory, Paşabahçe Glassworks, was founded in 1935. It was at first administered by the French company Stein, but in 1936, the factory was transferred to Turkish Glassworks, Inc. The Second World War broke out a couple of years later, which made the importation of glass, together with other commodities, difficult; this caused new workshops to be built in İstanbul to manufacture glassware and bottles by using broken glass as the basic raw material. These workshops changed owners very often and also ceased production from time to time (Bayramoğlu, 1976).

Several private enterprises were built in the successive periods. For instance, the Gökyiğit Factory was built in 1944 in İstanbul for the manufacture of glassware and articles of illumination, the Bottle Factory in Cubuklu was also built in 1944, the Türkgenç Lamp and Bottle Factory was built in Cibali in 1950, the Net Glass factory of glassware and articles of illumination was built in 1958. Similarly, during 1960s and 1970s, some other private enterprises as well as smaller workshops emerged in İstanbul and various cities of Anatolia (Bayramoğlu, 1976).

There had been attempts to challenge the monopoly position of Şişecam in the 1970s as well, the most outstanding of which was Denizli Cam. Although the firm was established in 1973, it took some time until it actually started production in 1981. It produced glassware and glass rods for chandeliers. It incurred losses for all the years it was in operation, the main reason for which was believed to be incompetencies in management. The company invested heavily in technological improvements in 1983 and increased its capacity when the second and third blast furnaces started operation in 1988 and 1989, respectively. Its main exports were glassware and glass rods mostly to the EU, USA and Japan. In 1994, a few years after, however, 51 per cent of Denizli Cam's shares were bought by Şişecam Holding reinforcing the latter's monopoly position in the industry (T.C. Başbakanlık Yüksek Denetleme Kurulu, 1994). Currently, the Turkish

Glassworks Inc. (Şişecam) clearly dominates the Turkish glass industry, owning all firms with the exception of a few in the glassware segment.

Sources of Advantage in the Turkish Glass Industry

Factor Conditions

Around 98 per cent of the raw materials used in the industry are domestic ones, and only some chemical materials like lead oxide and potassium carbonate are imported. The main reason for the apparent preference for domestic raw materials is the high cost of transportation, especially in the case of sand. Although raw materials are adequate in Turkey both in terms of quantity and quality, it is hard to say whether they are distinctive enough to provide a clear advantage to the Turkish glass industry. The costs of raw materials, however, are lower than those in the world market which probably owes a lot to the fact that Şişecam has its own supplier firm.

Average wages in the Turkish glass industry are relatively low compared to the main competitors. In fact, it is one of the lowest rates in the world as far as the glass industry is concerned. If, however, we also take productivity rates into consideration, then the apparent wage advantage of Turkey, especially relative to the competitors in the EU, diminishes since the productivity rate in the Turkish glass industry is approximately one seventh of the corresponding rate for the EU (Şişecam, 1992). Despite this, we can safely say that Turkey has a cost advantage in the glass industry stemming from low wages relative to some important competitors in Europe.

Here, it should be stated that average wages in the Turkish glass industry are in fact high relative to those in other Turkish industries. This is reflected in the answers glass industry workers have given to a survey conducted by Veri Araştırma A.Ş. When asked to prioritise their expectations from the union, for instance, they put job security in first place, improvements in the working conditions in second and training in third. Expectations of workers from the union regarding the increases in wages only took fourth place according to 1992 survey results, decreasing from the third place it captured in the 1990 survey (Kristal-İş, 1992a). This may partly be explained by the increasing trend in real wages after 1988, which, in the long-run, may threaten the advantage of the Turkish glass industry stemming from relatively low wages compared to major foreign competitors.

High wages in the glass industry relative to other industries in Turkey have been mainly achieved by the 'tough' union, Kristal-İş. There are several reasons for the strength of the union in the Turkish glass industry. One is the fact that the industry requires qualified employees who are usually more inclined to take part in the unions. Another reason is that there is practically only one employer and one union in the industry, which increases the bargaining powers of both parties. Since the first union was founded in 1947, the industry has faced several breaks in production due to labour-management conflicts. In fact, the whole history of the industry is full of grievances, layoffs and factory occupations. We can safely say that conflicts between managers and employees in the Turkish glass industry have been rather frequent and severe relative to the other industries.

When we examine the attitude of management towards this situation, we observe that increasing labour costs and the present attitude of the union are seen as the most important obstacles for the long-term competitiveness of the Turkish glass industry. In fact, the share of labour costs in gross value added is gradually diminishing indicating that the response of management to increasing labour costs seems to be a parallel increase in the emphasis on automation. This also explains the shift of worker preferences from wage increases to job security since job losses have started to go hand-in-hand with increases in automation.

Although the capital market in Turkey is far from functioning efficiently and the cost of capital is high, Şişecam does not face any difficulties in raising its capital requirements both from Turkey and abroad due to its credibility and good reputation in the domestic as well as international financial markets. Therefore, although it still imposes some constraints, the disadvantages of the Turkish capital markets are not as problematic for the Turkish glass industry as one expects.

As a Turkish exporter in the world market, firms in the glass industry have geographical advantages relative to foreign competitors in some mature as well as emerging markets. Countries of the Middle East and Eastern Europe as well as Greece and Italy are of special relevance in this respect.

Country infrastructure has crucial importance for the glass industry. A timely and guaranteed supply of raw materials, packaging services satisfying international standards, and a well-functioning and widespread railway and port system are amongst the first infrastructure-related factors to consider as far as the glass industry is concerned. As a concrete example, we can take the case of railways. It is well-known that most of the West European countries have well-functioning railway networks. Corporations like Heye Glas and Flachglas have the advantage of railways entering right into their factories. For the case of Turkey, the railway system, which has been ignored for decades, is far from satisfying the needs of the industry.

Relatedly, as opposed to previous plans, necessary investment has not been made until very recently for Tekirdağ port, which is quite near the most important flat glass factory of Turkey. Under these circumstances, the company has to use İstanbul port, Haydarpaşa, which adds an otherwise avoidable item to the total costs. In fact, Şişecam has calculated this additional cost burden as around 3 per cent (Şişecam, 1992).

Another disadvantage for the Turkish glass producers is the high cost of energy. Although this is a problem for all of the Turkish manufacturing industries, it has special importance for glass producers due to the high portion energy captures in the total costs in this industry. A comparison of energy prices in some of the OECD countries gives an indication of the extent of this problem. As an example, we can compare energy prices in France and Turkey, which is particularly important since France's Duran is the major competitor of Şişecam in the glassware segment. France has a cost advantage over Turkey in all of the three categories of energy used, namely, electricity, fuel-oil and natural gas. In fact, in all of these categories, energy prices in France are nearly half those in Turkey. Higher tax rates for energy in Turkey compared to France and many other competitors are largely responsible for this situation (TİSK, 1995).

Two other crucial issues concerning the role of energy in the glass sector are its reliability and continuity. It is quite rare in Western Europe to have the electricity supply cut off, but this continues to be a problem for Turkey. Şişecam estimates the amount of time lost due to cut-offs in the electricity supply just in the İstanbul region as 1.1 per cent of the total production time per year. The resulting loss is calculated as approximately 3 per cent of annual production (Şişecam, 1992).

Another problem related to the disadvantages the Turkish glass industry faces stemming from deficiencies in the infrastructure is the lack of a well-functioning system of glass recycling. In the EU, in accordance with environmental regulations, recycling systems have been established, enabling savings from both raw materials and energy. These savings are not negligible given that one tonne of recycled glass can replace 1.2 tonnes of raw materials and save 100 kg fuel oil. An overview of glass recycling in Europe reveals that the rate of recycling in Turkey is rather low at 30 per cent only, as compared to the European average recycling rate of 42 per cent.

The importance of innovations and, therefore, that of research and development is undeniable in the glass industry. The share of research and development expenditure in the turnovers of the glass producers in the Western Europe and Japan amounts to 2-2.5 per cent, whereas the related figure for the Turkish glass industry remains around 0.3 per cent. In this respect, Şişecam highlights that in some other nations such as France, the share of government support for research and development expenditures of firms is around 20 per cent. Low research and development expenditure and lack of government support for research and development are, therefore, important drawbacks for the Turkish glass industry, causing Şişecam to be dependent on foreign firms in terms of major developments in technology (Şişecam, 1992). This, of course, has its costs. Pilkington, for instance, restricted Şişecam's exports to certain countries for a while in accordance with the contract signed when Şişecam imported float glass technology.

Furthermore, Turkey lacks any private or public institutions conducting specific research for the glass industry, which are considered as specific and advance factors in Porter's classification. Although there are some universities offering post-graduate programmes in glass and related subjects, it is hard to say that they are of first-class quality by world standards. Relatedly, since Şişecam has a good reputation, it has no difficulties in accessing the necessary economic information about markets, technologies, and competition, which, according to Porter (1990a), can be an important mechanism for factor creation.

In summary, as far as the factor conditions are concerned, it can be said that the Turkish glass industry has a relatively advantageous position compared to its main competitors in basic and generalised factors with low-cost and good quality raw materials, a very favourable geographical position, low-cost unskilled and semi-skilled labour, and easy access to debt capital. The industry, however, faces severe disadvantages regarding the advanced and specific factors with inadequate infrastructure with specific properties, lack of specific research institutions, and difficulties faced regarding research and development. Given that, according to Porter, advanced and specific factors are more important and sustainable sources of competitive advantage, this situation poses a threat to the Turkish glass industry in the long-run.

Demand Conditions

When we examine the sizes of the major segments in the world market, we see that in terms of dollar value of production flat glass is the most important segment, followed by lighting products of glass, fibre glass, glass containers and glassware, in order of importance. In terms of volume of production, however, the glass containers segment is the leading one, whereas flat glass and glassware segments come as the second and third, respectively (ICEF, 1992). When we have a look at the situation in the Turkish glass industry, we see that it more or less resembles trends in the world market. The most important segment is flat glass both in terms of quantity and value of production. The glass containers segment comes second in terms of production volume, whereas it is the glassware segment that captures the second position in terms of value of production. As far as exports are concerned, however, flat glass again holds its position in first place in terms of quantity exported, whereas, this time, it is the glassware segment which comes first in terms of value of exports (The United Nations, *International Trade Statistics Yearbook*, 1993).

A quick look at the growth rates shows that almost all segments in the Turkish glass industry, resembling the situation in most of the middle-income developing countries, grow at a rate of around 7-10 per cent per year. The related rates for the developed countries, on the other hand, are around 3-4 per cent. This, of course, has some relation to the sectors the glass industry can be associated with such as the construction, food, pharmaceuticals, tourism and auto-manufacturing industries, which are more likely to be still growing at relatively high rates in developing countries.

Although demand for major glass products in the domestic market grows faster than it does in developed economies, this does not change the fact that most new product developments are taking place in developed nations, and it usually takes some time until new products reach developing countries like Turkey. Furthermore, it is hard to say that Turkish customers are anticipatory of the likely developments in the world glass industry. In fact, Şişecam itself has to create demand in the domestic market for the new products that have emerged in the developed countries, although by doing so it takes the risk of paying for all externalities involved. The Şişecam executives express some concern about that issue especially regarding the extremely cheap imports from Eastern Europe and Indonesia as well as unfair competition from small firms that have no unions and imitate the products of Şişecam.

There are a number of independent buyers in the Turkish glass industry eliminating the risk of being trapped into the comfort of serving one or two guaranteed customers only. When we compare the standards of foreign versus domestic customers in terms of product quality, product features and product-related services for the Turkish glass industry combined, we see that in the past some differences did exist with foreign customers having more sophisticated demands than the domestic ones. Since the late 1980s, however, this discrepancy has disappeared, and now, both foreign and domestic customers are equally demanding. We should, however, state that there is an exception to this -the glassware segment, where Turkish customers are traditionally very demanding.

Another important category Porter (1990a) proposes for demand conditions is the influences of domestic firms on foreign needs. Given that Şişecam holds approximately 4 per cent of the glassware market, second to France's Durand, it has an effect on foreign demand in this segment. Particularly, the brandname 'Paşabahce' is well-established with a reputation of combining aesthetics with quality.

Apart from some apparent historical reasons mentioned in previous sections, several other factors have also contributed to the exposition of foreigners to Turkish tastes, reinforcing the international competitiveness of several Turkish industries including the glass industry. A large number of Turks live abroad for instance, especially in Europe, with more than two million just in Germany. In this respect, it is interesting to observe that Germany is the most important importer of the Turkish glass industry in the glassware and flat glass segments, and it comes third as an importer of Turkish glass containers. The very competitive Turkish tourism sector has also a lot to contribute in terms of creating an opportunity both for sales and for publicity of Turkish products. In addition, Şişecam, which is a successful firm in general, is very active in marketing as well. It takes part in almost every fair and exhibition as well as in contests of design for glass products, organises some itself (for instance, the International Symposium of Anatolian Glass Art, İstanbul, 1988), and has marketing and sales subsidiaries abroad.

In summary, as far as the home demand conditions are concerned, the Turkish glass industry has the advantage of having a large, rapidly growing and dynamic domestic market. Domestic customers, however, are neither less nor more sophisticated than foreign ones, meaning that although this dimension of home demand does not create a problem for the Turkish glass industry, it does not suffice to provide a lead either. Finally, it is difficult to say that domestic customers are anticipatory of likely developments in the world glass market, which is apparently a disadvantage for the Turkish glass industry.

Related and Supporting Industries

One of the most interesting results of Porter's more than one-hundred industry case studies is the presence of supplier and/or related industries that are also internationally competitive. Figure 3.1 shows the internationally successful Turkish industries that can be associated with the glass industry.

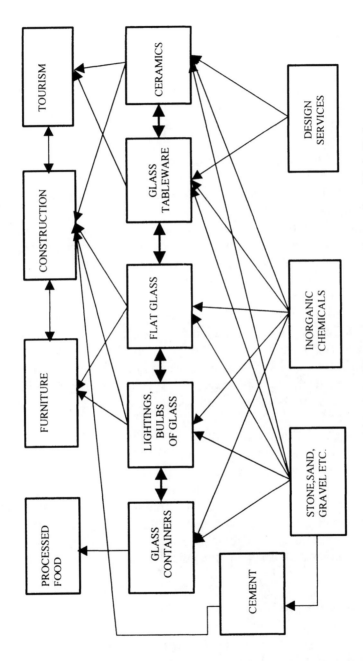

Figure 3.1 Internationally Successful Turkish Industries Related to the Glass Industry
Source: Author's estimates based on cluster charts (see Table2.2 and Appendix A1) and field interviews

We can safely say that most of the industries for which the glass industry supplies inputs (e.g. process food, construction, etc.) are very competitive in international markets. The housing/household cluster, which includes most of the glass products constitutes the fourth largest cluster of the Turkish economy. Regarding the main input suppliers, Şişecam has overcome the problems created by the lack of internationally competitive supplier industries by following an internalisation strategy. It is also possible to consider these supplier industries as relatively competitive in international markets although vertical integration has been a compulsion rather than an option for Şişecam under the circumstances.

Due to its similarities with the glass industry, such as close ties with the construction industry and having the advantage of being a long 'tradition' in the lands of Anatolia, the ceramics industry certainly deserves some special attention. The ceramics and glass industries both provide inputs to the construction industry; in this regard, especially the flat glass and ceramic tiles segments can be considered as complementary. In terms of ornaments and tableware, however, the products of the two industries are clearly substitutes for each other. Another related industry that has a lot in common with the glass sector is the cement industry. The Turkish ceramics and cement industries are both competitive in international markets and enjoy a rapidly growing domestic market. Furthermore, the 'stone, sand, gravel' segment provides inputs to both, and for both of them the construction industry is an important customer.

Apart from ceramics, the plastic tableware segment is also amongst the substitutes of the table glassware segment. The glass containers segment faces tough competition from the plastic and metal containers sectors. These substitutes of glass products are also relatively competitive in international markets.

In summary, Porter's hypothesis that internationally competitive industries of a nation are related to each other, and, therefore, tend to cluster together finds support from the case of the Turkish glass industry. Almost all of the Turkish industries that can be associated with the glass industry are relatively competitive in international markets. One exception is the lack of internationally competitive supplier industries, which has been overcome by the company through vertical integration.

Firm Strategy, Structure and Rivalry

Porter (1990a) considers the association between vigorous domestic rivalry and the creation and persistence of competitive advantage in an industry as the strongest empirical finding of his research. The case of the Turkish glass industry, however, puts a question mark to this hypothesis given the fact that Şişecam is basically a private monopoly in the industry.

It is unnecessary to repeat the entire industry history here, but, as a summary, we should state that Şişecam's dominance in the industry is undeniable, and it has been so throughout the history of the industry in the Republic of Turkey. Some firms have tried; in fact, some (the latest attempt is being made by Kütahya Porselen, a firm from the ceramics industry) are still trying to enter into the industry, but most of the time it has turned out to be the case that they have either ceased to survive or Şişecam has bought them after a while (e.g. Denizli Cam). Among the firms trying to enter into the industry, there are both totally new ones and the ones established by the companies operating in other industries such as the ceramics industry.

The case of the Turkish glass industry is, in other words, quite interesting in that it is still competitive, although there are hardly any domestic competitors, with one firm Şişecam holding more than 90 per cent of the market. Furthermore, it was even competitive when the domestic market was highly protected, although the company tremendously improved its competitive position in the international markets after liberalisation. The possible explanation for this situation may be the nature of the industry. In particular, the existence of economies of scale, the continuous production requirement, together with the necessity of a step-wise increase in capacity compels firms in the glass industry to compete in international markets as well. These structural characteristics of the glass industry, in a way, help offset the problems stemming from the lack of domestic competition in the industry and, even to a certain extent, the effects of the presence of import protection measures. To be able to sell their products in the international markets they have to be competitive anyway. Even a large home market may not be sufficient under the circumstances, since firms probably prefer to diversify their risk by selling abroad as well, instead of relying solely on the domestic market.

Due to its above mentioned structure, large firms are dominant in the glass industry, both in Turkey and in the rest of the world. Şişecam is vertically (activities ranging from the supply of raw materials to the marketing of the final products) and partially horizontally (e.g. İstanbul Porselen is a firm operating in the ceramics industry) integrated. It is a privately-owned domestic firm. It prefers to organise its international activities in the form of an 'export department' though it has sales and marketing subsidiaries in several other countries.

As far as company policies are concerned, we can say that the long-term goal of the company is stated as being the leader in the world glass market in terms of quality and cost rather than sales volume or quantity produced. Priority is given to the domestic market since the philosophy dominant amongst the top management is that it is crucial to be strong in the domestic market before entering into international markets. This emphasis on the domestic market is compatible with Porter's approach, which gives special importance to the attributes of the local market (like home demand) for a sustainable success in international markets.

Şişecam tries to overcome the previously mentioned research-related disadvantages by its own investment in research; it has a well-functioning and productive research laboratory, for instance. Specifically, in the glassware segment where the need for innovation is especially high, the innovation rate for Şişecam is quite satisfactory with one innovation per day, but still lower than France's Duran's, the leader in this segment, which has an average rate of 1.6 innovations per day (Şişecam, 1992). Over time the emphasis on research and development programmes has shifted from the improvement of management techniques to process and product development as well as the improvement of marketing techniques in accordance with the changing environment and customer needs. The company also finances research projects that may have direct or indirect impacts on the glass industry and sponsors students studying in the glass-related departments of universities. To compensate for the lack of specifically skilled personnel for the industry, Şişecam has developed on-the-job and off-the-job training programmes; some workers are trained abroad if necessary.

In summary, the managerial capabilities of Şişecam executives can be considered as amongst the most important strengths of the Turkish glass industry. The existence of an active and adoptive management team, together with a strong union, for instance, has resulted in a company implementing the recent developments in participatory management such as quality circles and share-distribution schemes designed for the employees. The real advantage the strength of the company brings as far as the managerial capabilities are concerned, however, shows itself in the way it faces several challenges and deals with the problems caused by the inadequacies in the country infrastructure. Specific examples include its vertical integration strategy to compensate for the lack of internationally competitive supplier industries, its own attempts to promote recycling of glass products, its vigorous training programmes and its attempts to create demand in the domestic market for new products. To conclude, for this element of the diamond, we can argue that managerial capabilities provide an important lead for the Turkish glass industry, whereas being a competitive industry despite the lack of domestic competition can be partly explained by exposure to international competition and the structural characteristics of the industry.

The Role of Chance

Arguably the most important factor that can be considered as a 'chance' event for the Turkish glass industry is the tradition of glassmaking in the lands of Anatolia throughout the ages. It is also a fortunate fact that it was founded in the early years of the Republic and was supported and protected by the government for a long period of time during which it found an opportunity to develop from an infant industry into one of the most competitive industries of the Turkish economy.

Recent political changes in the world, especially the emergence of the new republics from the former USSR, and the conversion of the Eastern and Central European countries into market economies, have created opportunities as well as challenges for the Turkish glass industry. The former republics of the USSR mostly provide opportunities due to historical and geographical proximity to these developing markets, which have the potential for a rapidly growing demand for glass products as well as the availability of relatively cheaper inputs. The possible effects of the conversion of the Eastern and Central European countries into market economies, however, are twofold. On the one hand, they provide potentially attractive markets for the Turkish glass industry, whereas, on the other hand, the likelihood of tough competition from these countries poses serious threats for the Turkish glass industry both in the domestic and international markets. Needless to say, some chance events stated above are favourable whereas others create some burdens for the Turkish glass industry. On average, however, it seems that the favourable ones are outbalancing the unfavourable ones.

The Role of Government

The Turkish glass industry has been protected for a long period of time. It should be, however, stated that this was a reflection of the general economic development policy followed until 1980 rather than a specific targeting for the glass industry. After 1980, import protection measures started to be relaxed together with the encouragement of exports but, like the import protection measures of the previous period, these were not industry-specific policies either. One exception may be the restriction of imports and the facilitation of exports of some intermediate inputs and raw materials which may have more relations with some sectors relative to the other ones. The inputs the Turkish glass industry uses, however, as has been stated before, are 98 per cent domestic. It is, therefore, hard to say that there has been an import protection policy specific to the glass industry. The same argument is valid for government subsidies, foreign direct investment and tax policies as well, which are not targeted to specific industries.

There have been, however, close ties with the government and Şişecam since it was founded in 1935. In fact, the foundation of the company itself was initiated by the government. It is also well-known that the glass industry is quite good at lobbying the government, the last example of which is the anti-dumping regulations designed mainly as a response to the dumping practices of the Eastern European producers. Another example of this may be the special credit insurance rates the Turkish Export-Import Bank applies for the Turkish glass industry, the reason for which is stated as the 'good' relationship between Şişecam and the government.

Inadequacies in the regulations related to the copyrights of trademarks cause some burden for the company, since both importers and small domestic producers that operate without the pressure of unions imitate the products of Şişecam (especially in the glassware segment) and sell them at lower prices. Until recently, the government failed to take the necessary precautions regarding these matters. The problem has just been solved by the adoption of laws protecting the trademarks in accordance with the customs union with the EU, though the complete implementation of the new regulations will probably take some time.

Another issue concerning the role of government has already been discussed in detail previously while examining the factor conditions. The essence of the situation is that the government to a large extent controls energy prices and holds them at relatively high levels. This, predictably, increases the input costs of all energy-intensive industries including the glass industry, putting it in a disadvantaged position against its international competitors.

Similarly, as mentioned before, inadequacies in the infrastructure that have special importance for the glass industry, such as the lack of a well-functioning railway system and insufficient capacity in the ports (e.g. lack of containers), together with the more general government-related problems affecting many industries, such as a slow bureaucracy and unstable political and economic environment, pose serious problems for the Turkish glass industry.

In summary, we can describe the role of government as a source of competitive advantage in the Turkish glass industry as a rather direct one in the beginning, since it was the government that initiated the foundation of the industry and protected it for a long period of time. This protection has its positive effects via the infant industry argument, but it also has its costs as it caused the industry to develop the habit of lobbying the government. In terms of other issues related to the role of government, we can say that the industry suffers from the disadvantages caused by the deficiencies in the country infrastructure, a poorly functioning bureaucracy and an unstable economic and political environment.

Concluding Remarks

Borrowing from Krugman (1991), 'history [indeed] matters' for the Turkish glass industry. It grew out of a tradition in Turkey, a country located in a region that witnessed the discovery and development of glassmaking throughout the ages. If we, however, remember Porter's (1990a) argument that the determinants play a major role in locating where inventions are most likely to occur, we can even elaborate on the reasons for the very emergence of glassmaking in that particular area by using the diamond framework. First of all, there was plenty of high quality sand in the Mediterranean coasts, which is the single most important ingredient in glass production. Given that the region was the centre for the major civilisations at the time, the likelihood that there were qualified craftsmen and enough technological accumulation to produce the first products in the area was also quite high. These together mark the first element of the diamond: favourable factor conditions. It is also interesting to observe that the region was well-known for its earthenware products as well: a closely related industry. The rationale that the area was home to the major civilisations of the time can also be used to support the potential for a relatively large and sophisticated domestic demand. One can also imagine the presence of a rivalry among the producers competing to satisfy the needs of their customers. Although it is hard to say that these explanations satisfy all of our queries regarding the emergence of the industry in that particular region, it is still impressive to see that the 'diamond' helps us organise our thinking about the birth and subsequent development of an industry in a systematic way.

In recent times, relying upon this tradition of glassmaking in the region and the good prospects of demand for glass products, the Turkish government initiated the foundation of a large-scale glass industry. It should be stated, however, that the 'potential' was there, leaving us with the following question: Why couldn't it develop by itself then? It is simply because the level of technological competency and economic conditions in Turkey at the time did not permit the development of a large-scale glass industry by the private sector alone. More specifically, capital accumulation in the country was not sufficient to allow the exploitation of this opportunity by the newly emerging Turkish bourgeoisie. Although founded by the attempts of the government, however, Şişecam has been a private company acting quite independently from the government, and certainly is far from being similar to a state enterprise.

Having summarised the historical context, we can now turn back to the diamond to see if it works in explaining the later developments. Although we can say that basically it pinpoints a positive sign in favour of the diamond framework, the examination of the Turkish glass industry makes us question some of the strong arguments Porter (1990a) puts forward concerning the sources of competitive advantage. Regarding the 'firm strategy, structure and rivalry' determinant, for instance, it is interesting that we have a quite successful firm where there are hardly any domestic rivals in the market. The structural characteristics of the glass industry; mainly the existence of economies of scale, the continuous production requirement and the necessity of a stepwise increase in capacity, all favouring large-scale production, help us understand the high level of concentration in the industry. The exposure of the industry to international competition, on the other hand, may help offset some disadvantages of not having vigorous domestic competitors. The other part of this element of the diamond, the firm strategy and structure, is one of the most outstanding advantages of the Turkish glass industry. Strong managerial capabilities can be seen in the way the company tackles the problems and faces the challenges, as well as in the modern management techniques applied.

Another interesting area concerns the role the government plays in the case of the Turkish glass industry. We see that in the beginning, the degree of government involvement in the industry was really high; in fact, it was the government that initiated the foundation of the industry and protected it for a long period of time. In other words, especially in the beginning, the role of government is more direct in the Turkish glass industry than Porter (1990a) assumes in his diamond framework. Its relatively close ties with the government, however, do not change the fact that the Turkish glass industry suffers from the deficiencies in the country infrastructure, political and economic instability, poor regulations and a badly-functioning bureaucracy.

In light of our analysis, we can summarise what we have learnt from the case of the Turkish glass industry. First of all, we have understood that the diamond indeed provides us with a framework around which we can organise and systematise our thinking regarding the sources of competitive advantage. We have also seen that even without domestic rivalry it is still possible to be competitive in international markets given that some sort of exposure to international competition and pressure exists on the firms operating in the industry, and the structure of the industry favours large-scale production. Another thing we have learnt is that given that there is a potential, a more 'direct' involvement of the government, even in the initiation of an industry, has a chance to work in a developing country setting. Yet another important finding we derive from the analysis of the Turkish glass industry is that 'firm strategy and structure' can be of crucial importance and that some firms can create 'miracles' out of severe disadvantages. As Porter (1990a) suggests, pressure and challenge seem to be effective in pushing companies to be more proactive and creative in solving their major drawbacks.

4 The Turkish Construction Industry

The importance of the construction industry is obvious given that it is one of the largest sectors in the economies of many countries, especially if the country in question is in the process of industrialisation (Stallworthy and Kharbanda, 1985). The apparent reason for this is that almost all types of investments require some sort of construction activity. Furthermore, construction is considered as a 'locomotive' sector in that it leads and stimulates other commercial activities. As a result, construction services account for a considerable portion of GDP in many countries in the world, and the related figure for Turkey is around 6-7 per cent for recent years (*Construction Europe*, 1995). The share of the construction sector in the total employment of Turkey, which exceeds 4 per cent (Giritli et al., 1990: 420) is also undeniably high. The success of Turkish contractors in international markets has attracted world-wide attention (see, for instance, *ENR*, 1984: T1-12). The total value of work undertaken by Turkish contractors abroad has amounted to US$33 billion. The latest figures compiled by TCA show that the share Turkey captures in the international construction market reaches 10 per cent. The contribution of Turkish construction companies abroad to the Turkish economy as a source of foreign exchange earnings has amounted to one billion dollars annually for the preceding decade (i.e. 1980s) corresponding to around 10 per cent of total Turkish exports (T.C. Başbakanlık, 1995), and is envisaged to reach a yearly average of two billion dollars for the present decade (Gürer, 1995). International construction activities also contribute to the economy by generating additional employment opportunities. Currently, the number of Turkish workers employed abroad by both Turkish and foreign contractors has reached about 100,000. Apart from this fact, Turkish contractors operating abroad make an indirect contribution to the economy via their imports of inputs as well as consumer products from Turkey (Kaynak and Dalgıç, 1992).

Development of the Turkish Construction Industry

Tekeli and İlkin (1993: 209) argue that in the 1930s the newly founded Turkish Republic to a large extent offered a suitable environment for the development of local contractors by satisfying three prerequisites. First, there was a huge demand for construction activities, especially for infrastructure projects. Second, the necessary institutional structures as well as technological accumulation and cadres were more or less existent. Finally, the use of domestic debts to finance construction projects was made possible in the early 1930s, removing an obstacle that used to block the development of a local construction industry.

During the 1930s, most of the large-scale projects completed for the Turkish government were designed and implemented by foreign contractors. In these large projects, young Turkish engineers were highly active as site and office staff of the foreign contracting firms, taking this opportunity as a kind of on-the-job training (Gürer, 1995). The Turkish government, in the mean time, was highly motivated by the desire to decrease Turkish dependence on foreign technology. Accordingly, apart from favouring local contractors, it took an active part in increasing the supply and quality of engineers by launching a programme to educate technical personnel in foreign countries (OECD, 1988). All these resulted in a gradual increase in the share of domestic contractors in the Turkish market (Tekeli and İlkin, 1993).

The Turkish contractors' failure to form proper professional organisational structures is another issue of special interest as far as the Turkish construction industry in the 1930s and early 1940s is concerned. Most of the firms at the time were confronting their problems on an ad hoc basis. They were equally unsuccessful in establishing a proper sectoral organisation. The last noteworthy feature of the period that we should take into consideration is the nature of the relationship between the contractors and the government in the pre-World War II era, which was based on mutual trust, support and understanding. This is particularly important given that the government was virtually the only customer for the construction industry during this period (Tekeli and İlkin, 1993).

Although the emergence of the construction business right after the foundation of the Republic does obviously deserve special attention, it was not until the end of the Second World War when the Turkish construction industry really began to develop. Especially between 1950 and 1970, the industry grew remarkably with the help of several factors. First of all, huge infrastructure investments could be made during this period thanks to the USA government and other development funds given to the country after the war. Second, Turkey's entry into NATO initiated various military installation projects. Third, the period witnessed a massive urban migration fed by the rapid economic development and the social and political evolution it brought about. This resulted in extensive urban development programmes with large amounts of small-scale residential construction, which created a suitable environment for small-sized construction firms. In-house research and development units of two public agencies created in this period, namely the Highways Directorate and the State Waterworks, played important roles in developing technical manpower capacity in that some executives and technical staff from these agencies established their own private-sector firms later (OECD, 1988). In fact, it was this period during which most of today's important construction companies were founded (Tavakoli and Tulumen, 1990), and construction started to be a big business (Gürer, 1995).

In contrast to the rapid growth in the early 1970s during which Turkish construction companies were still trying to meet the huge demand for private housing as well as for public sector industrial projects, the economic environment of the mid-1970s posed enormous challenges to the construction industry. The country faced serious difficulties because of the embargo imposed after the Cyprus crisis in 1974 and continued to suffer economic problems which affected the construction industry like many other sectors until the end of the decade (Tavakoli and Tulumen, 1990). Under these circumstances, the boldest contractors started to go abroad. The large firms such as STFA and Enka were the pioneers.

In fact, this depressed home market coincided with the recession in the world caused by the surge in oil prices. This, ironically created an opportunity for the internationalisation of the construction companies since both oil-rich countries of the Middle East and Africa, and developing countries making use of the relatively cheap funds easily obtained from international financial markets to which these petro-dollars flowed contributed to a boom in demand for construction services. For the Turkish contractors, 'the enormous Middle East and North African markets were the closest and easiest to enter, and in 1975 the Turkish-Libyan Joint Economic Co-operation Protocol paved the way for Turkish contractors in Libya and for the gaining of valuable experience of working overseas' (Giritli et al., 1990: 416). Apart from the huge demand for construction services in the region caused by enormous wealth from the sale of petroleum and natural gas, there are some other factors that initially attracted Turkish construction companies to the Middle East and North Africa. Geographic proximity, a common cultural and religious heritage to Turkey, similar construction needs to that of Turkey, and a similar economic development path followed are among the most important ones (Kaynak and Dalgıç, 1992: 61-2).

In the late 1970s, Turkish contractors developed rapidly overseas and earned a reputation for being able to undertake low-technology projects quickly and at a low cost. Later on, parallel with their growth overseas, they developed an ability to tackle more complex projects both in their domestic market and abroad, and they started to act as prime contractors, a further improvement from their initial position as subcontractors.

According to an OECD study (1988), the 1980 liberalisation in Turkey affected the engineering services firms in two ways. First, some small firms disappeared with the increasing competition while some stronger ones joined conglomerates. Second, the larger companies decided to take more advantage of the buoyant Middle East markets. Rapid economic development in Turkey in the early 1980s started a massive building expansion as well. During the period, most of the domestic contracts were won by Turkish contractors. Financial, engineering, consultancy and construction services for the Atatürk Dam, for instance, the sixth largest in the world, were totally accomplished by Turkish firms (Gürer, 1995). As a result of this success, in both international and domestic markets, ENR ranked Turkey's construction industry as the eighth largest internationally as of 1984, just behind Germany.

In the following years, however, like construction industries everywhere, the Turkish construction industry ran into a drastic decrease in orders from the Middle East. This, together with the payment problems with Libya, the world oil crisis, the Iran-Iraq war, the Gulf crisis and an increasing tendency towards favouring local contractors everywhere in the world caused a serious contraction for the construction firms. Turkish firms were a bit lucky to have a number of domestic projects they could turn to in the meantime while searching for other opportunities abroad (Reed, 1985). An agreement made between Turkey and the Russian Federation in 1984 changed the destiny of the Turkish contractors during this difficult period and helped them recover from the crisis. The Turkish government decided to import Russian natural gas, but payment was made via a special payment system according to which 70 per cent of the annual payments were cleared through Turkish goods and services. Accordingly, Turkish contractors began to undertake projects in Russia starting from 1987. By winning the contract for the construction of around 15,000 homes in Russia, which were built using German loan facilities, to house soldiers returning from the former East Germany, they made use of the opportunity to establish themselves in this emerging market. They, in fact, impressed the Russians who had an opportunity to sample and appreciate the quality and efficiency of the Turkish contractors (Gürer, 1995).

The beginning of the 1990s, therefore, was an important turning point for the Turkish construction industry. A comparison of distribution of the works of Turkish contractors abroad on the basis of countries reveals that before 1990, classical markets for Turkish contractors were North Africa, the Middle East and Gulf countries. In North Africa, Libya was the dominant country, in the Near East, it was Iraq, while Saudi Arabia came first among the Gulf states (Kaynak and Dalgıç, 1992). After 1990, Turkish construction firms were handling contracts in the Russian Federation and the other former republics of the USSR, in addition to the Middle Eastern and African countries.

The most striking feature of the geographical break-down of the work of Turkish contractors is the dominance of one country. It was Libya before 1990 and the Russian Federation afterwards -both having shares of around 50 per cent. Up until 1989 the Russian Federation accounted for around 2 per cent of international work carried out by Turkish contractors whereas by 1995 the figure had increased to almost 54 per cent (*Construction Europe*, 1995). Another interesting development is their success in Germany, which was in a way a pilot case for Turkish contractors trying to enter into the European market. Although concentration on the Russian market still continues, Turkish contractors seemed to be diversifying the countries they work in by searching for new markets in Europe, Asia and the Far East.

A comparison of the distribution of work abroad on the basis of field of activity, on the other hand, shows that in the pre-1990 period, almost half of the work done abroad was related to 'housing' while 'infrastructure' took the second place. Since 1990, 'housing' continues to be the number one field of activity for the Turkish contractors abroad, though its share has diminished by more than 10 per cent while the shares of 'building', 'irrigation', 'hotel/hospital' and 'industrial facility/refinery' have increased considerably. In other words, we observe that Turkish contractors have been engaging in a wider range of activities in the 1990s than in the previous period (TCA and UIC-Turkey, 1994).

Sources of Advantage in the Turkish Construction Industry

Factor Conditions

The widespread use of a bid and tender system makes costs and prices the major competitive factors in the international construction industry. Among the factors that may contribute to the ability of the firms to undercut their competitors on price are lower labour costs, superior labour productivity, lower material costs, lower transportation costs for equipment and personnel, less costly financing and/or willingness to accept a lower rate of return (OECD, 1992).

Turkish construction firms prefer to employ Turkish workers. The reasons stated by my interviewees for hiring Turkish workers are threefold. First, they are willing to work for less than any equal counterparts from most other nations. In fact, they earn only about 60 per cent of their Korean counterparts' pay, which is a country also known to enjoy an advantage stemming from low-cost labour (Kaynak and Dalgıç, 1992). The same is true for skilled personnel and engineers in that a first rate Turkish engineer costs the same as a third-rate American engineer (Stallworthy and Kharbanda, 1985). Apart from that, they are very efficient, hard working, mobile and competent by international standards. Furthermore, they are able to adopt to new climates easily, and are prepared to work and live in harsh conditions which may be difficult to accept, say, for an American or German worker (Reed, 1985). Lastly, by taking their own labour to their projects abroad, Turkish contractors believe they avoid possible communication (language as well as cultural incompatibility) problems that may otherwise emerge. Regarding this issue, one of my interviewees argues that the ease of communication and ability to anticipate the likely performance of workers are more important than the other reasons since otherwise it would be perfectly possible to employ Pakistani or Indian workers who in fact demand even less. In short, considering the combined effect of these factors, the Turkish labour force becomes a major asset for Turkish contractors operating abroad (Tavakoli and Tulumen, 1990).

As far as the quality of Turkish engineers and architects is concerned, it is quite difficult to make a generalisation since it varies enormously from college to college. It is, however, undeniable that there are several universities in Turkey whose civil engineering and architecture faculties are world-class. All of my interviewees agree on the supreme quality of educational standards achieved by several universities in Turkey, especially in the Middle East Technical University and Istanbul Technical University. Practical orientation, however, remains weak, even in the top colleges (DPT, 1993a).

The advantages Turkish contractors enjoy related to human resources, however, are tempered by several problems. The first one, as mentioned above, is a lack of practical orientation. Another problematic area is that since the authority needed for the mid-level supervisory positions is not well-defined, we observe an underutilisation of engineers undertaking such duties. A lack of systematic training (both standard education and on-the-job training) for mid-level positions is considered to be mainly responsible for this. Occupational schools that would teach how to cope with new technological developments that affect the industry and would give practical as well as theoretical education are badly needed (DPT, 1993c).

Although it depends on the type of work done, Turkish contractors usually prefer to use materials and equipment from Turkey in their projects. When the project requires a type of equipment that is difficult or not feasible to obtain from Turkey (e.g. elevators, air-conditioning etc.), or when the type of equipment is specified in the contract by the client or the creditor, they then use imported materials, usually from the EU. The reason for their predominant preference for the inputs from Turkey is their satisfactory quality with a competitive price. The type of work does matter, however, in that around 80 per cent of the materials used in housing construction comes from Turkey whereas around 90 per cent of inputs used in road construction is imported from other countries.

The recent developments in the international construction market have increased the relative importance of technology, and also of financing, as two determinants of international competitiveness. To be able to win contracts, it is becoming increasingly a must for construction firms to provide a financing package for the client through arrangements with commercial banks or their own governments. This is described by my interviewees as a major disadvantage for Turkish contractors in international markets. In fact, financing difficulties often restrict them to the contracts with no financing requirements. Of course, these are, at the same time, projects for which competition is really intense. Reasons for financial problems are manifold. Letters of credit provided by Turkish banks are expensive, costing as much as 4.5 per cent of a contract's value against no more than 1 per cent in Europe, and furthermore they are less credible than those from other countries, which are covered by insurance or state guarantees (Reed, 1985). Moreover, Turkish firms lack insurance, which will protect them in case of any risk of devaluation or political changes in the client country (Giritli et al., 1990). The same difficulties cause troubles in the domestic market as well. Although there is, for instance, a huge demand for housing, no properly financed and officially registered mass housing market yet exists in Turkey (*Construction Europe*, 1995). Given that government support is inadequate and if there is any, it is very slow, what contractors usually do, in order to overcome this problem, is to form joint-ventures with foreign companies, especially for large projects. For the smaller ones, they use their owners' equity instead. Build-operate-transfer (BOT) systems, pioneered by the former president of Turkey, Mr Turgut Özal, which took their place in the literature as one of the most innovative international project financing techniques, also emerged as a way to overcome such financing difficulties.

Turkish contractors are weak not only in finance but in technology as well. In fact, like some other service sectors, overall research and development intensity in the construction industry is very low with research and development expenditures averaging less than 0.1 per cent of net industry output in most countries (OECD, 1992). While most construction technology is available through licensing, innovation in construction methods and proprietary rights for new technologies can, of course, add to competitiveness (OECD, 1992). Unfortunately, as in other sectors of the economy, research and development conducted in the construction industry is rather limited in Turkey. A noteworthy related characteristic of the Turkish construction industry is that the strength of firms remains 'person-specific' in that it is manifested in the capabilities of their personnel and, thus, vulnerable to turnovers of that personnel (OECD, 1988). We should, however, state that some construction companies do have connections with the universities. Some fund research projects and give scholarships to the students studying in the related fields, which can be considered as an indirect way of supporting research and education in the industry.

None of the interviewees had any complaint about the difficulty of accessing relevant information. They instead stated that the required information was to a large extent available, and they did not have any problems in reaching either technical information or information about projects and markets. It seems also that this is not a problem in the domestic market if we can believe a sarcastic remark made by one of the interviewees: 'There have been so few new projects in the domestic market recently that it is almost impossible not to hear about them'.

In summary, an overall evaluation for the factor conditions reveals a relatively advantageous position for the Turkish construction industry. Especially as far as the basic and generalised factors are concerned, the industry enjoys considerable advantages thanks to low-cost, competent, hard-working and self-sacrificing Turkish workers, cheap and good quality materials, and a quite favourable geographical position near the important markets for the international construction industry. Turkish contractors, however, suffer a severe disadvantage due to financing difficulties, which are becoming increasingly important in the world market, especially for larger projects. Although this problem forced the industry to find creative solutions like the BOT system to find remedies for their drawbacks, the situation is likely to pose serious threats for the further development of the industry. Regarding advanced and specific factors, a well-educated army of engineers is the first thing to note, which constitutes a valuable asset for the Turkish construction industry. Disadvantages in technology cease to be so determining though they are still arguably important, given the low technology intensity of the construction industry. Turkish constructors do not encounter many obstacles while trying to reach the required information, and there are some, though few, connections among the universities and industry participants. To conclude, factor conditions, both with respect to basic and advanced as well as general and specific factors, are to a large extent favourable for the Turkish construction industry with the exception of financing difficulties.

Demand Conditions

Confirming Porter's (1990a) hypothesis, the international construction industry is somewhat specialised with firms being strongest in technologies important in their home market. Just to give a few striking examples, Japanese firms are leaders in high speed railroads, seismic design and bridge construction whereas Swiss and Austrian firms are advanced in ground stabilisation techniques and tunnelling technology (OECD, 1992). The case of Turkey gives further support to the argument in that Turkish exports of construction services reflect the pattern of demand in Turkey's domestic market, which is dominated by housing and infrastructure projects. Although the demand for houses is skyrocketing together with the rapidly increasing population and urbanisation, and Turkey's infrastructure programmes are very ambitious, serious doubts concerning how they might be realistically financed remain. We, nevertheless, expect further change in Turkey towards greater industrialisation and urbanisation, making it rather hard to postpone investments in the domestic market, despite financial difficulties. Apart from housing and infrastructure, hotel construction emerges as another area in which success at home seems to be paralleling that abroad. The country's booming tourism sector certainly helps Turkish constructors gain some experience in this segment. It is also confirmed by the interviews I conducted that during recent years infrastructure has captured a considerable share of domestic demand with motorways constituting a dynamic market while housing remains bright as usual.

Having this picture for the domestic market in mind, it becomes no surprise that the countries where Turkish contractors are active resemble Turkey as a developing country. The Russian Federation, for instance, the most important client for the Turkish contractors in recent years, is badly in need of infrastructure, housing stock, public buildings and hotels, a quite similar demand pattern to that of Turkey (Gürer, 1995). The demand structure in the rest of the world, especially in the developed countries, however, is changing, and it is envisaged that a better management capability and the ability to work with high technology will be key factors in the international construction environment, posing a threat for the Turkish contractors in the long-run, who still to a large extent depend on labour-intensive projects.

Porter (1990a) argues that the nature of home buyers, particularly whether they are more sophisticated and demanding relative to the foreign ones, is of crucial importance in both creating and sustaining competitive advantage. A comparison of the standards of foreign versus domestic customers shows that standards in the domestic market match, even exceed, the ones of the major foreign clients, say Russia, for instance. Many interviewees described the average quality required by Russian customers as 'below average' as compared to the ones required in the Turkish domestic market. It should be, however, mentioned that my interviewees have stressed the increasing level of sophistication in the Russian market in recent years. They usually agree that Turkish firms are capable of doing high quality work, and that in fact everybody wants high-quality work but it all depends on the financial means of the client in the end. The required quality in the Middle East, another important market for the Turkish contractors, for instance, is considered to be quite high mainly because they have money, and firms from Western countries usually undertake the design and consultancy phases of the projects above a certain level of quality. Another related issue is that the current contract awarding mechanism employed by the Ministry of Public Works and Settlement requires conformity with the 'typical projects' they have on their hands, which apparently aims to guarantee a minimum level of quality, but at the same time is seen by some contractors as limiting, even discouraging the technological development process (DPT, 1993c). In short, we indeed observe a pressure for higher standards and quality in the domestic market, especially relative to the countries where Turkish contractors operate (e.g. Russia). This, however, does not change the fact that it is the developed countries that lead the industry in terms of quality and technological developments as it is evident from the continuous reference to Europe by my interviewees when asked about quality or technology.

In summary, it is undeniable that the home market is important for Turkish contractors though local demand has been stagnant in recent years, even described as depressed by some scholars (e.g. Kaynak and Dalgıç, 1992: 70). Turkey, however, is a developing country with a rapidly increasing population, which makes investments, especially in infrastructure and housing, essential. The nature of the domestic market, therefore, gives Turkish contractors an important lead while working in other developing countries where they have an opportunity to make use of their experience accumulated over the years in Turkey. Other attributes of home demand like the sophistication or anticipatory nature of home buyers, however, do not suffice to provide an advantage for Turkish contractors, but they do not put them in a particularly disadvantageous situation, either.

Related and Supporting Industries

Deriving from Porter's (1990a) study, we expect the industries that are suppliers for and/or somewhat related to the Turkish construction industry to be also competitive in international markets. The firms operating in the Turkish construction industry are linked to a large number of supplementary industries such as glass, steel, wood, cement, bricks, ceramics, sand and clay (Kaynak and Dalgıç, 1992); all of which are amongst the most competitive Turkish industries (see Table 2.2 in Chapter 2, and Table A1.1, Table A1.2, and Table A1.3 in Appendices).

The technical excellence and reliability of the construction equipment used certainly affects the competitiveness of construction firms. American and Japanese construction firms, for instance, enjoy the advantages brought about by their competitive construction equipment industries in winning overseas contracts (OECD, 1992). The construction equipment industry is in fact dominated by a few firms. The structure of the industry until the late 1970s is best described as an oligopoly involving a number of international players led by Caterpillar. Together with the entrance of Komatsu, however, the industry structure evolved towards a duopoly. Other competitors responded via consolidation and rationalisation of operations, globalisation of strategies, segmentation of products and markets, and strategic alliances to be able to return to a more stable oligoplistic structure (Rukstad, 1993). Although such moves definitely affected trade, Caterpillar and Komatsu continue to be the most important players in the industry. When we examine the situation in Turkey, we see that the industry mainly includes Turkish companies that are dealers for these giants; Borusan Makina is the dealer for Caterpillar whereas Sabancı is for Komatsu's (*Construction Europe*, 1995).

Another related industry that is of special importance for the construction industry is design engineering and consultancy services. In sharp contrast to the outstanding performance of the Turkish construction industry, the competitive position of the Turkish design engineering and consultancy services is weak. One reason that blocked the development of the independent design engineering and consultancy firms is the inadequate and fluctuating domestic demand that makes it insecure for the firms to concentrate on that segment only. Another fact is that construction firms first started to internationalise as subcontractors to foreign firms during the 1970s, which delayed the development as well as the internationalisation of design engineering and consultancy firms. Design engineering and consultancy firms also suffered because of such reasons as lack of capital and organisational or co-ordinational problems. Moreover, it took some time for the Turkish government to realise the importance of the design and consultancy engineering services; in fact, it was not until 1992 that the Ministry of Public Works and Settlement prepared a regulation to help the industry improve its competitive position, both in the domestic and international market. The relatively poor placed competitive position of the Turkish design engineering and consultancy firms signals problems for the long-run, given that during the design phase, firms have the opportunity to affect the further phases of the project and promote the use of materials and/or contractors from their own country (DPT, 1993a).

In summary, the hypothesis that internationally competitive industries of a nation tend to be related to each other finds a somewhat mixed support from the case of the Turkish construction industry. Turkish firms, for instance, are not amongst the important competitors in the engineering design and consultancy services industry, and the construction equipment industry is mainly dominated by the foreign affiliates of a few transnational companies. The construction materials industry, on the other hand, is very competitive internationally and dominated by local private firms. Similarly, the presence of highly competitive supporting and related industries like glass, ceramics, and iron and steel indicates a potential for the development of a self-reinforcing cluster.

Firm Strategy, Structure and Rivalry

There is no doubt that the competition amongst the Turkish contractors is cut-throat, both in the domestic and international markets, confirming one of the strongest empirical results of Porter's (1990a) study that intensity of domestic rivalry and the creation and persistence of competitive advantage in an industry go hand in hand. A typical example is the vigorous competition observed amongst the Turkish contractors to win the contracts, which were awarded to a Turkish contractor in connection with the natural-gas barter agreement with Russia. It is a really dynamic sector with firms growing, and new, smaller entrants quickly replacing the old ones. Competition concentrates on price, quality and references of the company, in order of importance. Since the competition is very intense, some firms may tender incredibly low prices.

When we explore the attitude towards collaboration in the Turkish construction industry, we observe that joint ventures are considered to be the most important form of collaboration because they provide good learning opportunities as well as access to domestic and foreign markets. Subcontracting, which can be regarded as another collaborative mechanism, is more common in local projects though it is becoming more important in exports of engineering services as well. Firms may also engage in project-specific joint ventures with both local and foreign partners (OECD, 1988). The forms of collaboration stated above, however, are more related to the nature of the industry rather than attempts to decrease or eliminate competition in the industry.

In fact, as has been mentioned before, according to Tekeli and İlkin (1993), the least successful area for Turkish contractors, in the early years of the development of the industry, was their failure to come together and form organisations to voice their problems and look after their interests. Later, however, this situation changed drastically with the foundation of the Turkish Contractors' Association (TCA) in 1952. While in the beginning it was a businessman's lobbying club serving the needs of the distinguished contractors, it gradually, especially after the late 1980s, emerged as an important professional institution recognised as the representative of the construction sector both at home and abroad. The second important organisation of Turkish contractors, the Union of International Contractors (UIC) - Turkey, was founded in 1991 since an apparent need arose to deal with the problems of the contractors operating abroad, which obviously deserved separate attention after the increasing involvement of Turkish contractors in international markets (TCA and UIC-Turkey, 1994).

When we examine the structure of the Turkish construction industry, we see that Turkish construction firms are relatively small by international standards. Exceptions, of course, remain. ENKA, for instance, became the tenth largest in 1986 amongst the top international contractors list of ENR. Furthermore, companies like Enka, Alarko, Doğuş, Gama, STFA, Botek and Tekfen are large enough to have their shares listed on foreign stock exchanges (notably in Germany) (*Construction Europe*, 1995). Predictably, those contractors active abroad are usually relatively bigger than the ones whose major area of interest is the local market. Turkish construction firms are rather centralised. Owner managers are usually professionals themselves, and it is not rare for them to be involved in practical work supervising the details personally. It follows from this that the internal organisation of Turkish construction firms is usually not that formal. This is partly related to the firms' relative youth as well as to the fact that managers are often the founders of the firm. The widespread use of subcontracting in the construction industry in general also contributes to a lack of attention to formalisation since it gives an organisation a capacity to undertake work beyond its scope in terms of size and specialisation (Giritli et al., 1990).

This picture, however, has been changing, especially since firms became increasingly active in the international market. Kaynak and Dalgıç (1992) argue that Turkish construction companies went through four stages during their internationalisation process. Initially they were low-cost bidders to win projects, then they aimed at making use of more efficient business opportunities to maintain profitability. Afterwards, they concentrated on creating economies of scale, and lastly, they became global companies whose activities are diversified. Now, conglomerates dominate; in fact, Turkey's main construction companies are typically part of wider industrial and financial diversified entities (*Construction Europe*, 1995). Among the other industries they operate in are banking, tourism, marketing, automotive, construction materials and cement production. It is, in other words, difficult to grasp a pattern in their diversification although construction related industries and tourism frequently appear as the most popular areas. Construction, however, seems to remain as their major area of activity. The two important reasons for the overwhelming extent of unrelated diversification in the industry are the dwindling nature of demand in the construction industry in general and the unstable economic and political environment of Turkey in particular.

Turkish firms' heavy dependence on the international market is undeniable. In fact, construction firms from Yugoslavia, Turkey, Switzerland and Italy have traditionally been among the most dependent on foreign work in the ENR survey of the top 250 firms (OECD, 1992).

With regard to the strategies commonly used by Turkish contractors, we can cite the conclusion Kaynak and Dalgıç (1992: 69-70) derive from their interviews with the executives of Turkish contractors, which states that 'survival' is the most important strategic objective, not a surprise in an environment of ongoing instability. In another study, Giritli et al. (1990: 418) find out that the most frequently used methods, by the Turkish contractors, to penetrate a market are the prospects and opportunities created within the sphere of joint economic co-operation agreements (the Turkish-Libyan JEC and the Turkish-Iraqi JEC), or barter terms (the Turkish-Soviet co-operation projects), and military construction projects (Turkish contractors have found a niche in Libya for such projects). In addition, the labour shortage in some countries like Saudi Arabia make it possible for developing countries like Turkey to undertake large construction projects in such countries. They usually prefer to be independent contractors. The contracts undertaken in Libya between the years 1978 and 1990, for instance, show the following pattern: 81.2 per cent of Turkish firms worked as independent contractors, 15.3 per cent as a partner to a joint venture, and the remaining 3.5 per cent as a subcontractor (Kaynak and Dalgıç, 1992: 63).

Although Turkish contractors complain about the contracting domestic market, they still consider it as important. One of my interviewees states that 'the domestic market is even more important in that the foreign markets you operate in may not be that reliable in the long-run as we have learnt from the case of Iraq. Now, we want to enter into the more stable markets of Western countries, but their demand is not that high given that they have the necessary infrastructure as well as strong construction firms. Thus the competition is tough'. Another manager I interviewed, on the other hand, says that 'our target market is wherever we find jobs, and in fact, it is not so difficult to change markets for contractors'.

Gürer (1995), the president of both TCA and UIC-Turkey, argues that the success of Turkish construction firms in the international markets is perhaps unique since they mostly depend on their ability of organisation, power of enterprise and courage of taking risks. Kaynak and Dalgıç (1992: 68-69) reach similar conclusions as a result of their interviews; Turkish construction companies which are willing to undertake risky construction projects, prefer initiating rather than imitating the moves of others, have a desire to seek market opportunities on a global scale, and have longer planning horizons compared to other sectors. In fact, the extent of their courage in risk taking is beyond the imagination of many Western companies. To quote Ali Rıza Çarmıklı, Chairman of Libas: 'We arrived in Libya in early 1975 with nothing more than our curiosity and a tourist visa [...] We returned with US$200 million worth of orders' (Stallworthy and Kharbanda, 1985). The importance attributed to the entrepreneurial spirit of Turkish contractors by my interviewees is striking. Some argue that they cannot see any other advantage so peculiar to Turkish contractors.

Distinguishing managerial characteristics of Turkish contractors is not limited to their courage in taking risks. Their communication skills, both interpersonal and interorganisational, the latter including the relationships with local and foreign governments as well, are also considered to be a major asset. They know how to deal with the bureaucracy. In fact, my interviewees state that most of the projects Turkey undertake abroad are won as a result of established contacts there. Good relationships both at home and abroad are at the same time a reflection of their sensitiveness to social issues. In this regard, Kaynak and Dalgıç (1992: 69) argue that 'major Turkish construction companies tend to have strong nationalistic feelings. [...] They felt obliged to repay Turkey for educational opportunities and wished to see Turkey raised to international standing and credibility. Managers see the extension of their business outside of Turkey as socially motivated rather than economically'. As a result of my interviews, I also got the impression that, confirming the findings of Tekeli and İlkin (1993) for the early periods of the Republic, executives of the construction firms believe that they have a mission, and they assume an important part in the development process going on in the country.

In summary, like in the glass industry, managerial capabilities of Turkish contractors can be considered among the most important strengths of the Turkish construction industry. The only weak point of the Turkish contractors as far as this 'corner' of the diamond is concerned may be their over-dependence on a single market, which was Libya before 1990 and became Russia afterwards. They look for other opportunities, however, especially in the East Asia and Europe, and do not consider it hard to change markets. The results revealed by our analysis concerning the last element of this category, domestic rivalry, are also in line with Porter's (1990a) predictions in that rivalry among Turkish contractors is very intense indeed, not just in the domestic market but in the foreign markets as well. To conclude, for this element of the diamond, the case of the Turkish construction industry provides a comfortable support for Porter's (1990a) hypotheses.

The Role of Chance

The most outstanding event that can be described as 'chance' for the Turkish construction industry is without doubt the construction boom in the Middle East and North Africa in the 1970s, following the oil shock. The Turkish contractors were next door to these important construction markets. Apart from geographic proximity, there is an undeniable psychological proximity stemming from a common heritage, cultural and religious ties. The importance of such factors should not be underestimated given that, for instance, the holy cities of Makkah and Medina of Saudi Arabia are closed to non-Moslems. Şarık Tara from ENKA states that 'we know how to fight against bureaucracy, we have patience, and Western contractors do not understand this' (Reed, 1985). In fact, for this market, Turkish contractors can be attractive joint-venture partners for Western companies, and it is even considered that it may provide advantages to have the Turkish contractor 'up front' (Stallworthy and Kharbanda, 1985).

Another favourable chance event for the Turkish construction industry took place more recently with the disintegration of the USSR. An enormous demand for construction emerged there and Turkish contractors were again lucky to enjoy the advantages stemming from geographical and cultural proximity.

Turkish contractors also had to face some unfavourable events taking place beyond their control. The Iran-Iraq War, for instance, created serious problems in a what used to be a good market for Turkish contractors as plans for most of the major projects were suspended. Similarly, Iraq's invasion of Kuwait created considerable troubles for some Turkish contractors. As of August 1990, the TCA estimated the related losses of Turkish companies as high as US$800 million, which was partly compensated for by a special package prepared by the Turkish Undersecretariat of the Treasury and Foreign Trade (Kaynak and Dalgıç, 1992). The aftermath of these two wars, however, ironically created some revival in the construction markets of the countries involved. In particular, the task of rebuilding Kuwait provides opportunities given the magnitude of destruction. Payment problems with Libya, which emerged after the US embargo, constituted yet another unlucky event causing headaches for Turkish contractors.

To conclude, if we try to derive the net effect of the chance events taking place beyond the control of the firms but affecting their performance, we can safely say that luck has been with the Turkish contractors most of the time.

The Role of Government

Although general debate over protectionism generally concerns manufacturing rather than service industries, industrial policies for services have started to attract more attention recently. To give a striking example, we see that the extent of intervention in South Korea is so excessive that in 1986 the government declared that it would reduce the number of overseas construction firms by a third (OECD, 1992). The Turkish government, on the other hand, does not have an integrated national strategy towards contracting overseas. Apart from failing to support contractors in their activities abroad to a notable extent, the government creates further problems for the industry. Bureaucratic obstacles that delay the assignment of personnel overseas, the contractors' inability to bring idle machinery back to Turkey due to import restrictions and difficulties workers face in the transfer of their remittances are just a few examples to mention (Reed, 1985).

Frequent changes in the regulations conducted by different governments, well-supported rumours of corruption in the awarding process of government contracts, and very high and unpredictable inflation rates making it difficult to prepare realistic bid offers undoubtedly create troubles for Turkish contractors. The regulations concerning the failure or delay of payment do not work properly or work very slowly. The contractors also express their disappointment since although it is the policy of the Turkish government to support sectors that are important exporters and/or create considerable employment for the country -and construction definitely fulfils both- they lack enough support from the government (DPT, 1993c).

Financing, which is the major factor disadvantage for Turkish contractors, relates to the role government plays for two reasons. First, an unstable macroeconomic environment resulting in oppressive interest rates makes it very hard to obtain the necessary funds through capital markets. Second, a major source of financing for the rest of the world, government funds, in the form of export credit for instance, cease to be a serious alternative for Turkish contractors since it is very limited indeed. We should, however, mention a noteworthy exception here, that is the BOT system as a creative solution to the financing problem which was introduced by the Turkish government and gained world-wide acceptance afterwards.

Other problematic areas related to or caused by the government include differences in foreign trade and customs regulations between the client countries and Turkey, which may result in troubles such as contractors not being able to export the machinery and investment goods they own at home. In fact, this problem can easily be solved by the help of bilateral agreements. Incompatibilities in the social security regulations and tax systems sometimes create problems too. Although required regulations are on the agenda, the progress is very slow. Another area to which the government has been rather slow to respond concerns the previously mentioned payment problem with Libya, which stopped payments in 1994 without stating any reason. Having suffered from such problems, TCA and UIC-Turkey are lobbying for the establishment of a risk insurance system which will insure them for political and economic risks including failure of a client to pay the receivable (UIC, 1996).

The general characteristic of state-business relations which is described as 'a love-hate relationship' by Buğra (1994), seems to be most heavily felt in the Turkish construction industry. They have many problems some caused by the state, or which have not been solved either because of simple negligence or inability or in some cases because of political reasons. The state, however, is definitely a major actor and the most important client in the domestic market. Turkish contractors, for instance, have to obey the regulations enacted specifically for the industry. The most typical example is that the Turkish Ministry of Public Works and Settlement uses a contractor classification system to control the nature and size of the projects a contractor may be allowed to bid on and issues a contracting licence and a technical proficiency certificate. The classification is based on past experience, and technological and the management abilities of the contractor. Government also affects the industry by controlling the contract awarding system. Prior to 1983, the lowest bidder was awarded the job in the public sector. This resulted in ultra-low bids and hence ever-lasting low quality projects, which was intolerable given the urgent need for transportation and energy investments. In 1983, government limited bidding to 20 per cent of government cost estimates except for the jobs open to international bidding. Under this system, every contractor automatically discounts 20 per cent, and contracts are awarded on the basis of the points given according to their financial strength, reputation, experience and reliability rather than cost. Since the enactment of the law, public projects have been completed more quickly and successfully (Tavakoli and Tulumen, 1990).

The Turkish government, in fact, has also provided support to the contractors from time to time. Tax incentives and tax rebates offered by successive Turkish governments during the early 1980s certainly provided a motive for the construction companies to go abroad (Kaynak and Dalgıç, 1992: 70). Moreover, contractors operating abroad are favoured by a corporate tax exemption. More recently, the previously mentioned natural gas barter agreement with the Russian Federation changed their destiny by facilitating their entrance to this emerging market (Gürer, 1995). Ankara has also had a similar deal with the Bosnian government initiating an agreement requiring that the US$20 million loan Turkey will provide for Bosnia would be used to finance the work of Turkish contractors to secure their entrance into this promising market (*Turkish Daily News*, 1996). Apart from these, it is undeniable that many of the top Turkish construction companies have traditionally enjoyed close ties with the government (*Construction Europe*, 1995). Of course, the fact that the only client was the state at the beginning of the development of the industry has contributed to the formation of this close relationship between the big firms and government (Tekeli and Ilkin, 1993).

It was not until 1992, however, that the government started to take their concerns seriously into account in a systematic way. In that year, a body responsible from the 'Consultancy to the Prime Ministry for International Contracting Services' was founded to analyse their demands and complaints, and solve their problems one by one. It seems to have been working quite well, though slowly. Payment problems with Libya, for instance, have been almost solved as of today. The conflicts between SSK, the major social security organisation of Turkey, and Turkish contractors have been settled down. An information centre for the international contracting services has been founded. A considerable reduction has been achieved in the required red-tape to get an incentive, and an opportunity to use a low-interest credit for those undertaking projects in the former USSR has been provided (T.C. Başbakanlık, 1993).

To conclude, there is no doubt that government is an important actor in the construction industry. Apart from being an important client, the government does affect the competitiveness of construction firms by its attitude towards the industry. Due to the particularly important and active role the government plays in construction, the industry suffers from the general incompetency of the government relatively more than the other sectors do. Deficiencies in the country infrastructure, a slow bureaucracy and dwindling economic and political environment put the industry in a disadvantageous position. As far as the government support for the industry is concerned, it can be said that the Turkish government failed to form a coherent and a systematic policy towards the industry although the situation has started to change recently. In fact, it is stated by my interviewees that there is a considerable improvement in the attitude of the government towards the industry, especially since the 1980s. The extent of government support, however, still lags a long way behind the ones provided by the EU and Korean governments. It is, therefore, hard to state that the degree of government support is enough to provide a clear advantage for the Turkish construction industry in international markets, despite the promising improvements taking place in recent years.

Concluding Remarks

As Demirel, the president of Turkey, who is a civil engineer himself, puts it Turkey has been in the process of 'construction' since the foundation of the Republic in 1923. The newly founded Republic with a huge demand for construction activities indeed paved the way for the development of the industry. It was not until the end of World War II, however, when the Turkish construction industry really began to develop, mainly thanks to the massive infrastructure investments of the period. This rapid growth in demand levelled off in the mid-1970s, and Turkish contractors found themselves confronted with the only option available: going abroad. The depressed home market, in fact, coincided with the booming demand for construction services, following the surge in petroleum prices, in the oil-rich and infrastructure-poor countries of the Middle East and North Africa. These geographically and culturally close markets gave Turkish contractors the valuable chance of gaining experience in working overseas. Later, they made good use of this experience when they had the opportunity to undertake projects in another promising market, the former republics of the USSR. As stated previously, the total volume of work undertaken by Turkish contractors abroad has reached approximately US$33 billion and Turkish contractors are among the top ten exporters of construction services.

If we combine the analysis presented in this chapter with the latest developments in the world market, we come up with the following picture. The relative importance of the competitive factors in the industry seems to be changing in favour of the ability to provide the necessary technology and financing in a single service package. Together with this is the increasing importance of the design engineering and management services. The important role attributed to the international relations and economic interests, and hence to the government are also of special interest. For many cases, in other words, competing on the basis of cost alone seems to be not enough anymore. Keeping this picture in mind, it may be tempting to conclude that prospects for the Turkish contractors are not that favourable in the long-run given their heavy dependence on cheap labour employed in the geographically and culturally proximate markets. Our analysis, however, reveals that these are not the only advantages Turkish contractors rely upon. Apart from these 'factor conditions' and 'chance' advantages, there are advantages in 'demand conditions' and 'firm strategy, structure and rivalry' as has been discussed in detail above. Furthermore, Turkish contractors achieved their success despite economic and political instability and without a notable government support. This, of course, does not mean that they do not suffer from some disadvantages. On the contrary, in particular financing problems and the relatively lagging position in design engineering and consultancy services pose serious threats for the future development of the industry.

In light of the analysis conducted above, we can argue that the diamond for the Turkish construction industry seems to have the potential of being a self-reinforcing and well-functioning one though considerable disturbances remain. Finally, regarding the diamond framework, we can state that the combination of factors shaping the advantage in the Turkish construction industry points a positive sign in favour of the diamond without raising much challenge to the framework.

5 The Turkish Leather Clothes Industry

The leather industry is widely accepted as one of the key sectors of the Turkish economy in terms of its production and export performance as well as its contribution to employment. The recent growth of the industry is very impressive with an annual rate of 9 per cent between the years 1984 and 1992, well above the corresponding overall industrial average of 5-6 per cent (Vakıfbank, 1995). Moreover, the industry creates considerable employment opportunities due to its labour-intensive nature. The number of registered employees in the leather clothes industry alone is estimated to be around 70,000 (DIE, 1994b).

Another outstanding aspect of the industry is its high export orientation. In fact, exports of leather and leather products constitute around 7 per cent of the country's total exports. Leather exports of Turkey reached a peak in 1987 at US$825 million, and since then have levelled off at around a yearly average of US$700 million (Vakıfbank, 1995). These figures, however, do not include the sales made to tourists visiting Turkey, which are estimated to be at least half, and probably as much as these official export figures. The most important export markets for Turkish leather producers are the EU and the Russian Federation. In terms of subsectors, 85 per cent of Turkish exports of leather products comes from the leather clothes industry, in which Turkey has become one of the most important exporters in the world market (DPT, 1996). Trying to understand the reasons is the subject of this chapter. There has been, however, a decline in the relative position of the industry in world markets since the late 1980s, and our second task in this chapter is to explore the reasons behind that loss in position. The answers given to these two will in turn clarify whether the underlying sources of advantage are the ones hypothesised by Porter (1990a).

Development of the Turkish Leather Clothes Industry

Like the glass industry, the leather industry has grown out of a tradition in Turkey. İstanbul, just after it was conquered by the Ottomans, emerged as a centre of leather making. It was, in fact, Sultan Mehmet (1450s) himself, the conqueror of İstanbul, who encouraged the foundation of a leather industry in Kazlıçeşme where the industry was located for the following 540 years until its move to Tuzla (*Deri*, 1995d). The technology employed at the time was supreme relative to those of other countries. It was not uncommon for foreigners to come to Turkey to learn specific methods of processing leather or producing some specific dyes (Adnan, 1935). When the Empire began to lag behind, however, the leather industry could not keep up with the technological developments, and hence ceased to prosper.

This lagging position of the leather industry went on in the early years of the Republic as well. During the etatist period, Sümerbank, a state founded giant, emerged as a major entity producing leather products, especially footwear. After 1950, together with the inclination by the government towards more liberal policies, the sector started to develop gradually. During the following decade, the planned period, although the industry in general and leather clothes production in particular continued to prosper, the emphasis was still on the domestic market (Özçörekçi, 1988). Leather clothes production was overwhelmingly a home-production activity scattered around the country. In the beginning of the 1970s, Germans encouraged Turkey to engage in leather production more extensively due to its geographic proximity to Europe and the relatively cheaper labour force. Turkish producers learnt how to improve their business from Germans and sold most of their final products to them. They did not have any difficulties in finding customers, and enjoyed an easy and comfortable life for a while during which exports in the industry were fuelled (*Deri*, 1995b). At that time, however, the capacity of leather producers was not that large, which resulted in exporting low-quality goods as well, and thus caused a bad reputation in terms of quality in this newly entered market. Meanwhile, international competition began to intensify, especially together with the increasing presence of South Korea in the leather clothes industry. Political and economic difficulties Turkey faced in the second half of the seventies hit the leather clothes industry too, contributing further to the negative picture described above (Küçükbali, 1983). Leather clothes producers of the time found it extremely difficult to compete with the cheap products of South Korea, Thailand and Argentina. Some of the small firms had to shut down, and considerable falls in the Turkish exports of leather clothes were observed until 1979 (Küçükbali, 1983).

The situation, however, started to change in the early 1980s; first, domestic demand increased as a result of rising income levels and changes in consumer tastes in favour of leather clothes. Then, by making good use of the export incentives and tax rebates, offered after liberalisation, leather clothes producers started to increase their export performance enormously

(Küçükbali, 1983). The industry recovered fairly quickly, and in a short period of time became one of the sectors in which Turkey had an important place in world markets. In fact, in one year, from 1980 to 1981, Turkish exports of leather clothes increased by more than 80 per cent (Vakıfbank, 1995).

The rapid increase observed in the exports of leather products in the 1980s did not endure for long, and a considerable decline in the Turkish share of world leather clothes exports, from more than 20 per cent in 1985 to around 7 per cent in 1992, was observed, the reasons of which are twofold. Internal reasons include the time lapse and hence production lost during the move of the leather factories from Kazlıçeşme to Tuzla. The municipality required the leather manufacturers to stop production in the late 1980s until the new industrial district was completed in 1994 because of the environmental pollution associated with the industry. Accordingly, starting from 1994, leather production factories in İstanbul shifted from Kazlıçeşme, their original and traditional area of geographic concentration to Tuzla Leather Industrial Zone. It was, however, far from being a well-organised move, and poor handling of this situation caused considerable losses in production as well as permanent closure of some factories. The fall in exports is certainly a lot to do with the abolition of most of the export subsidies in the late 1980s and the increasing labour costs in Turkey as well. They both damaged the price competitiveness of labour-intensive leather products (Vakıfbank, 1995). The latter relates to the second set of reasons, the external ones, in that new entrants with lower labour costs, like Pakistan, China and India, can offer more competitive prices than Turkish producers. Other external reasons include the decreasing demand for leather products from EU countries and considerable support for the key competitors from their governments. Having stated the reasons, we should also mention that decrease in exports has been partly offset since the late 1980s by the emergence of the 'Laleli market' in İstanbul which has been fuelled by Russian tourists. Due to the new trade regulations in the C.I.S. aimed at limiting their imports, however, Laleli market, where most of the direct sales to the visitors from these countries occur, is threatened (*Deri*, 1995e).

Around 80 per cent of leather and leather products exports are from the İstanbul region. The Russian Federation, Germany and France top the list as importers of Turkish leather products. The overall trade picture for the Turkish leather industry is such that Turkish leather processing industry imports chemicals and raw leather, and sells the processed leather to leather products manufacturers, who in turn export most of their final products. Considering its total leather production, and its imports of raw leather and exports of leather products, Turkey is an important country with a strong image in the world leather industry (DPT, 1996).

Sources of Advantage in the Turkish Leather Clothes Industry

Factor Conditions

The inputs used in leather clothes production and their approximate shares in total costs are as follows: processed leather 65 per cent, labour 15 per cent, accessories 6 per cent, administration 14 per cent. As is evident from these numbers, processed leather is the most important item followed by labour as far as the production costs are concerned (Vakıfbank, 1995).

The Turkish leather clothes industry utilises domestic processed leather. The only items imported are some accessories. The leather processing industry, however, imports almost half of the raw leather they further process. Two basic inputs of leather production are raw leather and chemical substances with raw leather constituting the bulk of the total cost (Vakıfbank, 1995). Specifically, in leather processing the raw material accounts for 50-60 per cent of the total cost, while labour comes second accounting for 10-20 per cent followed by chemicals amounting to 6-15 per cent of the total cost (ILO, 1992b).

Until the 1960s, Turkey used to export approximately 70 per cent of its hides and skins production, either in the form of raw or semi-processed leather. Imports of raw leather were negligible until 1982 when related import restrictions were totally abolished (Küçükbali, 1983). In the following years, however, domestic demand for raw leather increased enormously, consuming all domestic supply and even requiring a considerable volume of imports. In fact, domestic demand increased so much that raw leather exports of Turkey almost stopped. Moreover, from 1985 onwards the Turkish government, like many others in the world, required special permission be given to enable companies to export raw leather in order to discourage raw leather exports and save this valuable material for the local leather industry. Even though almost all of the domestically produced raw leather stayed in the country as a result of the precautions taken, demand for raw leather continued to increase, paralleling the development of the industry. As a result, although Turkey is among the top ten producers of raw leather in the world, more than 50 per cent of raw leather consumed by the Turkish leather industry is imported (Vakıfbank, 1995). Imports, however, are becoming more and more difficult given that similar export restrictions to that of Turkey are common among other countries as well, and thus total supply of raw leather in the world market is not expected to rise to a large extent (DPT, 1991a). This will probably force Turkey to increase its imports of semi- or fully-processed leather too, signs of which already exist in the current import figures.

Animal husbandry, which goes hand in hand with leather production, has been an important activity in Anatolia throughout the ages. The current state of animal husbandry in Turkey, however, is not promising in that not all slaughtering is formal and registered. It is, however, known that Turkey has a considerable animal population, in fact the greatest in Europe. Nevertheless, the share of animal husbandry in the total agricultural sector remains relatively small in Turkey, around 35 per cent, whereas it is around 65 per cent in many developed countries (Vakıfbank, 1995). Apart from being seen as secondary to other agricultural activities, animal husbandry in Turkey is not well-organised, and specialisation is very rare (*Deri*, 1995d). Most of the animal husbandry activities are concentrated in rural areas and are undertaken by poorly educated peasants (Özçörekçi, 1988). Apart from damaging the level of quality attained, this certainly increases the errors and losses stemming from human mistakes (DPT, 1991a). Due to such errors committed, raw leather becomes a US$0.8 product in Turkey, whereas average unit price in the rest of the world is around US$2 (DPT, 1996).

In recent years, plenty of cheap raw leather from Russia and the C.I.S. countries has been imported. The quality of this leather, however, is rather low. The main reason for importing raw leather in fact seems to be the insufficient domestic supply rather than the quality or price concerns (Vakıfbank, 1995). The customs union with the EU, however, is expected to increase competition (DPT, 1996). As a result, modern slaughtering complexes in the cities are likely to replace gradually the uncontrolled and inferior ones in the villages and small towns, a process which seems to be already underway (DPT, 1991a).

The labour-intensive nature of the industry provides Turkey with an advantage. The labour cost in the Turkish leather industry, however, is increasing continuously (Vakıfbank, 1995), posing threats to the industry in the long-run as the competition from countries with even cheaper labour forces like Pakistan, India and China intensifies in price sensitive segments. Another issue that should be considered is the relatively lower productivity of Turkish leather workers, which sweeps away a part of the advantage of being relatively cheaper (DPT, 1996).

Although developing countries are now the leading producers and exporters in the industry, research and development activities are still dominated by developed countries. Technological developments specific to the industry have, with few exceptions, originated in Western Europe, especially in Italy and Germany, and in the United States (ILO, 1985a: 33). As compared to the EU countries, the level of technology in Turkey is lagging, making the labour-intensive nature of the industry more visible in the Turkish case. In terms of subsectors, Turkey utilises a moderately-developed technology in leather processing and the leather clothes industries, and a low-level one in the footwear segment (DPT, 1988). Research and development activities seem to be rather concentrated on the firms supplying the leather chemicals and in some sectoral associations. There is however an undeniable improvement, which is clearly manifested in the fact that Turkey has started to upgrade from a country that imports technology to one that exports it and establishes leather factories in other countries like the C.I.S. (DPT, 1996).

Unfortunately, research and education institutions could not show a parallel development to the one that the industry experienced during 1980s. There are attempts, however, such as the establishment of the Pendik Leather Research Institution. As far as the universities are concerned, the oldest department is the Aegean University Leather Technology Department. Currently, it is the only department offering both undergraduate and graduate programmes in leather technology. In 1985, the İstanbul Technical University started a two-year-long undergraduate programme on leather processing. The university offers a night programme in the same subject as well, which was founded under the auspices of the Turkish Leather Industrialists' Association. There are seven other such two-year-long programmes, but the quality of the graduate technicians is usually rather low. Moreover, some high schools have started to offer specific education for the leather industry as well, most of which is related to leather clothes. One example is Rüştü Uzel Anatolian High School, which has a reputation for good quality, due to its close contacts with Germany. Unlike relatively well-developed textile engineering programmes, there is not a programme offering a degree in leather engineering in Turkey, and the interested students may attend chemical engineering departments and specialise in leather instead.

Although the number of institutions specific to the industry seems large, it should be stated that the majority of them were founded in recent years resulting in a serious shortage of qualified teaching personnel, and their quality leaves a lot to be desired. Moreover, the level of university-industry co-operation still remains limited despite such attempts as the participation of leather industrialists in education as lecturers in the areas of their expertise, and the establishment of the Technology Development Foundation and the University-Industry Co-operation Council.

Financing problems, reflecting a general obstacle for the businessmen in Turkey and creating troubles for many industries, are considered to be one of the weakest points of the leather industry as well. In the financial structure of the firms in the Turkish leather industry, short-term debts have a dominating importance. Debt-ratios for the firms in the industry are high, the main reason of which is simply the fact that other means of financing, like the owner's equity, are limited for the small and medium enterprises which are dominant in the industry. In the Izmir region, for example, financing sources of a typical firm are as follows: 25 per cent owners' equity, 30 per cent banks (mainly Halk Bank specialised in small and medium enterprises), and 45 per cent export credit from Eximbank (DPT, 1996).

The low circulation rate of working capital pushes the firms in the Turkish leather industry to small-batch production, creating a disadvantage in the international markets. Firms need higher working capital, reasons of which are manifold. First, it is an export-oriented industry, and the time lag between the shipment and the actual payment for that product can be rather long. Second, manufacturers need raw leather throughout the year whereas supply of raw leather is concentrated in several months. A need for higher working capital further increases with the import requirement created by the inadequate domestic supply of raw leather (Vakıfbank, 1995) and the need to cope with the seasonal fluctuations in demand for leather products.

To conclude, it is difficult to argue that factor conditions, as defined by Porter (1990a), are on average favourable for the Turkish leather industry. Raw materials availability and quality, for instance, which were probably the main advantages that made the industry develop in the beginning (*Deri*, 1995b), no longer provide an advantage. Instead, the situation is turning into a disadvantageous one since finding good quality and reasonably priced raw materials is a real problem for the Turkish leather producers, and it is becoming even more difficult as a result of the restrictions limiting the world supply. Shortage of qualified personnel and weaknesses in research and development are other obstacles preventing the further development of the industry. Better financing mechanisms are also badly needed. The only advantage regarding the factor conditions is the relatively cheap labour force, which is by no means guaranteed to endure in the long-run. In fact, the industry is already being threatened by competitors from countries with even cheaper labour forces. The Turkish leather clothes industry is, then, an interesting case, as far as the Porter (1990a) ideas are concerned, since it lacks a clear advantage in factor conditions.

Demand Conditions

Domestic demand for leather products has been increasing enormously especially since 1984, though it follows a rather cyclical pattern with occasional dips. Overall, however, between the years 1984 and 1992, domestic demand for leather products increased by almost 75 per cent. This is a tricky issue, however, since with regard to the leather clothes and accessories industry, this rise in demand is mainly attributable to the sales made to tourists, especially to those coming from the C.I.S. (Vakıfbank, 1995). When we compare the rate of increase in demand for leather products in the domestic market with the one in the rest of the world, on the other hand, we see that the former is still rather slow causing the industry to be dependent on exports to a large extent (DPT, 1988). Most of the imports of finished products come from EU countries, reflecting Turkish customers' belief that they supply higher-quality products (Vakıfbank, 1995).

Production in the Turkish leather industry is divided among the subsectors as follows: 30 per cent leather processing, 30 per cent leather clothes, 5 per cent accessories, and 35 per cent footwear (Vakıfbank, 1995). Leather clothes and accessories, however, constitute the bulk of Turkish leather products exports with a share of 85 per cent, although this share is diminishing as a result of the recent improvements achieved in the footwear industry (Vakıfbank, 1995). In the rest of the world, the footwear segment is usually the strongest. Currently, almost the whole leather sector in Turkey has been established according to the requirements of the leather clothes industry which is not considered to be healthy in the long-run given that the supply of sheepskins and lambskin, which are overwhelmingly used in leather clothes production, is limited in the world, and increasing competition both for raw materials and final products is likely to make the situation even worse (*Deri*, 1995a). Within the leather clothes industry, Turkish producers overwhelmingly target the middle-class, addressing both price and quality concerns of the customers.

In brief, attributes of the domestic demand do not put Turkish leather clothes producers into an advantageous situation relative to their foreign competitors. The rate of growth of domestic demand is lower than that of foreign demand. Segment structure in the Turkish leather industry is also dramatically different from the one common in many countries of the world in that leather clothes dominate in Turkey whereas it is the footwear sector that is the pre-eminent industry in the rest of the world. Apart from the latter, which may cause problems for the Turkish leather clothes industry in the long-run, especially in terms of availability of raw materials, attributes of domestic demand do not put the industry into a particularly disadvantageous situation.

Related and Supporting Industries

Although the leather clothes industry, and leather making and footwear manufacturing are distinct economic activities, there are important linkages amongst them. Apart from being related to each other, all subsectors of the leather industry are also linked to many other industries such as leather substitutes, chemicals and machinery (DPT, 1996).

After 1980, we observe considerable improvements in terms of mechanisation, number of factories, exports and quality in he Turkish footwear industry, which has been until very recently characterised by craftsmanship. The export performance has been improving; specifically, it increased from US$1.3 million in 1980 to US$90 million in 1992. This is in fact still low considering the potential advantages Turkey has in footwear production stemming from its being a relatively low-wage producer close to the EU, a large domestic market and several internationally competitive related and supporting industries (Vakıfbank, 1995). In other words, although the leather footwear industry is among the relatively more competitive industries of Turkey (see Table 2.2 in Chapter 2 and Appendix A1) and seen as having a good potential for growth (DPT, 1996), Turkey's above mentioned potential advantages have not yet been exploited successfully.

Leather processing too was a craftsman's and artisan's job until the 1950s when some mechanisation started to emerge. In particular, in the 1970s, considerable improvements were achieved in product type and quality as well as the quantity of production. The bulk of (90-95 per cent) the processed leather is consumed within Turkey. The rest is exported, especially to Italy (DPT, 1996). The Turkish leather processing sector is well-developed, and Turkey is considered to be among the top five countries in terms of experience, technology and production capacity in the industry (DPT, 1996).

Leather substitute materials have been made available with properties similar to those of leather in practically every category of leather production although characteristics of leather have been proven to be very difficult to reproduce. Their easy care and cost advantages make leather substitutes increasingly popular. It is, however, argued that leather should hold its position on performance and quality rather than attempt to compete with synthetics on a cost basis (Thorstensen, 1993). The Turkish leather clothes industry as well faces strong competition not just from man-mades and imitation leathers but from other substitutes like the products of the textiles industry, which has, predictably, a lot in common with the leather clothes industry and is very competitive internationally.

Although furskin production is among the relatively competitive industries in Turkey in each of the four years analysed in this study (see Table 2.2 in Chapter 2 and Appendix A1), the fur industry in Turkey is less developed when compared to the leather industry. One reason is that domestic demand is rather low for the industry because of Turkey's relatively mild climate and lower per capita income. Another reason is the popularity of imported fur products in the early years of the development of the industry. Moreover, since domestic production is not enough, fur producers import their raw materials, which cost a lot due to high customs duties (DPT, 1991a). Recently, as a result of the increasing demand from the Russians, numerous new firms have been founded, and competition has intensified. Since it is a labour-intensive industry, Turkey has a potential to be an important exporter in this sector (DPT, 1988). The quality of Turkish fur products are quite satisfactory; in fact, only second to Spanish products according to one manager I interviewed.

Regarding the leather goods and accessories industry, which embraces such items as ladies' handbags, wallets, purses and belts, we see that the origin of the industry in Turkey comes from the subcategory of 'saddlery', a traditional art for Turks dating back to centuries ago when they made use of such items on their horses. The industry in Turkey overwhelmingly consists of small-scale firms. Since their demand for processed leather is in small quantities, they face difficulties in obtaining good quality and soft leather. The industry is labour-intensive, and methods of production are more or less the same all over the world. The industry is involved in heavy competition both from domestic and foreign competitors, especially from South American and Far Eastern countries. The sector also faces stiff competition from the industries offering substitutes like plastics, textiles and aluminium products. Despite these, imports of the industry do not reach a considerable level while exports are continuously increasing, and the competitive prospects for the industry are promising.

Almost all machinery used in the sector used to be imported in the beginning. Now, there are some internationally competitive firms producing the machinery that the industry needs, but on a small-scale. They started

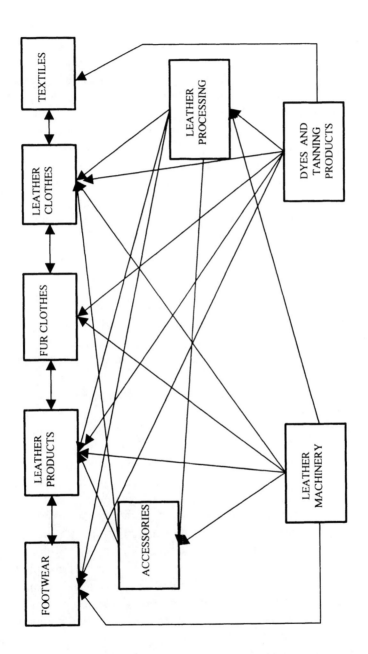

Figure 5.1 Internationally Successful Turkish Industries Related to the Leather Clothes Industry

Source: Author's estimates based on cluster charts (see Table 2.2 and Appendix A1) and field interviews

production by imitating imported machinery in the first place. Now, they can compete with Italian leather machinery producers (Vakıfbank, 1995).

With regard to the firms in the chemicals industry, we see that there are several joint ventures of foreign and Turkish firms like Türk Henkel A.Ş. and BASF Sümerbank Türk Kimya, and the rest are domestic firms (DPT, 1996). A good potential exists for the chemicals industry, especially for dyes, but a considerable development is seen unlikely because the producers can get good quality leather chemicals at reasonable prices from Europe, particularly after the customs union.

To conclude, most of the related and supporting industries of the Turkish leather clothes industry are internationally competitive, with several like fur, leather processing, textiles, and leather goods and accessories holding strong positions in international markets, and some others like footwear having a good current performance, and a potential for further development (see Figure 5.1). The leather clothes industry has a lot in common especially with the textiles industry, which is maybe the most competitive and dynamic cluster in the Turkish economy. The importance and contribution of chemicals and leather machinery industries, which are currently developing, in the success of the Turkish leather clothes industry is also undeniable. It is, in other words, possible to see signs of a well-developed cluster that the Turkish leather clothes industry relates. The only exception seems to be the lagging animal husbandry sector whose improvement will definitely help the leather clothes industry.

Firm Strategy, Structure and Rivalry

We see a fragmented structure in the Turkish leather clothes industry with a large number of small and medium enterprises. The industry is to a large extent dominated by the domestic private sector firms; in fact, the share of the private sector is almost one-hundred percent. Off-the-record production is rather common (Vakıfbank, 1995).

Family firms dominate. It is quite normal to see many relatives working in the same factory (Yelmen, 1994). In this respect, the reply of one of my interviewees was quite interesting when asked about with whom he recommended that I should conduct a similar interview: 'You can interview my father who works in the same factory and has an important position in one of the sectoral associations and/or my uncle who owns another leather factory and also holds a position in one of the sectoral organisations'. It is indeed rare to see firms employing professional managers who are not members of the family and/or not technically competent. As regards the latter, one manager I interviewed stated that if a person is not technically competent, s/he is usually not considered to be a good candidate for executive tasks, and employing such a person can be a 'waste of money'. Recently, however, the number of professional cadres has started to increase as an attempt to address developments like increasing labour costs, and the greater importance of quality and marketing.

Geographic concentration and industrial districts are especially common in the leather industry (e.g. in Italy). If we consider the leather industry as a whole, we see that geographic concentration holds in Turkey as well, even in terms of subsectors. Those producing processed leather gathered around Tuzla, Bursa, Bolu, Gerede and Çorlu, whereas the Uşak region is known as producing processed leather for clothes. Shoe bases and uppers producers, on the other hand, concentrate in the Denizli region. In İstanbul, however, it is possible to see all subsectors of the leather industry (DPT, 1996). In fact, İstanbul accounts for almost 80 per cent of total leather processing capacity, and two-thirds of total leather exports. This localisation is, in a way, a must in that most of the time leather producers are encouraged or even required to operate only in places that are permitted by the government. This is of course related to the environmental concerns which urge firms to position themselves together outside the city centres and share the cost of cleansing the created pollution (Vakıfbank, 1995).

All over the world, the industry is known for its substandard working conditions. In the history of labour-management relationships in the Turkish leather industry, conflicts are often encountered. In 1965, for instance, disputes resulted in a lockout decision in 54 factories. This tense relationship still continues, especially in the İstanbul region. In fact, the extent of this problem is such that it has caused some leather producers to move out of Tuzla (1995a).

It is also argued that the strong union in the İstanbul region, in a way, creates an 'unfair competition' case for the leather producers of Tuzla (Yelmen, 1995a). The fact that only firms in industrial zones have the burden of paying for the treatment complexes is another source of unfair competition. Turkey is in the process of employing full-treatment projects in the leather industry. As a result, there are currently firms and industrial districts utilising treatment complexes by European standards on the one hand, and others scattered around the country with no such ideas at all (therefore do not have to face the additional costs associated with the district) on the other (Vakıfbank, 1995). This is a factor affecting the costs considerably and thus creating unfair competition among the firms in the industry.

The Turkish leather clothes sector is a dynamic industry with many new firms being established, mostly through spin-offs. Firms are in tough competition with each other. The intensity of that competition in fact causes complaints among those who believe that they should learn to co-operate when necessary and compete with producers from other countries instead. In this respect, Koşar (1995c), the president of the Association of Leather Industrialists, introduces the example that as a result of tough competition among Turkish leather producers in obtaining raw skins and hides from the Russian Federation, the prices of these items increased considerably.

Recently, world-class leather fairs have begun to be organised in Turkey. The most important one is the International Leather Days Fair which is held in İstanbul annually. It is the third biggest leather fair of Europe and Asia (*Deri\Leather*, 1996). Ezgi Ajans, the agency that organises the Fair, states that they aim at making it the third best international leather fair world-wide after the Hong Kong and Paris fairs (*Deri*, 1996). Ezgi Ajans has also undertaken the bulk of the information disseminating task in that it is the Turkish regional distributor of the major leather publications available in the world. It is also responsible for publishing the sectoral periodical of the Association of Leather Industrialists, *Deri* (means 'leather' in Turkish).

Turkish leather clothes producers are highly dependent on a few markets, namely Germany and Russia, which makes them very vulnerable to fluctuations of demand in these countries (Vakıfbank, 1995). It is only recently that they have started to look for new opportunities, one likely candidate being the Far East, in particular China. They are however rather slow, and according to some even late. Italians are, for instance, already in the Asian market foreseeing the falling demand in Europe well in advance (*Deri*, 1995b).

With regard to their strategies concerning the diversification of activities, we observe that firms usually prefer to concentrate in the leather industry. Engaging in businesses in other industries is rare. Backward vertical integration, however, is quite common in that we often see leather clothes producers having leather processing factories as well.

As a positive sign, there is a tendency towards high quality and high value added segments. This has been mostly triggered by the intensity of competition in more price sensitive segments, following the entry of countries like India, Pakistan and China into the international market (Koşar, 1995b). Resembling the Italian businessmen, creativity and fashion are becoming more and more important for Turkish producers. As a result, they are getting more attention from the emerging markets. In China, for instance, Turkish leather is well-known for its image of quality (Koşar, 1995d). In fact, the managers I interviewed argue that Turkey competes with Italy in terms of quality. The relative importance given to price and quality may, of course, differ according to the target market; price, for instance, becomes the number one concern for the domestic as well as the Russian market whereas quality and design are ahead of price as competitive variables in the European market.

As far as this 'corner' of the diamond is concerned, the Turkish leather clothes industry like the previous industries I have analysed so far has benefited from the advantages that entrepreneurial skills of Turkish businessmen bring about. Lack of a long-run orientation may be considered a weakness, but it should be kept in mind that it is difficult to conduct long-run plans in a country where both economic and political instability exists. The environment in Turkey, which encourages companies to stay small, matches the needs of this industry where the attributes of demand are rapidly changing. Rivalry amongst Turkish leather producers is also intense; in fact, so intense that it disturbs some industry participants. The Turkish leather clothes industry, therefore, enjoys a comfortable advantage with regard to this determinant of competitive advantage.

The Role of Chance

Probably the most outstanding 'chance' event for the Turkish leather clothes industry is the emergence of a high demand from the Russian market since the late 1980s. Mahmut Yeşil, president of the Çorlu Association of Leather Industrialists, states that 'the Russian market is a kind of chance that nations can catch sometimes in their history. [...] For the Turkish leather industry it generates as much yield as recorded exports' (*Deri\Leather*, 1996). The Laleli district of İstanbul, which is Russians' favourite shopping place, had some trouble in meeting demand in the beginning. Later, Zeytinburnu district emerged as another important centre of trade. Now, both Laleli and Zeytinburnu collect substantial earnings from the Russian traders. This is mainly considered to be an off-the-record economy. Hakki Matraş, current president of ITKIB-Leather (*Deri\Leather*, 1996), states that 'our official exports were US$700 million last year [1995]. However, it is said that according to estimations export-oriented sales in Laleli were about US$3-4 billion'. Increases in customs and state taxes recently enacted by the Russian government, and economic and political instabilities in this country, however, have damaged this market.

Among other chance events, we can include the contacts lost during the Gulf Crisis, the customs union signed with the EU which has had positive effects on the leather clothes industry so far, the favourable geographic position which is close to important markets for the leather clothes industry, China's entry into the market as a lower price competitor which is a threat for Turkish leather clothes exporters, the recent jump in raw leather prices, and recent economic stagnation in Europe together with its ageing population which have considerably reduced the demand for leather products from this market (Vakıfbank, 1995). Moreover, some countries from the C.I.S. have started to establish their own leather clothes industries which threaten Turkish producers (DPT, 1996). On average, if we contrast the impacts of the negative and positive chance events that have been taking place beyond the control of the firms in the Turkish leather clothes industry, we see that most of the time chance has been with the Turkish leather clothes producers. Here, it should also be mentioned that time, contacts and production lost during the move from Kazlıçeşme to Tuzla, which can be considered as a 'negative chance event', definitely hurt the industry. This issue gives, however, interesting insights concerning the attitude of the government towards the industry, hence I prefer to discuss it in the following section.

The Role of Government

Since the very beginning of the Republican period, the importance of the industry has been appreciated. This is evident from the fact that the industry was pronounced to be of special importance together with the textile industry in the 1924 İzmir Economic Congress (Vakıfbank, 1995). During the mid-1960s, the industry enjoyed clear support from the government whose policies especially aimed at shifting the industry towards the leather clothes sector. Later in the 1980s, the industry was one of the best users of export incentives and tax rebates offered together with liberalisation.

The support of the government for the industry is, nevertheless, considered to be far from being sufficient when compared to the ones the main competitors from Pakistan, India, South Korea and China enjoy (Vakıfbank, 1995). Apart from finding the incentives insufficient (Vakıfbank, 1995), leather producers also complain about the difficulties they encounter in collecting the relevant receivable from the government (Koşar, 1995a). For instance, one of my interviewees mentioned a case that they started to establish a factory in the eastern part of Turkey, where they could make use of the incentives provided for investments in this area according to the regional development programme of the government, but they could not collect the promised incentives and had to abolish the investment when it was half complete.

Relatedly, incentives aimed at encouraging animal husbandry, which is an otherwise ignored area in Turkey, are considered not to be sufficient. Given the serious problems the Turkish leather clothes industry faces in obtaining enough good quality raw leather from the domestic market and its need to import half of the required raw leather, it becomes apparent that like many other governments in the world, the Turkish government should also support the animal husbandry sector and should encourage meat rather than live animal exports (Vakıfbank, 1995). Better control mechanisms and education for those engaged in this activity would be helpful as well (DPT, 1991a).

Another issue related to the role of government is the political and economic uncertainty and instability in Turkey, which affects all sectors but especially hurts the ones engaging in exports. In fact, engaging in trade is considered as 'bold', or even 'irrational' sometimes, since it is difficult to see even a few months ahead. Moreover, while there are 'ways' to operate in the domestic market without paying any taxes (off-the-record), there is little incentive to export where everything is recorded. The relatively lagging position of the footwear industry is also explained by following this logic. If you are a small firm, you can play with the system and can stay off-the-record. If you are big however you get attention. The system, in other words, encourages you to stay small. Then, it becomes difficult for such 'artisan' type of manufacturers to engage in export activities, not just because such activities are recorded but also it is difficult for them to compete in international markets with the larger shoe-making factories (*Deri*, 1995a).

Handling of the move to Kazlıçeşme is particularly interesting in understanding the attitude of the government towards the industry. Many producers learnt about it from the newspapers. The then İstanbul municipality decided to remove their factories without asking about their opinions concerning the details about the time and place they should move. When the leather production complexes were being built in Tuzla, which took some time from 1986 to 1994, leather manufacturers in Kazlıçeşme were not allowed to continue their production because of environmental concerns (Vakıfbank, 1995). Yelmen (1994), who is regarded as the 'father' of the leather industry in Turkey, believes environmental concerns are just an excuse and not enough to explain this hostile attitude without however openly specifying any other possible reason. He implies that it was probably the political gains the officials hoped to acquire by doing so (Yelmen,

1994). The ideal would be, of course, a planned and pre-agreed move following the full construction of the new industrial district without interrupting the production process.

There are also some, though few, positive things to say concerning the role of government in this industry. A special customs tax exemption applies for the imports of raw leather though recently they have started to apply a 6 per cent customs tax for certain imports. Value added tax rates are also lower for leather products: only 1 per cent. Leather producers also made use of special incentives designed to encourage them to move to the organised industrial zones. Starting from 1993, the leather industry is considered to be one of the 'industries that are of special importance'. Like the other industries in this category, the leather industry can also make use of such export incentives as customs tax exemption for the machinery they need to import, tax discount incentives for investments, and export credits. These are believed to have positive impacts on the industry (Vakıfbank, 1995). Furthermore, although it is far from functioning perfectly, there are live animal exchanges in Turkey from which the industry benefits, whereas raw leather exchanges are yet to be established (DPT, 1991a). A free zone for leather, which is helpful for securing the continuous and reliable supply of raw leather needs of Turkish leather manufacturers, has been founded, and it has been in operation since 1994 (Vakıfbank, 1995).

In summary, although the importance of the industry has been recognised since the foundation of the Republic, a clear government policy favouring the industry seems to be a very recent phenomenon. The government changes frequently, and it fails to keep a consistent policy towards specific industries. Apart from the government-related problems that affect all sectors by bringing instability and uncertainty into the business environment, there are some occasions in which the leather industry particularly suffered. The most typical example is, of course, the attitude of the municipality during the move from Kazlıçeşme to Tuzla. The role government plays in shaping the sources of advantage in the Turkish leather clothes industry is, therefore, not an active one and does not provide an advantage for the industry in international markets. Although there is some support in the form of export incentives, they are only recently started to be well-organised and are still not that extensive as compared to the government support firms of some other countries like South Korea enjoy.

Concluding Remarks

Products of the leather clothes industry are not a necessity; they are even considered as luxurious items. Demand for them increases with rising income levels and relates to changes in fashion. Both were favourable in Turkey during the liberalisation period of the early 1980s during which the industry made good use of the export incentives and tax rebates offered. The Turkish leather clothes industry, which already had a firm base in Turkey dating back to the times of the Ottoman Empire, as a result, developed enormously. In an incredibly short period of time, Turkey became one of the top exporters of leather clothes in the world; in fact, it was only second to South Korea for the most of the decade. The Turkish share of world leather clothes and accessories exports peaked in 1985 with more than one fifth of world leather clothes exports coming from Turkey. Towards the end of the decade, however, the industry experienced a decline in its position relative to the main competitors.

The most interesting issue we have learnt from the case of the Turkish leather industry with the help of our analysis is that the competitive position of the industry persists although initial advantages stemming from cheap and good quality raw materials, and low-cost labour have disappeared to a large extent. The industry has, in other words, faced the challenge, and managed to survive and remain competitive, though we observe a decline in its relative position. Furthermore, there are other, 'external factors' such as decrease in demand from the EU and 'uncontrollable factors' like the damages created during the move to Tuzla, behind that decline. Given this achievement, prospects for the Turkish leather clothes industry seem to be good, especially if we think of it together with the signs pointing that the industry is moving towards more rewarding segments where quality and style are the key competitive factors rather than price.

Regarding the diamond framework, we can conclude that the case of the Turkish leather clothes industry provides clear support concerning the roles of two determinants, 'related and supporting industries' and 'firm strategy, structure and rivalry' as well as the 'chance events' whereas it puts question marks with respect to others. Specifically, factor conditions cease to provide a clear advantage any longer, domestic demand conditions are not particularly favourable, and it is difficult to argue that the government facilitates the functioning of the industry 'diamond', or that a well-organised and particularly helpful government policy towards the industry exists. The industry, nevertheless, remains highly competitive.

6 The Turkish Automobile Industry

Like construction, the automotive sector also relates to, and drives along, a large number of other sectors. Furthermore, it is considered to be critical to the industrialisation efforts of developing countries. The world's largest manufacturing industry, capturing more than 10 per cent of GNP in many developed nations, is of crucial importance for the Turkish economy as well. In fact, the Turkish automotive industry is one of· the youngest in the world with a history of around 30 years, as opposed to the industry's world history of one-hundred years. Despite its short history, it is considered to be one of the most strategically important sectors of the Turkish economy, a position which is, in fact, well-justified: its contribution to employment, for instance, amounts to half a million when those working in the automotive parts and components, service outlets and motor vehicle insurance industries are included (DPT, 1993d). It follows two giant industries of the Turkish economy, food and beverages, and textiles, in terms of production capacity (Renda, 1995). The industry captures a considerable share of GDP -11 per cent in 1993 (DPT, 1993d). The value-added of the industry is high, and it facilitates the spread of recent technological developments to related industries. Between the years 1987 and 1992, the industry attained the highest growth rate of all Turkish industries with an annual average of 12.5 per cent (Bayraktar, 1995). Turkey, in addition, is responsible for almost 1 per cent of world automobile production, which is enough to place it among noteworthy producers. All this, however, does not change the fact that Turkey is a net importer of automotive products. The Turkish automotive industry, in other words, has a poor record when its relative position in the world markets is considered (Bayraktar, 1995). This chapter aims to explain why.

Development of the Turkish Automobile Industry

Azcanlı (1995: 31) states that the reasons for the relative lagging position of the Turkish automotive industry can be traced by looking back through its history, particularly focusing on the lack of attention to technological developments. The first cars Turks used were imported from Europe in the

117

times of the late Ottoman Empire and in the early years of the Republic. The first automotive firms of Turkey were, therefore, the dealers of the foreign corporations. Between 1923-1927, both Ford and Chrysler had become established in the newly founded Turkish Republic (*Ekonomist*, 1995b). Later in 1929, the Ford Motor Company started to assemble parts in İstanbul to sell in Turkey as well as in the then USSR and the Middle East. Low demand stemming from the low development level and low purchasing power in these regions, coupled with the depression of the early 1930s, however, caused this first assembling plant, İstanbul Ford Motor Co., to soon stop production. As a result, although world automotive industry was developing rapidly, Turks were stuck with their horse-powered vehicles until the first half of the 20th century (Azcanlı, 1995).

After the World War II, the Turkish economy gained some impetus with the help of the Marshall Plan which, among other things, facilitated the entry of tractors into Turkey since it attributed special priority to the development of the agricultural sector (Azcanlı, 1995). Without a well-developed plan, however, all sorts of tractor brands were imported, making it difficult to find the spare parts or repair the broken ones. This attitude, which was not peculiar to the automotive industry, soon resulted in foreign exchange shortages, and assembling became a necessity. The first tractor assembly plant in Turkey, Türk Traktör Fabrikası, which imported most of its parts and components, was founded in 1954 under the Mineapolis Moline license (Özşahin, 1989). The first local jeep production was performed by Türk Williys Owerland A.O. in the same year, which was the first private sector involvement in the automotive industry. 1954 also witnessed the establishment of a truck company, Federal Türk Kamyonları Fabrikası, under the license of Federal Truck. Later in 1959, Otosan, which is a Ford Motor Co. and Koç Ticaret A.Ş. partnership, producing mainly trucks and automobiles, was founded (Azcanlı, 1995).

Until the mid-1960s, the Turkish automotive industry consisted mainly of a few assembly plants of imported parts, working under the license of foreign firms (OSD, 1985). In 1964, the 'Regulations of the Assembly Industry', which marked a milestone for the Turkish automotive industry, were issued. This directive is, in fact, widely considered as the origin of today's Turkish automotive industry. Its rationale was parallel with the import substituting philosophy of the time (Azcanlı, 1995). The main objective was to transform the initial stage of assembly operations into full scale local manufacture. Accordingly, the local content was encouraged to increase (Duruiz and Yentürk, 1992: 63). The most outstanding result was the immediate increase in the number of firms in the automotive industry (Azcanlı, 1995).

The production of the first Turkish automobile, Anadol, was started in 1966 by Otosan. Later, however, Anadol ceased to continue production since it could not cope with the advances in technology. Again in 1966, Otomarsan started to produce buses and trucks under the Daimler-Benz AG license (Azcanlı, 1995). Following Otosan and Otomarsan, two important automobile producers, Tofaş (a Koç and Fiat partnership) and Oyak-Renault (an Oyak and Renault partnership), were founded in 1968 and 1969 respectively. In 1971, the former started to produce Murat-124 and the latter Renault-12, and these two models dominated the Turkish automobile industry for a long period of time (*Ekonomist*, 1995b). Their introduction coincided with the extension of import restrictions imposed to cover automobiles. 1975 and 1976 are often regarded as the golden years of the Turkish automotive industry which was protected and supported throughout the period 1964-1980. The period between 1977 and 1980, however, is considered to be stagnant, which stems from a combination of reasons such as energy crisis, exchange rate shortage, and an unstable economic and political environment (OSD, 1985).

In 1984, a new import regime was enacted, through which finished car imports were made possible. Local producers would however still be protected with the help of custom duties, and some special funds would be deducted from the imported cars. The new import regime, which replaced the 'Regulations of the Assembly Industry' and marked the start of the reflection of liberalisation on the automotive industry, aimed to improve the competitiveness of Turkish automotive products, and by so doing prepare the industry for the customs union with the EU (Azcanlı, 1995).

The lack of a consistent long-run strategy for the industry, together with the preservation of some protective measures, resulted in a distorted structure with too many firms, some of which were operating below capacity most of the time. The limited purchasing power of customers further contributed to the overall picture by restricting potential demand. Operating below the optimum level results in higher costs of production and makes Turkish automobiles relatively more expensive (OSD, 1985).

As can be seen from Figure 6.1, the number of automobiles sold in Turkey, nevertheless, increased considerably from a yearly average of around 65,000 cars in the pre-1990 period to above 200,000 thereafter. Rising income levels and a growth in the use of consumer credit were believed to be the two major reasons for this increase in sales, which peaked

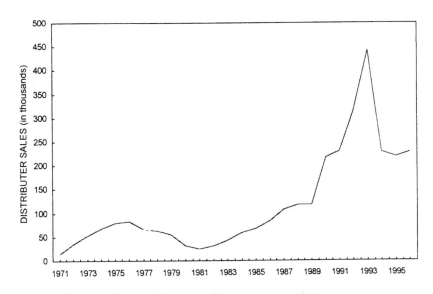

Figure 6.1 Automobile Sales in Turkey (1971-1996)
Source: Unpublished company data, Tofaş, 1997

in 1993 at around 440,000, but later decreased again to around 228,000 in 1994, to 218,000 in 1995, and 229,000 in 1996 (Tofaş, 1997).

The export interest of the industry has always been low, and the domestic market has been the driving force of production (Duruiz and Yentürk, 1992). A recent increase in the export performance of the industry is associated with tough economic conditions and intensifying competition at home as well as export incentives. Exports of the industry, however, still remain rather low although considerable rises are expected in forthcoming years. Exports are mostly targeted to developing countries, especially Egypt, the Turkic Republics of the C.I.S., Russia and recently to Europe, especially France, Germany and Italy (Bayraktar, 1995).

While exports of the industry continue to expand only gradually, the increase in imports is strikingly high. Sales of imported cars, for instance, increased by 182 per cent between 1995 and 1996 (*Ekonomist*, 1996). The share of imports in total automobile sales of Turkey reached 24 per cent in 1996. The main countries responsible for Turkish automotive imports are the East European countries, Germany, Japan, South Korea, Russia, France, the USA, UK and Italy (Bayraktar, 1995).

High potential demand for automobiles in Turkey as well as its favourable geographic position, coupled with the ongoing protection provided for the automotive industry and the recent customs union agreement with the EU, have resulted in increased interest by the foreign giants in establishing automobile firms in Turkey. GM, for instance, established a line to produce the Opel Vectra in 1990. Toyota made the decision to invest in 1992, and production started in 1994. These were soon followed by increasing interest from Honda, Mazda, Hyundai and Kia, which subsequently declared their investment decisions. Existing firms are, however, rather sceptical about the local market getting increasingly crowded, which further intensifies the competition fuelled by the customs union with the EU. They express their concerns about the extent to which the domestic market can absorb that many firms. According to them, some firms are already suffering from excess capacity, and it is a mistake in government policy to support and give incentives to the establishment of new firms despite there being an export requirement for a certain period of time for newly established car makers. New entrants, on the other hand, argue that the industry will gain impetus and export drive as a result of the recent developments. To support their view, they use the projections of demand for passenger cars in Turkey which show that it will reach 700-800 thousand cars towards the early 2000s, and, therefore, that the Turkish market can absorb 7-8 car manufacturers, each having around a 100 thousand car producing capacity (*Para*, 1995b).

In summary, the automobile industry in Turkey has enjoyed high protection levels for a long period of time. The sector has, however, gained some dynamism since the mid-1980s, with diminished import restrictions and new foreign investments. The consequent increase in competition has pushed the industry participants to improve their productivity levels and quality as well as product diversity (Duruiz and Yentürk, 1992). The Turkish automobile industry seems to have been experiencing a take off especially since the beginning of the 1990s, mainly stemming from the rise in income levels and spread of consumer credit schemes.

Sources of Advantage in the Turkish Automobile Industry

Factor Conditions

The major inputs in automobile production are sheet iron, steel, spade, aluminium, rubber, dye, plastic, insulation equipment, glass, pipes and electronic equipment (DPT, 1991c). Given that there are many firms, and a great variety of vehicles are produced in the industry, it is rather difficult to come up with a healthy cost structure analysis. On average, however, the share of the major items in total cost typically shows the following pattern. Imported materials capture 28 per cent of total costs whilst the figure is 45 per cent for local materials, 5 per cent for labour, 4 per cent for general expenditures, 3 per cent for depreciation, 9 per cent for financing, and 3 per cent for sales and management. Among imported materials, high quality steel and some chemicals come first (DPT, 1991c). In Turkey, costs are relatively higher mainly because of higher input and financing costs, which are obviously enough to sweep away the advantages derived from the relatively cheap labour -around 35 per cent cheaper than European counterparts (Bayraktar, 1995). If we also consider the high tax and profit rates, and low capacity utilisation rates in Turkey, we reach a cost figure which is 10 per cent higher than those attained by the European Union countries (Renda, 1995).

Regarding the productivity concerns, we can, on average, say that the level of productivity attained by the Turkish automotive industry, is rather low relative to the countries enjoying the benefits of fully-automated production. Most of the steps in the welding operation, for instance, are performed manually in Turkey whereas 90 per cent of this operation is automated in the leading countries (Renda, 1995).

Both research and development and sector-specific education facilities are of special importance for the automotive industry given its technology-intensive nature. Automobile companies are, in fact, amongst the research and development focused in the world. The Turkish automotive industry is predictably one of those industries suffering most from the relative lack of emphasis on research and development in Turkey. If research and development activities in the automotive industry are classified into three groups: product development; production technology development; and scientific research, we see that the focus in the Turkish automotive industry is on the former two. In fact, it is concentrated on the selection of the vehicle to be produced and the subsequent adaptation of it to the specific conditions of Turkey, such as the climate or customer preferences (DPT, 1991c).

The most important industry-specific education unit is a graduate programme run by the İTU (İstanbul Technical University): the Mechanical Automotive Programme in the Mechanical Engineering Faculty. There are also two-year-long undergraduate automotive programmes in Sakarya and Marmara Universities. The mechanical engineering departments of İTU and

METU have some relations with the industry as well. The number of such institutions as well as their relations with the industry are, however, limited although the educational quality attained by some is considered to be of a satisfactory level (Azcanlı, 1995). Uludağ University is, for instance, located in Bursa where the automotive industry is geographically concentrated yet it has poor relations with the industry. One manager I interviewed argues that industry is ahead of universities in general, and the practical as well as technical educational levels of universities, on average, leave a lot to be desired.

The automotive industry requires not only a large amount of initial investment but also continuous investments thereafter to be able to introduce new models and keep up with technological developments (Bayraktar, 1995). In the case of Turkey, this poses a clear disadvantage, since capital is relatively more expensive. Related disadvantages are not limited to investment requirements and may affect the demand side as well, since poor financing mechanisms definitely worsen the sales prospects in a country where potential demand is high but income levels are low.

In summary, our analysis of factor conditions suggests that, for this element of the diamond, the Turkish automobile industry suffers severe disadvantages. Apart from being relatively more expensive, major inputs are of lower quality compared to imported ones. Although labour is still relatively cheap in Turkey, labour productivity in the automobile industry does not compare well to that of European countries, sweeping away the advantage stemming from the lower wages. Inefficient, poorly functioning financial mechanisms pose additional problems for Turkish automobile producers. The situation becomes even more pessimistic when we also take research and development activities. Another source of trouble concerning the factor conditions is the poor infrastructure in Turkey. In short, apart from one exception, cheap labour, it is hard to say that the Turkish automobile industry can derive much advantage from the factor conditions.

Demand Conditions

Economic growth and the rapidly increasing population in Turkey have triggered the urbanisation process and resulted in a need for more and better transportation facilities. When we examine the transportation policy of the government, we see that motorway transportation has been clearly favoured since the 1950s. The share of motorway transportation was about 50 per cent and railway transportation was 42 per cent in 1950, whereas by 1985 related shares were 92.6 per cent and 6.6 per cent respectively, which obviously shows a tremendous increase in favour of motorways (T.C. Sanayi ve Ticaret Bakanlığı, 1987a). Moreover, public transportation facilities could not be developed properly, which resulted in a constantly increasing demand for automobiles. Demand for automobiles in Turkey is, however, still rather low, which is evident if we compare the per capita car figures of Turkey with those of many other countries. In 1993, for instance, the number of people per car in Turkey was 39, whereas the related figures for some other countries were much lower; specifically the average figure for Europe was 4.90, for North America 2.50, for South America 15, for Asia 58, for Africa 79, and the world average was almost one third of that for Turkey: 12 (Demirci, 1993). The potential demand, in fact, is believed to be much higher. This potential, however, cannot be exploited totally because of still low per capita income levels in Turkey, excessively high tax rates on automobile products and high energy prices coupled with the lack of a well-developed consumer credit market (T.C. Sanayi ve Ticaret Bakanlığı, 1987a).

When we examine the growth of demand for automobiles in Turkey, we observe that there is a cyclical pattern in that it continuously increases until 1976, after which a period of diminishing sales starts, covering the hard years of the late 1970s, and going on until 1981 during which sales start to rise again. The demand for automobiles, however, only reached one hundred thousand in 1987, followed by rapid increases until 1993, a year marking the peak in sales with around 442 thousand cars. Then we again observe a fall of almost a half, to around 230 thousand cars in the latest figures (Tofaş, 1997). Under these circumstances, demand projections forecasting 700-800 thousand car sales in Turkey by the year 2000 (DPT, 1993d), seem rather unrealistic, although some increase is expected after the unusually tough conditions of recent years.

In terms of the segment structure, if we consider the automotive industry in general, we see that in the beginning the emphasis was on tractors and commercial vehicles, while, as time passed, it shifted towards automobiles (Bayraktar, 1995). Currently, the latter clearly leads the industry as the largest segment. For the automobile industry, in particular, small, cheaper and fuel-efficient cars seem to be preferred recently, resembling the trend in many countries of the world.

As mentioned several times throughout this study, Porter (1990a) argues that the nature of buyers, particularly whether they are more sophisticated and demanding relative to the foreign ones, is essential in both creating and sustaining competitive advantage. It is, of course, hard to say that Turkish customers are relatively more sophisticated and demanding given that, until recently, Turks have been only offered the outdated models that were in use in developed countries in the 1970s. In recent years, however, this has been changing in response to decreasing protection levels and intensifying competition as well as rising income levels in that we observe a pressure for higher standards and quality. Relatedly, we should also state that in Turkey owning an automobile is considered as a type of investment activity (Duruiz and Yentürk, 1992). It is, in addition, regarded as a luxury (Bayraktar, 1995).

To conclude, in terms of the attributes of home demand as defined by Porter (1990a), it is not so easy to detect an advantage for the Turkish automobile industry. More specifically, although Turkey is a developing country with a rapidly increasing population and has a considerable potential demand, the number of cars sold in relation to the population is still much lower than the world average. With regard to the other attributes, Turkish customers are probably less, certainly not more, 'demanding' and 'sophisticated' compared to many foreign customers as far as automobiles are concerned. The segment structure of home demand more or less resembles, but follows rather than leads, that of developed nations. In short, attributes of domestic demand do not put automobile producers of Turkey into an advantageous situation relative to their competitors. It may even be argued that the needle points to the negative side although, following the recent changes, one can reasonably expect that a rapidly growing home demand together with increasing concerns for quality may provide a good chance of turning home demand conditions into an important advantage for automobile producers in Turkey.

Related and Supporting Industries

For many countries in the world, including Turkey, the automotive industry has taken a catalyst role in the development of other industries, including: the motorway vehicles industry; the parts and components industry; the iron and steel industry; the chemicals industry; the electronics industry; the ceramic industry; the road construction industry; the aluminium industry; the petroleum industry; the dye industry; the robotics industry; the defence industry; the tire industry; the plastic industry; and the glass industry.

The development of the automotive parts industry in Turkey has been triggered by the assembly industry. Difficulties in importing parts stemming from foreign exchange shortages, and local content requirements were especially helpful for the early development of the industry (Dumanlı, 1987). Currently, however, only 10-30 per cent are considered to be satisfying European standards in terms of quality. In fact, ToyotaSA has decided that 80 per cent of component producers in Turkey do not satisfy their quality levels (Renda, 1995). There are, on the other hand, some positive signs. Although imports still outweigh exports, the export performance of the industry is, for instance, improving considerably (Bayraktar, 1995). The industry, in fact, exports automotive parts to more than 40 different countries. For example, Opel of GM in Germany, a company and a country both known for their competitiveness in the automotive industry, uses parts produced by the Turkish automotive parts industry (DPT, 1993d).

When we review the competitive situation of the commercial vehicles industry, we see that Turkey has good prospects in this sector since it is relatively more labour-intensive. If we, for instance, examine the current situation in the truck industry, in which firms either have foreign capital involvement or operate under the license of a foreign firm, we observe that in terms of technology and quality truck producers have reached a level at which they can compete even with their parent companies. The same is true for buses and tractors (T.C. Sanayi ve Ticaret Bakanlığı, 1987b).

With regard to tires, the situation is brighter in that leading tire manufacturers of the world have been investing in Turkey, usually in the form of joint ventures (e.g. Sabancı-Bridgestone partnership) and are exporting the tires they have produced in Turkey all over the world (Özşahin, 1989). Lastly, we should mention our next case study, the Turkish flat steel industry, which provides major inputs to the automobile industry and is competitive (see Chapter 7).

In brief, deriving from Porter's (1990a) argument that the internationally competitive industries of a nation tend to cluster together, we do not expect to see so many internationally competitive Turkish industries around the automobile industry given its lagging position in the world market. This hypothesis is indeed confirmed by the Turkish automobile industry since most of the industries that it can be related to have poor records in the international market. Exceptions like glass, ceramics and steel, however, remain. One last issue that should be clarified here is the fact that most of the closely related industries to the automobile industry operate under foreign licenses. Given their ownership structures, it then becomes tricky to say, for instance, that Turkey is competitive in bus or tractor industries since both appear among the competitive industries of Turkey for one of the four years I have studied ('tractors' in 1985 and 'buses' in 1992). I prefer to address this problem, which is one of the mostly criticised parts of Porter's (1990a) study, while discussing the ownership structure in the following section.

Firm Strategy, Structure and Rivalry

There are currently seven automobile manufacturers in Turkey: Tofaş (Koç-Fiat), Otosan (Koç-Ford), Oyak-Renault, Opel (GM), ToyotaSA (Sabancı-Toyota-Mitsui), Assan-Hyundai and Honda. The number of car producers is expected to increase even further given the intentions of Kia and Mazda (*Ekonomist*, 1996).

When we examine the sales patterns of the two leading automobile producers (see Figure 6.2) in Turkey between the years 1971-1996, we see that Tofaş is still the industry leader with a market share of around 30 per cent, although Renault has come very close, reaching a share of 27 per cent in 1996. We should, however, state that despite these two companies still dominating the Turkish car manufacturing industry, their shares show a decreasing trend in recent years. They, for instance, together captured almost 60 per cent of the market in 1996, which is high but represents a fall from their combined share in the early 1980s which exceeded 90 per cent. In the meantime, the share of imports, which reached 24 per cent in 1996, is especially noteworthy (Tofaş, 1997).

Until recently, in other words, domestic competition was not that intense. Tofaş and Renault were enjoying a comfortable life and high profits and offering a few outdated models, knowing that Turkish customers had no choice but to buy them in a protected market. It was not uncommon for a customer to wait several months for the delivery of the car. For a long period of time, Turkish customers did not know any other model apart from Otosan's Anadol and Taunus, Tofaş's 'bird' series and Renault's Toros (*Ekonomist*, 1996). The profits of Turkish car manufacturers, although showing a decreasing trend recently, are still high; the rate of profitability to turnover in the Turkish automobile sector in the last three years, for instance, has been 15 per cent on average, compared with a figure of 10 per cent in many industrialised countries (Capital - Turkey, 1996). Competition in the domestic market is, however, definitely getting tougher with diminishing protection levels and a number of threatening new entrants. Although quality has improved considerably since the early 1980s and is approaching European/OECD standards (Hillebrand, 1986), Turkish automobiles still have problems related to noise, emission, safety and standardisation (Renda, 1995).

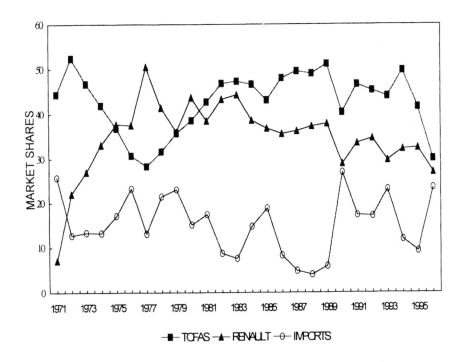

Figure 6.2 Market Shares in the Turkish Automobile Industry
(1971-1996)
Source: Unpublished company data, Tofaş, 1997

Taking a closer look at the individual companies may improve our understanding of the sources of advantage in the Turkish automobile industry. The leader of the industry, Tofaş, was founded in 1968 by the initiative of Mr. Vehbi Koç, who believed that Turkey should not be content with just assembling automobiles but establish its own automobile industry. The company now employs more than four thousand people (Tofaş, 1997) and has a capacity to produce 250 thousand cars per year. Investors estimate that Tofaş has a value of US$1.7 billion. According to Jan Nahum, the general manger of Tofaş, there is not another automobile factory of this scale in the region until you reach South Korea and Japan. It is, in other words, undeniable that given the conditions of Turkey it is a giant company (Buğdaycı, 1996).

Oyak-Renault, the second largest automobile manufacturer in Turkey, on the other hand, was founded in 1969. Otosan, a Koç-Ford partnership and the producer of the first Turkish automobile 'Anadol', has lost much of its initial position in the market, and now it has a share of around 4 per cent. Koç-Ford partnership has, however, recently reinforced by the decision to establish a new factory in Turkey. The main focus will be on exports, and the estimated cost is US$550 million (*Radikal*, 1998). The other two, Opel (GM) and ToyotaSA, are relatively new in the market; in fact, they started production in 1990 and 1994 respectively (Azcanlı, 1995). The former has an annual production capacity of only 10,000, whereas the latter can produce 200,000 cars per year (Tofaş, 1997).

Car manufacturers are geographically concentrated in the Marmara region to a large extent, Gebze and Bursa being specifically preferred locations. In terms of size, Turkish car manufacturers are regarded as too small to be competitive (Duruiz and Yentürk, 1992). In terms of technology, since all firms operate under a foreign license, assembly technology compares well with European and American standards (Bayraktar, 1995). There are, however, several factors limiting the employment of superior technology in Turkey. Expensive licenses, the high cost of investment in full automation, the expectation of rapid changes in technologies, the relatively low labour cost in Turkey, restrictions dictated by the limitations of the parts and components industry, purchasing power and even the education level of customers, and the quality of motorways are just a few factors to remember (DPT, 1991c). These can be plausible explanations for slowing the introduction of brand-new models as well as full automation.

As I have emphasised previously, Turkish automobile producers are often criticised for producing old-fashioned cars and selling them at high prices in a protected market. Moreover, the introduction of new models is slow (Özşahin, 1989). However, the situation has been changing in recent years. Companies have begun exploring alternative means of improving their positions in the market and stimulating consumer demand. Unsatisfied customers, new entrants and the diminishing protection seem to have forced companies to compete more intensely and increase their concerns for quality, technology and product diversity (Duruiz and Yentürk, 1992). These concerns are predictably reflected in their strategies as well. Since 1980, for instance, model changes, which were the exception rather than the rule until the end of the 1970s, have become more frequent. Product innovation, or at least some upgrading of the existing model range, has become important (Hillebrand, 1986). Another example is the establishment of special financing deals, pioneered by Koç Holding (has shares both in Tofaş and Otosan), which have created the opportunity for consumers to purchase their cars at low interest rates (Capital - Turkey, 1996).

A few examples from the responses of a company, for instance the market leader Tofaş, to the recent changes in its environment can improve our understanding of Turkish car manufacturers. Tofaş has been undergoing a restructuring process and trying to correct its poor image as well as its bad relationship with the government. The company executives believe the company's poor image stems from the fact that most of the old cars currently in use are products of Tofaş, and the company is usually judged by them, despite the recent improvements achieved (Buğdaycı, 1996). The company has its own research and development unit, which has been in operation since 1996 and was established despite the opposition of the parent company Fiat. The company also has plans for further investments, modernisation and introduction of new models (Buğdaycı, 1996). Their last model 'Tempra', for instance, has brought modernisation, especially in microelectronics, not only in Tofaş itself but in the components industry as well. Despite recent improvements, however, we should state that Tofaş is still behind, though quite close to, its parent firm Fiat and other leading international firms in terms of technological capability (Duruiz and Yentürk, 1992).

Regarding the role of entrepreneurship in shaping the advantage in the Turkish automobile industry, we can safely state that Turkish entrepreneurs have always been interested and active in the automotive sector from the very beginning. In fact, the very first step was accomplished by A. Ferruh Verdi who, together with his brother, fuelled the foundation of the automotive industry in Turkey by producing the first assembly jeep. Vehbi Koç, founder of Tofaş and probably the most outstanding entrepreneur not just in the automobile industry but in Turkish business history, performed intensive lobbying activities both in Turkey and abroad to establish an automobile factory in Turkey. He, together with Bernar Nahum, another assertive entrepreneur, managed to persuade Ford which rejected similar offers from countries that were at the same development stage as Turkey at the time, and that is how Otosan was founded. Similarly, another entrepreneur, Yalman, succeeded in persuading Chrysler to produce trucks in Turkey (Azcanlı, 1995).

Another interesting issue that the examination of the Turkish automotive industry raises is the problem of locating the source of competitive advantage in an industry dominated by multinational enterprises. If we review the ownership structure in the Turkish automotive industry as a whole, we see that without exception, passenger cars, the subject matter of this chapter, are produced under foreign license, and the share of foreign capital varies between 30-100 per cent amongst different companies (Bayraktar, 1995). Turkish partners of passenger car manufacturers are usually private sector holding companies, still, however, retaining their family enterprise structure which is the dominant managerial type for many Turkish enterprises (Dumanlı, 1987). As mentioned previously, a protected market and the financial weakness of Turkish firms, together with the favourable geographic position, have drawn the attention of more foreign investors to Turkey (Bayraktar, 1995). In addition to Toyota, two others, Honda and Hyundai, have recently started production. They are likely to be followed by Mazda and Kia as has been mentioned above.

With regard to the role of multinationals and foreign direct investment (for a summary of criticisms about that issue see Chapter 1) in shaping the competitive advantage in a country, Porter (1990a) states that the ideal is to make the nation the 'home base'. He argues that before including an industry among the competitive industries of a nation, we should first determine whether the firms operate as branches of a multinational company or whether they can be associated with the host nation without any difficulty. Predictably, Porter (1990a) thinks that they should be excluded in the former case.

In his Canadian study (Porter and The Monitor Company, 1991: 72) Porter further clarifies his attitude towards inward foreign direct investment as well as the role of multinationals in shaping the competitive advantage in a country's industries. He argues that the question is not whether inward FDI or MNEs are good or bad, but rather what they prefer to do in a particular country. He classifies FDI activities into three according to their aims: those sourcing basic factors; those trying to gain market access; and those shifting their home bases to another country. Porter believes that the latter offers the widest set of benefits to a nation. When we consider the Turkish automobile industry, the last FDI wave in the industry, starting from the foundation of Opel-Turkey by GM, and followed by those of Toyota, Hyundai and Honda, as well as the intentions of Kia and Mazda, can be more easily fitted to the classifications defined by Porter. These firms have been operating or are expected to operate as branches of their parent firms. They may fit best to the second category, 'market access', in that their entry seems to have been triggered by tariffs or non-tariff barriers in Turkey, a country which offers an attractive growing market for automobile producers and good access to important nearby markets such as the EU, the Middle East and the C.I.S. The relatively cheaper labour cost in Turkey, included in the first category of Porter's classification, may also have an effect. The motives behind their entry into the Turkish market, however, do not seem to be limited to these. The existence of an established automotive industry, both assembly and components, as well as a pool of qualified technical and managerial personnel, and entrepreneurs, have definitely contributed.

The importance of such factors becomes more obvious when we turn to the analysis of more established firms, namely Tofaş (Koç-Fiat), Otosan (Koç-Ford) and Oyak-Renault. In the case of these firms, it is rather difficult to say they are just branches of the multinationals they are linked to. This is, in fact, evident from the fact that their very establishment, especially for Tofaş and Otosan, was triggered by Turkish entrepreneurs rather than the MNEs themselves. Although models are designed in the parent company and, thus, key research and development take place there, Tofaş does choose what to produce and adopts it to the Turkish market. In short, we should repeat that attraction of foreign investors to produce automobiles in Turkey cannot be only explained by the foundation of some branches to serve a protected market, or to tap on the cheap labour. This is clearly manifested by the analysis of more established firms in the industry which do not so easily fit with one of Porter's classifications, and arguably they are not branches of multinationals but new firms in and of themselves. Tofaş, for instance, is not a branch of Fiat, but rather a firm that prefers to operate under foreign license mainly because it could not afford the required investment to develop its own model when the industry started to emerge in Turkey in the 1960s. Porter's treatment of MNE and FDI, therefore, appears to be somewhat inadequate. In fact, the issue of ownership in the automobile industry has become so complicated that some (e.g. Wells and Rawlinson, 1994) believe it no longer makes sense to say, for instance, 'the Turkish automobile industry' since it is, in fact, 'the automobile industry in Turkey'.

In light of the preceding discussion, we can conclude that as far as this 'corner' of the diamond is concerned, the Turkish automobile industry, like the previous industries I have analysed so far, benefits from the advantages offered by the managerial abilities and entrepreneurial skills of Turkish businessmen. In terms of domestic rivalry, however, we observe that two leading companies, Tofaş and Oyak-Renault, have led an easy life for a long period of time although this situation has been changing recently with decreasing protection and new entrants. In short, the Turkish automobile industry is on average more likely to derive advantages from the factors included in that element of the diamond given that competition is intensifying, causing existing companies to upgrade. Our analysis of the industry, especially the ownership structure, on the other hand, reveals that Porter's treatment of MNEs and inward FDI in shaping the sources of advantage in an industry proves to be inadequate.

The Role of Chance

Maybe because this is a technology-intensive industry, and they are all deterministic engineers, my interviewees were quiet when asked about the impact of the events taking place beyond their control but still affecting the industry. One of my interviewees mentioned the failure to develop a Turkish brand for the automobile sector during its early years of establishment as an unfortunate event. Others think that the existence of a high potential domestic demand for automobiles is a chance for the industry. They all, however, agreed that maybe the most important factor in this respect, whether it is considered a natural resource or chance event, is the favourable location of the country. It is widely accepted that Turkey has an intrinsic advantage with regard to transportation, stemming from its favourable geographical position. From here, we can argue that the country's recent customs union with the EU, and its proximity to the newly emerging markets of the C.I.S. as well as East Europe have contributed to the increasing attention towards Turkey given by the leading foreign automobile manufacturers. As an exaggerated advertisement slogan puts it 'Turkey is not the centre of the world, it is just located there' (Buğdayci, 1996).

The customs union with the EU, however, has brought problems in that the automobile industry is the hardest hit by decreasing protection levels. Assuming gradually intensified competition will push firms to upgrade, this may well turn into an advantage as well. Impacts of chance events, in other words, are on average more likely to be favourable for the Turkish automobile industry, provided, of course, that a smooth transition and restructuring will take place following the recent challenges.

The Role of Government

While assessing the role of government in shaping the sources of advantage in the Turkish automobile industry, starting with an overview of the import protection history may be helpful. Such a review reveals that until recently, protectionist policies, achieved through tariffs and quotas, have restricted foreign competition. The protectionist policies and overvalued exchange rates are considered to be responsible for the concentration on the domestic market and the resulting small-scale production as well as low productivity (Duruiz and Yentürk, 1992). The policies were vague until 1964, which was the year the 'Regulations of the Assembly Industry' were issued. The protection the Regulations brought about went on until the liberalisation (the early 1980s). In 1984, imports of parts and components were liberated to a large extent, and signals for automobile industry itself were given by a gradual decrease in protection levels. Tariffs for cars were slightly reduced, and some quantitative restrictions on imports were abolished. The government also permitted large-scale imports of used cars. Since imports increased too much, however, it later had to introduce a new levy to limit imports of used vehicles. The purpose was to push the industry to start preparing for the customs union with the EU; although considerable protection via tariffs was maintained (Azcanlı, 1995). In 1989 particularly, many protective measures were further relaxed (*Ekonomist*, 1996). Another related development after liberalisation is the reduction obtained in red-tape, especially in the import and driving license procedures (Azcanlı, 1995).

The protective rates for motor vehicles are, nevertheless, always above the industry average in Turkey, despite their undeniably diminishing trend. Nominal protective rates for the Turkish economy in general, for instance, have been calculated as 42 per cent for 1981, 16 per cent for 1985, 9 per cent for 1989, 15 per cent for 1991, and 13 per cent for 1992. The corresponding rates for the automotive sector, on the other hand, are 39 per cent, 37 per cent, 29 per cent, 30 per cent and 29 per cent respectively. The rates for automobiles only are even higher, and, furthermore, it is not possible to detect a decreasing trend. They, in fact, increased from 93 per cent in 1989 to 99 per cent in 1992 (Turhan and Tanrıkulu, 1992). We, of course, observed a decrease after the customs union in 1996 to around 33-59 per cent depending on the type of car. A 'Special Consumption Tax' on imported cars, however, was employed after the union in order to give some time to the industry for adjustment (Capital - Turkey, 1996).

According to the agreements, Turkey will be able to apply higher protection levels (now 27-33 per cent) than the EU levels (10 per cent for automobiles, 11 per cent for light commercial vehicles) towards the third countries until the year 2001. The industry demands further protection stating that the Turkish automobile sector is a young industry. In particular, they have serious concerns about cheap imports from the former Eastern Block countries. Specifically, they demand a further protection for 22 years after the customs union against third countries for automobiles (DPT, 1991c). If their demand is not met, they expect a fall in local production that may amount to as much as 60 per cent (Renda, 1995).

The policy of the local development of the industry, pursued throughout the period 1964-1980, definitely contributed to the development of many related industries and qualified personnel (T.C. Sanayi ve Ticaret Bakanlığı, 1987a), although for some time automobiles were considered as luxurious and this prevented the use of some incentives. Since 1990, however, the industry has been included among the 'industries with special importance', and, thus, it has been able to make use of the incentives and supports specific to these privileged industries. Investment incentives, customs exemption on some imported items, and discounts in taxes and energy bills are just a few examples of such incentives (Azcanlı, 1995; Bayraktar, 1995).

Another government policy that indirectly but considerably affects the automotive industry, which has been mentioned while discussing demand conditions as well, is the transportation policy. In sum, we can say that the emphasis, which was on railways between 1923-1950, shifted in favour of motorways thereafter, and Turkey almost forgot about other means of transportation (T.C. Sanayi ve Ticaret Bakanlığı, 1987a). Several factors responsible for the overwhelming current dominance of motorways in Turkey have been identified ranging from the great number and the scattered nature of cities to the argument that it was dictated by developed countries. It is also argued by one of my interviewees that the reason is political in that government rightly wanted the automotive industry to prosper since it creates considerable employment and contributes to the development of other sectors as well. No matter what the reason is, today Turkey has an inefficient public transportation system, and an almost non-existent railway system, making transportation highly dependent on motorways, which can be considered as an advantage for automobile producers since it increases the demand for cars.

Taxes deserve special attention in an examination of the Turkish automobile industry since they amount to almost 50 per cent of the price of a car in Turkey. The related figure for Europe is 25 per cent maximum, or lower (around 15-20 per cent) for many countries. In Turkey, value-added tax is higher for automobiles, and there are some additional taxes like motor vehicles tax, vehicle purchasing tax and pollution tax. These, of course, decrease the demand for automobiles and, thus, pose an obstacle for firms aiming to operate at full capacity (Azcanlı, 1995). Apart from restricting demand, these taxes also serve as an enormous source of revenue for the government. The argument that the local producers lack the necessary capacity to satisfy the demand if the government decreases taxes does not seem justifiable in the long-run, for which a policy that arranges a step by step decline in taxes can be formulated.

Another issue of criticism for the government relates to its attitude towards new entrants. Some argue that it damages the existing companies when the government lets or even encourages the entry of new firms into the industry. Jan Nahum, the general manager of Tofaş, for instance, implies that there are too many automobile producers in Turkey by stating that there are five automobile manufacturers in Germany, three in Italy and two in France. Only Japan may be an exception, but its production amounts to 5-6 million per year (Buğdaycı, 1996). We should, however, keep in mind that new entrants are usually branches of the leading multinationals which brings us back to the issue of the pros and cons of inward FDI. Given that they are initially subject to local content and export requirements, the advantages they bring are likely to outweigh their disadvantages, from a purely short-run perspective. In the long-run, their effect largely depends on the state of local industry; that is, whether or not local producers are able to compete with them.

The practice of allowing imports of used vehicles without custom duties started as a considerate move to enable Turkish workers abroad to bring in their cars when they return to Turkey. In practice, however, it was largely abused, especially after being extended to cover some commercial vehicles as well (DPT, 1991c). The 1984 regulation allowing the use of this practice was often regarded as having made Turkey Germany's scrap heap. It was also criticised as causing unfair competition. Not surprisingly, as a result, it was abolished at the end of the year (Azcanlı, 1995).

This issue came onto the agenda again when preparing for the customs union with the EU, and it was in principle agreed that Turkey would retain the right to control the importation of used vehicles[1]. In 1996, however, the government decided to introduce the regulation again, this time organising it in such a way that not only Turkish citizens abroad but also the ones in Turkey could make use of the opportunity. This predictably caused disturbance among the industry participants, who, including union representatives, engaged in intensive lobbying activities but could not prevent the government from putting it into practice. Even the rumours and expectations about such a regulation caused a considerable fall in demand for automobiles since customers preferred to postpone their purchasing decisions (*Ekonomist*, 1996).

One of the most important issues related to the role of government in the automobile industry is the lack of a master plan and, hence, a consistent policy towards the industry. In 1987, the government organised a Council of Industry meeting, and the automotive industry was among the ones invited. Although the meeting was regarded as being highly successful, hopes and expectations of a master plan could not be fulfilled. Instead, policies concerning the industry have continued to be rather ad hoc and inconsistent. Industry participants have been rarely consulted before vital decisions about the industry are made. A typical example may be the above mentioned issue of importing used cars. The general negative attitude towards the industry also creates disappointment among the industry participants. The industry has been indeed seen as an 'import-dependent assembly' for a long time, which has affected the attitude of government as well (Duruiz and Yentürk, 1992: 63). A typical example is an anecdote told by İlkbahar, the president of the Automotive Manufacturers' Association and Otosan in which a high level government official has allegedly stated 'Your cars are crap, I will recommend Mercedes as my preference for the official car purchases'. İlkbahar points that they have to deal with this negative image among other things and reminds us that the Japanese even used to have marching songs for their domestic cars (DPT, 1993d).

In light of the preceding analysis, it is obvious that there is a tense relationship between the industry and government, although it is true that the industry has been protected for a long time. I have previously emphasised that excessive protection levels for a long period of time have caused firms to lead an easy life and develop a habit of lobbying the government whether or not they are successful in their attempts. Now, given the industry's contribution to employment and tax revenues, the social costs associated with its likely failure are, of course, hard to face. I should also emphasise that the role of government in the case of the Turkish automobile industry is a rather direct one. The initial foundation of the industry was triggered by the government's 1964 Regulations of the Assembly Industry, and the subsequent changes especially in the protection policies towards the industry, were, and still are, of crucial and determining importance for the industry. It is argued that despite relatively low labour costs in Turkey, when protection levels are equalised with the EU levels, the industry is likely to face difficulties. This is, in fact, a top issue in Turkey in that everybody is aware that protection levels should be reduced to reasonable degrees if not eliminated, which is unavoidable if the industry wants to face the challenge of competing internationally, and if we care about satisfying the customers which are currently destined to buy lower quality cars at higher prices. On the other hand, the industry has high value added, contributes significantly to government revenues and to employment, has a locomotive role for the development of many other industries, and is likely to have good export prospects in the long-run (Turhan and Tanrıkulu, 1992). In short, given that the present structure of the industry cannot persist over time, the government should formulate a smooth transition policy for the industry in order to minimise the social costs of the restructuring process (Hillebrand, 1986). Such a well-thought out transition policy is, in fact, essential for the very existence of the automotive industry in Turkey.

Concluding Remarks

'The machine that changed the world' may also change the destiny of more than 500 thousand people working in the automobile assembly and related industries in Turkey. Since the industry is in the process of a major restructuring, cautious handling of this critical transition is of crucial importance. It is undeniable that during the relatively short history of the industry, Turkish automobile manufacturers have enjoyed high profits for a long period of time thanks to the high levels of protection provided. Recently, decreasing protection levels and an increasing number of new entrants, and the resulting intensifying competition have, however, started to destroy this cosy life and have brought about problems that have long been postponed, but had to be faced sooner or later. Companies have, however, gained some dynamism, in that the stiffer competition pushes them to improve their productivity and quality levels as well as product diversity.

Especially following the customs union with the EU, the industry has started to have conflicts with the government which thinks that automobile manufacturers have been enjoying abnormally high profits at the expense of the customers who are forced to buy lower quality cars at higher prices. The industry is, in other words, seen as a typical example of an infant industry that cannot grow up, and needs to be 'put into order' and 'disciplined'. The recent customs union with the EU provides this 'opportunity', according to the government. What the industry actually needs, of course, is not further clashes with the government, but a realistic handling of the situation which requires a well-planned transition period to minimise the social costs.

Having given a short synopsis of the industry, we can now return to the diamond. The first thing to note is that we have seen that the diamond can be used successfully in detecting the sources of disadvantage in an uncompetitive industry (see Chapter 8 for a discussion). The analysis of the industry with regard to its ownership structure, on the other hand, gives us a valuable opportunity to have a more detailed look at Porter's treatment of MNEs and inward FDI. Our analysis reveals that Porter's treatment of these issues proves to be inadequate.

Note

1   For example, a similar arrangement covering 25 years had been made for Mexico during its NAFTA negotiations. In case of the Turkey-EU agreement no time period was specified (Bayraktar, 1995).

7 The Turkish Flat Steel Industry

The existence and/or strength of the iron and steel industry in a particular country is often associated with the level of economic progress attained by that country. In particular, flat steel production is considered one of the major indicators of industrialisation. The industry ranks high in terms of its forward and backward linkages. Amongst its major customers, for instance, we see such giants as the automotive, construction and defence industries.

The iron and steel industry is one of the prime industries in Turkey capturing 10 per cent of manufacturing industry production (Duruiz and Yentürk, 1992). Its contribution to employment, which amounts to 43,000, is also substantial (Demir et al., 1993). The Turkish iron and steel industry is one the fastest growing amongst the developing countries; in fact, it was the fastest in 1987 with a rate of 18.6 per cent (Güçlü and Muslu, 1987). Latest figures place Turkey as the 15th largest crude steel producer in the world (Metal Bulletin, 1996).

In terms of export performance, the success achieved by the non-flat steel products segment is quite remarkable. In the early 1990s, for instance, Turkey captured almost 15 per cent of the world market in the hot-rolled iron and steel bars segment (SITC code 67326), second only to Italy. The flat steel products industry, on the other hand, experiences a negative trade balance. It is, nevertheless, considered to be competitive; Ereğli Iron and Steel Works (Erdemir thereafter), holding a monopoly in the industry, is highly profitable, exports to over twenty countries (Erdemir, 1995), and is listed amongst the top 100 steelmakers of the world (Metal Bulletin, 1996). The negative trade balance Turkey experiences in the flat steel products segment mainly stems from the high domestic demand; even though Erdemir operates at full capacity, it cannot meet the local demand. Given that a comprehensive expansion project has just been completed, and another one is on the agenda, it is quite likely that the industry will attain a better export performance in the near future.

Development of the Turkish Flat Steel Industry

Attempts by the government to establish an iron and steel industry in Turkey started immediately after the foundation of the Republic (Çelebi, 1979). As a first step, a General Directorate for Iron and Steel was formed in 1926. Its initiatives, however, were not so successful, and, as a result, the body was abolished in 1928. Soon thereafter, a small facility, consisting of two 20-tonne capacity Siemens Martin furnaces and a 2-tonne capacity electric arc furnace, and aiming to produce mainly military products, was built in Kırıkkale near Ankara. Production started in 1932; capacity was subsequently increased to 62,000 tonnes of hot metal and 50,000 tonnes of ingots and blooms. The performance of the plant was not so satisfactory (Szyliowicz, 1991: 50), and later in 1950 it was transferred to the Machinery and Chemicals Institution (MKE), another state-owned enterprise (Çelebi, 1979).

The aspiration of the Turkish government to establish an integrated iron and steel mill that would produce non-flat products became more concrete when it appeared in the First Industrialisation Plan, which allocated 23 per cent of investments to iron and steel (Çelebi, 1979). Karabük, a Black Sea town, was chosen as the location for the plant. Overall organisation of the project created tough competition between Germany and Britain (Szyliowicz, 1991), and the final contract went to the British firm Brassert. In 1935, a state economic enterprise (SEE), Sümerbank, was entrusted with the task of implementing the project. Construction began in 1938, and production started the following year (Çelebi, 1979) with an initial capacity of 150 thousand tonnes (Ata Menkul Kıymetler, 1995). It was soon separated from Sümerbank, and became a state economic enterprise in and of itself. Karabük iron and steel complex, which was designed to produce large sections and heavy plates, is amongst the first integrated iron and steel plants founded in a developing country (Çelebi, 1979).

Karabük, however, began to experience problems in the 1940s. Administrative issues, which were not accorded the required attention, constituted the major problematic area. Deficiencies such as poor location and the imbalances of the design, which were inherited from the project phase, made the situation even worse. Turkey's first venture into iron and steel as a result was not so successful (Szyliowicz, 1991). In fact, the problems were so severe that an evaluation report prepared by American experts in 1946, called the Thornburg Report, recommended that the plant should be closed (Çelebi, 1979).

Turkish authorities, however, preferred to modernise the plant and increase its capacity instead. Until very recently, the plant was supported by the state and did relatively well until 1989 when the government signalled that it considered closing it down. Some (e.g. Kansu, 1996) argue that the then government, in fact, wanted to get rid of the Karabük mill, and to justify this socially difficult task, it deliberately led the plant into losses. Karabük's shares in Erdemir, Turkey's second steel mill, for instance, were transferred to an entity responsible for privatisation in 1987, without any payments to the plant. The factory started to suffer huge losses, and in 1994, the government proposed either the closure or privatisation of the plant. In 1995, 51.8 per cent of the shares were bought by the employees, and the bulk of the rest by the Karabük residents, while the government did not want to have any shares at all. Following the take-over by the employees, the administration improved, and the company started to make a profit, leaving the question 'why wasn't that possible under government administration' unanswered (Kansu, 1996). It is, however, too early to conclude that this model is successful, especially given the fact that, at Karabük, steel is produced by open-hearth furnaces, and there is no continuous casting, which makes the plant outmoded (Hogan, 1991: 68-70).

The second integrated factory, Ereğli Iron and Steel Works, which is the only integrated flat steel producer in Turkey (the type of products constituting the subject matter of this chapter), was officially established in 1960 and started full operation in 1965 (Duruiz and Yentürk, 1992). In accordance with the project, one port and one dam were constructed in Ereğli, another Black Sea town (Çelebi, 1979). It carries the status of a joint stock corporation, although its foundation was undertaken by two state economic enterprises, Sümerbank and Karabük (TDÇİ), which together used to hold more than half of the shares. Specifically, establishing parties are the TDÇİ, Sümerbank, Ankara Chamber of Commerce, İş Bank and Koppers (Çelebi, 1979). Koppers Associates, which used to own 22.5 per cent of the shares, later sold its holdings (T.C. Sanayi ve Ticaret Bakanlığı, 1987c), and, in 1990, 5.5 per cent of the shares were sold to the public (Hogan, 1991: 68-70). The issue of privatising Erdemir by selling the rest of the shares owned by the government is also currently on the agenda.

Szyliowicz (1991) argues that the decision to build Erdemir was political rather than economical, and this created problems later, since careful economic analysis of the project was not carried out. Most serious of all, Erdemir started to experience financial difficulties in paying back its debts. The main reason for such problems was the small-scale of the plant. During the project phase, assuming that demand for flat steel products would not increase much in Turkey, the capacity was held relatively small for a steel mill, which prevented it from working efficiently (Çelebi, 1979). To solve the problem, an emergency programme of debt rescheduling was organised together with a major expansion plan. The proposed expansion was a major undertaking, and the World Bank and AID were willing to support it. Production of hot metal was expected almost to double, rising from 860,000 to 1,654,000 tonnes. It was envisaged to involve two stages, stage one taking place between 1972-76 and two between 1976-80. The Second Five Year Development Plan (1968-1972) required further expansion of Erdemir's capacity. This time, the motive was related to demand concerns to avoid a heavy dependence on imports (Szyliowicz, 1991). Recently, another major expansion that will improve the plant's competitiveness, apart from increasing the capacity, has been completed. This issue, that is the international competitiveness of Erdemir, and, thus, of the Turkish flat steel industry, will be further analysed when discussing the sources of advantage in the Turkish flat steel industry in the next section.

While Erdemir was struggling with its problems in the late 1960s, the government was busy with the other ambitious projects designed to provide a massive expansion in Turkey's iron and steel capacity. Work began on a third iron and steel plant, a plan for a fourth one was initiated, and a comprehensive modernisation programme was launched at Karabük (Szyliowicz, 1991: 156). After the above mentioned reimbursement difficulties experienced with the Erdemir project, neither the United States (financed Erdemir) nor the West European countries (financed Karabük) were willing to finance the third plant. The only country with any interest in the project was the USSR, which at the time was trying to establish friendlier relations with Turkey. The agreement was signed in 1969. It is interesting to see that some mistakes of the past were also repeated in this project. The size of the plant was again held small, for instance. This insistence on small-scale can be partly explained by such restrictions as the demand predictions, the availability of local raw materials and amount of financing provided by the USSR. Furthermore, the scheduled completion dates for the last integrated factory in Turkey, İskenderun Iron and Steel Works (İsdemir), which was to be located in İskenderun, on the Mediterranean coast of Turkey, proved to be rather unrealistic. Construction began in 1970, the first blast furnace could only start to operate in 1975, and the second in 1979 (Szyliowicz, 1991: 165).

In terms of ownership structure, İsdemir, like Karabük, is under the jurisdiction of the TDÇİ (Hogan, 1991: 68-70). With regard to its performance, we see that İsdemir in the late 1970s and early 1980s was a very uneconomic plant since it produced only a small percentage of its rated capacity of 2.2 million tonnes (Ata Menkul Kıymetler, 1995), and productivity levels were extremely low. It also suffered from the administrative and managerial deficiencies common to many other state economic enterprises in Turkey. As in the case of Erdemir, an expansion programme was designed to solve some of its problems (Szyliowicz, 1991: 165). Despite such efforts and its modern technologies, however, the İsdemir plant still performs poorly. The level of technological mastery as well as quality is low, and its workforce is too large (Szyliowicz, 1991: 185). A comparison of Karabük and İsdemir reveals that despite all its shortcomings, Karabük functions well relatively to İsdemir (Szyliowicz, 1991: 180).

Apart from these three integrated factories, there are eighteen private mini-mills operating in Turkey using electric arc furnace technology (Renda, 1995). The first mini-mill of this kind, Metaş, started production in İzmir in 1960. The first flat steel producer in the private sector is, on the other hand, Borçelik which is an Erdemir and Borusan partnership with some foreign involvement (Ata Menkul Kıymetler, 1995). The number of firms in the private sector has been increasing, paralleling the demand and the subsidies provided (Kartay, 1993). In fact, the investment in the electric arc furnace segment of the industry has been so great that it now constitutes almost 60 per cent of the total steel output of Turkey (Kansu, 1996), as opposed to 25 per cent in the early 1980s (Hogan, 1991: 68-70).

The historical review conducted above reveals that, by the end of the 1970s, Turkey had built up an iron and steel industry of considerable size, including three integrated mills, which operate blast furnaces as well as steelmaking and finishing facilities, and the electric furnace segment, which consists of companies that produce steel from scrap in electric furnaces (Hogan, 1991). Furthermore, seeing good demand prospects, the Fourth Five Year Plan called for building two more integrated plants meaning an addition of another 10 million tonnes to the country's capacity. The larger, of eight million tonnes capacity, never moved beyond the concept stage; the other, of only two million tonnes, was to be located at Sivas and called as Sidemir (Szyliowicz, 1991: 166).

Important political and economic changes, however, took place in Turkey in the early 1980s, which affected the iron and steel industry, including the decision not to proceed with the Sidemir plant (Szyliowicz, 1991: 188). These were difficult years for the iron and steel industry everywhere, as new producers entered the market creating excess capacity. Dumping became common, and prices were pushed to very low levels as governments protected their industries. Turkish plants were unable to compete in this environment (Szyliowicz, 1991: 187), and the DPT prepared a master plan, which recommended investments to modernise the plants. The quality of management was upgraded by placing qualified persons in key positions and creating an environment in which they can function properly. The government also moved to reduce the number of excess workers. These reforms went hand in hand with liberalisation policies, and the combined effects were remarkable; iron and steel production increased more between 1980-86 than it did between 1940-80 (T.C. Sanayi ve Ticaret Bakanlığı, 1987c). The trade balance in steel turned positive, and Turkey became an exporting country in that industry. The country now meets much of its own steel requirements locally and can even export systems such as rolling mills (Szyliowicz, 1991: 218). More importantly, these improvements happened while the industry was stagnant in many other countries of the world (Akın, 1993). Much of the sector's improved performance is associated with the change in the situation of İsdemir, where the level of production was so low that merely bringing it up to that of the other integrated iron and steel works produced a dramatic change in the sector's condition.

While most of the exports are non-flat products, scrap constitutes the bulk of the imports, most of which come from Southern European countries, Germany and Eastern Europe (Duruiz and Yentürk, 1992). If we concentrate on the trade of flat steel products only, we see that in 1995, Turkish flat steel exports amounted to 700,000 tonnes, still a long way behind the imports, which reached 2,641,000 tonnes in the same year, surpassing the total flat steel production of Turkey (Erdemir, 1995). The trade balance for flat products is, therefore, still negative.

If we review the current situation of the Turkish iron and steel industry, we see that the total steel production capacity in Turkey is over 16 million tonnes (Erdemir, 1995), and Turkey has one of the fastest growing steel industries in Europe (Hogan, 1991: 68-70). In 1994, Turkey was ranked as 15th largest producer in the world with 12 million tonnes of crude steel production (Renda, 1995), jumping from the 33rd place it captured in 1980 (Duruiz and Yentürk, 1992). This figure is, however, expected to increase further since the flat steel capacity in Turkey has recently reached 3.65 million tonnes (3.3 million tonnes Erdemir and 350,000 tonnes Borçelik). Flat steel production was 1,633,000 tonnes in 1995 (Erdemir, 1995).

Having provided a brief history of the industry's development in Turkey, I would like to proceed by describing two structural problems prevailing in the sector. In the Turkish iron and steel industry, there is a severe imbalance in the supply of the main product groups; the supply of flat steel falls short of, whereas non-flat production supply surpasses, demand in the domestic market. In 1994, for instance, 2.6 million tonnes of flat steel had to be imported to meet domestic demand, whereas almost 4 million tonnes of long steel, the surplus over consumption, had to be exported with difficulty. The share of flat steel products in total steel production is around 60-65 per cent in the European Union countries, while in Turkey it is only 20 per cent (Erdemir, 1995).

The main reason for this situation is the unanticipated increase in the demand for flat products in Turkey, following improvements achieved in the flat-steel using industries like the automotive, shipbuilding, durable consumer goods, can-making and machine tools industries. The main users of non-flat products are, on the other hand, the construction and transportation sectors, which improved as well, but not enough to consume all of the domestic production. Although it is known that the early stages of development require a lot of infrastructure, and, thus, construction, whereas, later, the types of industries requiring flat steel products (Sezgin, 1993) are expected to prosper, related bodies seem to have failed to predict the extent of their relative development patterns in Turkey.

Another structural problem that persists in the Turkish iron and steel industry concerns the share of integrated mills versus mini-mills. The share mini-mills capture in the total steel production of Turkey is 60 per cent, whereas it averages around 30 per cent for many countries. This fact, although mini-mills are considered to be more efficient and responsive to market forces, makes Turkey more dependent, thus more vulnerable, to changes in the world scrap supply, given that the mini-mills have to import the bulk of the scrap they need (Kansu, 1996).

Sources of Advantage in the Turkish Flat Steel Industry

Factor Conditions

Amongst the raw materials required for steel production, three -iron ore, coal and scrap- are highly important. Domestic iron ore and coal supplies are not sufficient either in amount or quality, and their costs are relatively higher. The high ash content of domestic coal, for instance, causes the blast furnace to function below the optimal effectiveness level. It is, therefore, not surprising that Erdemir imports more than half of its raw material requirements. In terms of quantity, imports outweigh domestic inputs (approximately 65 per cent vs. 35 per cent, respectively), whereas it is the reverse in terms of value (around 40 per cent versus 60 per cent, respectively) (DPT, 1995a).

An analysis of the cost structure of Erdemir reveals that input costs, labour costs and energy costs are amongst the most important cost items, in order of importance, for the main product groups (DPT, 1995a). The energy and input (mainly iron ore and coal) as well as financing costs are very high (Kunak, 1995), and government support, which can be essential to maintain a cost-price balance in the case of the iron and steel industry, falls short of that available to many foreign competitors (DPT, 1991b). As a result, costs of production, thus prices, remain near or even higher than those in Europe, despite labour cost advantages (DPT, 1995a: 35).

Given that it is an energy-intensive industry, extremely high relative energy costs in Turkey pose some problems for the sector. Two main energy inputs, fuel oil and electricity, are both more expensive in Turkey than many other countries (TİSK, 1995). Apart from high energy costs, the deficiencies in the country infrastructure also pose serious problems for the Turkish flat steel industry. The importance of a well functioning transportation system, especially of railways and ports, becomes clear, when we consider that both inputs and outputs are bulky items (T. C. Sanayi ve Ticaret Bakanlığı, 1987c). Turkey's rail system is however obsolete. Turkish government's decision to not build the link between the railroad and the major Zonguldak-Ankara route, because it is costly, definitely limited transportation possibilities for Erdemir. High transportation costs and the relatively small size of the port at Ereğli pose further constraints for the company (Szyliowicz, 1991: 192-3).

Financial difficulties, which put all industries into a difficult position in Turkey, are felt heavily in the iron and steel industry since the investment requirements are huge. As stated previously, current capacity falls short of domestic demand, and, thus, additional investment in the flat steel industry is badly needed in Turkey. Finding the necessary financing is, however, the most important obstacle, preventing an otherwise likely investment in the flat steel segment. Funds, especially on such a large scale, are in short supply in Turkey, and developed countries as well as the international organisations are not so willing to finance additional investments in iron and steel, given the excess capacity in the world market (DPT, 1995a).

In terms of productivity, we see that man-power productivity figures for Erdemir are very satisfactory. It ranks first amongst the Turkish iron and steel plants, and the figure for coke oven man-power productivity is higher than the related figure for many countries, for instance, the USA (Szyliowicz, 1991: 182). Furthermore, upward trends have been observed in productivity (Duruiz and Yentürk, 1992).

Although around 80-100 metallurgy engineers graduate each year in Turkey (T. C. Sanayi ve Ticaret Bakanlığı, 1987c), the company has experienced some difficulty in hiring qualified personnel, mostly stemming from its geographic position, though not to the extent that it blocks the operations of the plant (DPT, 1995a). Apart from metallurgists, the industry employs mechanical, electric and electronic engineers, the latter gaining special importance recently. There are also a few intermediate level technical schools offering casting-intensive programmes, but they cannot satisfy the needs of the industry either in terms of number or quality (T. C. Sanayi ve Ticaret Bakanlığı, 1987c). A need for an iron and steel institution, which would organise the accumulated information, data and experience, is also frequently expressed (T. C. Sanayi ve Ticaret Bakanlığı, 1987c).

Since 1976, the company has had its own research and development unit. Its activities, however, remained limited for some time, and some fifteen years elapsed until the research and development laboratory and documentation centre was eventually established in 1991. The centre serves the production, sales, purchasing and engineering units, and it has connections with the Dialog Information Services, Inc., USA (Duruiz and Yentürk, 1992). Key technology is transferred from abroad, and key research and development activities still remain limited. They instead mostly focus on product improvement in line with the demands of the customers.

In brief, an overall evaluation of the factor conditions for the Turkish flat steel industry looks bleak. Erdemir has to import a considerable amount of its major inputs, since, apart from being relatively more expensive, the domestic ones are either not sufficient in amount or of inferior quality. The industry, however, most severely suffers from financing and infrastructure problems, which definitely harm the competitive prospects of the industry. The states of both research and development and sector-specific educational institutions also remain weak. The only positive element regarding the factor conditions relates to labour. Labour costs are still lower in Turkey, and man-power productivity levels are satisfactory, providing an advantage. Even this advantage is however shadowed by the problem of excess labour, and it does not suffice to neutralise the disadvantages described above.

Demand Conditions

As has been stated previously, we see that the share flat steel captures in total steel production is around 20 per cent in Turkey, whereas the related figure is around 60-65 per cent for many developed countries (Erdemir, 1995). Demand for flat steel products is, however, high and shows an increasing trend. Moreover, projections show that Turkey's flat steel consumption will reach 7 million tonnes in the early 2000s, more than double the newly increased capacity of Erdemir (Erdemir, 1995). In fact,

Erdemir can meet only 70 per cent of the domestic demand, and the rest is imported (DPT, 1995a). Within the flat steel industry, there is a shift from basic steel products to specialty steels, paralleling the trend in the rest of the world (Szyliowicz, 1991).

There are plans calling for a new integrated flat steel plant as well as increasing Erdemir's capacity further (DPT, 1991b). Investment possibilities to increase this capacity are, as stated previously, bounded by the availability of financing. Despite the accelerated demand for flat steel products, per capita consumption figures for Turkey are still rather low. Although it jumped from around 70 kg/person in 1980 to around 160 kg/person in 1995, passing the world average of 140 kg/per capita, the figure still remains well below the corresponding one for developed countries which averages around 300-400 kg/per capita (Erdemir, 1995).

Regarding the nature of domestic versus foreign buyers in terms of being more demanding and anticipatory, my interviewees state that it is hard to detect a difference in that both domestic and foreign buyers are equally demanding. It is, however, possible to observe an increase in the quality consciousness of all buyers, especially so for the domestic car and pipe producers following the liberalisation, and later after the Customs Union.

As a result, when we review the attributes of home demand as defined by Porter (1990a), we cannot detect either a clear advantage or disadvantage for the Turkish flat steel industry. Although demand for steel products is growing fast and expected to increase further, per capita consumption is still considered to be low in Turkey. The segment structure in the iron and steel industry in general does not resemble that of the rest of the world in that the flat steel segment is smaller than the long steel one. Within the flat steel industry, however, there is a shift from basic steel products to specialty steels, paralleling the trend in the rest of the world. Lastly, it is hard to say whether Turkish customers are more or less sophisticated and demanding than foreign ones, or whether they are anticipatory of the changes in the world market. It is, however, true that both domestic and foreign customers are becoming more demanding. As a conclusion, then, we can state that the attributes of domestic demand do not provide a clear advantage for the Turkish flat steel industry; they, however, do not put it into a particularly disadvantageous situation, either. It is even possible to argue that demand conditions have a potential to provide a considerable advantage for Turkish flat steel producers, given that local demand is increasing and domestic customers are getting more demanding.

Related and Supporting Industries

The flat steel industry in Turkey provides the major inputs for the pipes and profiles, automotive, fuel storage and related equipment, tinplate industrial users, household and related equipment, agricultural machinery production, electrical machine production, shipbuilding, durable consumer goods, can-making and machine tools industries. The shares of the first three industries in flat product shipments of Erdemir in 1995 were 43 per cent, 8 per cent, 5 per cent respectively (Erdemir, 1995). As a result of the expansion recently completed, the cold-rolled production capacity has increased more, meaning that the shares of the automotive and durable consumer goods will probably rise.

As has been mentioned previously, after the early 1980s, non-flat steel production in Turkey far exceeded domestic demand, forcing domestic producers to export. This coincided with the increased export incentives of the early liberalisation period, and from the mid-1980s, as a result, Turkey began to enjoy a trade surplus in the industry (T. C. Sanayi ve Ticaret Bakanlığı, 1987c). The destination of exports shifted from the Middle East to the Far East, especially to China, starting from 1992 (Duruiz and Yentürk, 1992). The important competitors in non-flat products are Eastern European countries, especially the Ukraine, in the domestic market, and the EU, some Latin American and Eastern European countries, Japan, South Korea and Taiwan in the export markets (Renda, 1995). The removal of some key export incentives in the Sixth Plan era (1990-1994), however, put the industry into a difficult position, especially when firms had to compete with cheap and low quality products imported from the former Eastern Block (DPT, 1995b). Stagnation in the world iron and steel industry, high dependence on one market -China, and on one advantage -price, are other reasons explaining why the export success achieved did not endure for long (*Ekonomist*, 1995c). More recently, the industry has faced serious problems because of the Asian crisis. In short, despite the fact that the Turkish non-flat steel products segment experienced a rapid growth throughout the 1980s and especially in the early 1990s, it was mostly thanks to a vulnerable cost advantage and started to erode as the world market got more stagnant, many incentives were abolished, new markets began to saturate and the competition from other low cost competitors intensified.

With regard to the casting industry, we see that when compared with the EU countries, costs are more or less the same. Although an increasing trend is observed in exports, the potential of the industry is considered to be much higher, which cannot be realised because of financing problems, lower productivity rates, and relatively high input, energy (30 per cent higher) and freight (7 per cent higher) costs as compared to those of the EU countries (Alkan, 1993).

The seamed pipe industry gets the bulk of its inputs from Erdemir and has been increasing its exports recently. The technological level attained in the industry compares well to that of the main competitors (DPT, 1991b). Although the industry faces some problems like high financing, transportation and energy costs, it is competitive and regarded as having good prospects for the future (T. C. Sanayi ve Ticaret Bakanlığı, 1987c).

The only producer in the ferro-alloys industry, which is closely linked to the iron and steel industry, is a SEE, Etibank. Turkey is an important producer of ferrochromium in the world, which is used in the production of quality steel. Since the production of the latter is limited in Turkey, the bulk of the production in the ferrochromium industry is exported, especially to the USA and Japan. The competitive position of the industry mainly stems from rich raw material supplies as well as a high level of technological mastery. In fact, the technological level attained by the industry has come to a point that Turkish engineers are involved in consultancy activities in the Middle East and the C.I.S. (DPT, 1995c).

To conclude, if we review the cluster charts (see Table 2.2 in Chapter 2 and Appendix A1), we see that the 'materials/metals' cluster, one of the leading clusters of the Turkish economy, is mostly occupied by long steel products as well as metal manufactures and non-ferrous metals. Another interesting point that the cluster chart for 1985 in particular reveals with regard to the iron and steel industry is that Turkey succeeded in having one strong position in the related machinery segment -foundry moulds- although it ceased to appear in the 1992 chart. Apart from foundry moulds and long steel products, which had strong international positions and then lost some of their position in a short period of time due to their heavy dependence on cost advantage, a few export markets, and subsidies, which are relatively vulnerable and easy to replicate, we see two other closely related internationally competitive industries: pipes and ferro-alloys in the cluster charts. Substitutes also include some competitive industries like aluminium products, plastics, glass and ceramics. The casting industry is, on the other hand, considered to have good prospects for the future. It is hard to say, however, that the industries providing inputs to the Turkish flat steel industry, like the iron ore or coal industries are competitive internationally, neither is the transportation industry. The competitive structure of the automotive industry, which has been analysed in the previous chapter, is not that bright, either, despite the recent revival. There is, in other words, a mixed support for Porter's (1990a) argument that the internationally competitive industries of a nation tend to cluster together. Although the needle definitely points to the positive side, the evidence does not suffice to justify full support.

Firm Strategy, Structure and Rivalry

If we review the structure of the flat steel industry in Turkey, we see that Ereğli Iron and Steel Works (Erdemir) is the only integrated flat steel producer, which includes a harbour, dock, ore preparation facilities, coke plants, two blast furnaces, steelmaking facilities, rolling mills and utilities and maintenance shops. Apart from crude steel, its main products include cold and hot rolled sheets, plates and tinplate (Duruiz and Yentürk, 1992). After the very recent completion of a comprehensive expansion project, its capacity has been increased to 3 million tonnes of crude steel and 3.3 million tonnes of flat-rolled steel production (DPT, 1995a). Erdemir accounts for 16 per cent of crude steel production in Turkey (Erdemir, 1995). Borçelik Sanayi ve Ticaret A. Ş. (BORÇELİK) is another company that started flat steel production in 1994. It is a joint venture of Erdemir and Borusan with some foreign involvement (Ilva and Usinor Sacilor), producing cold-rolled sheets by getting most of the necessary semi-finished products from Erdemir. Borçelik has an annual capacity of 350,000 tonnes (Erdemir, 1995). Given that Borçelik has a limited capacity and is a joint venture of Erdemir, it is clear that Erdemir has a monopoly in the Turkish flat steel industry.

With regard to its ownership structure, Erdemir's situation differs from the other integrated steel plants of Turkey since it is legally a private sector enterprise. In fact, it is more appropriate to consider it as a mixed enterprise, since initially it was organised in such a way as to ensure that, even though the Turkish government would own over half of the shares, actual control would lie with the private Turkish and the American shareholders. Actually, what happened, however, is that, to cover the shortfall which amounted to US$13 million, almost three-quarters of the shares were owned by the Turkish government (Szyliowicz, 1991). Currently, putting the privatisation attempts aside, almost half of the company is owned by the government. It is amongst the biggest ten companies in Turkey, and it acts as a private independent company (Duruiz and Yentürk, 1992). Its management, for instance, can basically form its own policies in many critical areas such as setting its own price and salary levels. Moreover, decisions can be taken relatively quickly and easily since they only have to be approved by the board of directors, whereas, in state economic enterprises, decisions have to go from the plant to the General Directorate of Turkish Iron and Steel, then to the High Planning Commission (Szyliowicz, 1991: 186-7).

There have been occasions, especially during the 1970s, however, when it was treated like a state enterprise. Such practices as changing the board whenever there is a change in the government and political appointments of managers who lacked the necessary industrial experience as well as technical and managerial education, definitely made some mark on the managerial culture of the company. Another adverse effect of the past political interference in Erdemir is that the number of employees rose sharply resulting in extensive overstaffing. Szyliowicz (1991: 199-200) argues that Erdemir's organisational culture differed only in degree, though not in kind from the SEEs. Some of Erdemir's drawbacks, in other words, stem from its history.

Erdemir, nevertheless, has managed to maintain a relatively stable and strongly motivated managerial team and workforce that has enabled it to operate at a profit, despite this problematic history and deficiencies stemming from errors of the past. The extent of the improvement attained in its management is impressive indeed, as has been detected by a World Bank group which concluded that Erdemir's personnel is well experienced in operating the plant (Szyliowicz, 1991: 180). The management, for instance, initiated a programme trying to make life in Ereğli more interesting to be able to attract qualified technical and managerial manpower, which have been somehow reluctant to live in Ereğli, a town on the Black Sea coast (Duruiz and Yentürk, 1992). Erdemir's management has also been organising intensive on-the-job training programmes. In 1995, for instance, 281 employees participated in various training courses totalling, 174,252 training hours (Erdemir, 1995). A number of employees were sent abroad; the training programme for engineers conducted in Japan was particularly effective. The factory also conducts annual training sessions for engineers coming from other developing countries in collaboration with UNIDO (T. C. Sanayi ve Ticaret Bakanlığı, 1987c). Erdemir's management is also fast in mobilising their entrepreneurial skills, one example of which is the fact that they have been able to take advantage of the low cost of billets in the world in such a way that they imported, rolled and exported them, thus capturing the value added for the factory (Szyliowicz, 1991: 218). In short, Erdemir seems to have shaken off most of the shortcomings it inherited from the previous political involvement in the plant's administration. In fact, Erdemir is considered by many as Turkey's best iron and steel complex (Szyliowicz, 1991: 155).

Similarly, Erdemir has shown substantial progress in productivity and quality in recent years. Apart from managerial improvements, the completion of the recent expansion project has definitely contributed towards that progress. Its technology compares well to that of developed country firms, and the quality of its products is in compliance with international standards (Erdemir, 1995). It is a very profitable company, and its shares, which are viewed as a no-risk investment, are considered as an important factor affecting the share index in the İstanbul Stock Exchange. Expectations and news concerning the privatisation of the company permitted Erdemir to be very popular amongst investors.

When we review the strategies followed by the company, we see that the firm works on an order-based system, and, thus, consumer relations are of vital importance. Automation is selectively used. The aim is a well co-ordinated and integrated factory, not a fully-automated one (Duruiz and Yentürk, 1992). The main emphasis of Erdemir has always been on the domestic market. Its exports started in 1981 with 8,000 tonnes (T. C. Sanayi ve Ticaret Bakanlığı, 1987c), and later, they accelerated to reach around 15 per cent of the company's total production. Export destinations range all over the world; the EU, Middle East, the USA and the Far East are amongst the important markets (DPT, 1995a).

The Capacity Improvement and Modernisation (CIM) Project, which was launched in 1990 and intensified in 1995 deserves some special attention. The CIM Project, whose costs amounted to approximately US$1.5 billion, enabled the company to raise its annual capacity from 2 million tonnes to 3 million tonnes. The Project is a massive investment in that among other things it includes the construction of a dam and a natural gas distribution system (Erdemir, 1995). The main motive for launching such a project is predictably the high domestic demand. Apart from increasing the capacity, the project also aims at improving quality as well as decreasing the cost of the products, especially by lowering fuel and raw material consumption. Even though the increased capacity is aimed at the domestic market, an improvement in the export performance is also envisaged (Duruiz and Yentürk, 1992). Considering the consumption potential in Turkey, feasibility studies for a new investment project aimed at raising the production capacity to 4.5 million tonnes of flat steel is also on the agenda of Erdemir's management (Erdemir, 1995).

To sum up, our analysis for the Turkish flat steel industry reveals that the industry is more likely to derive advantage from most of the factors included in the determinant 'firm strategy, structure and rivalry'. One exception is the lack of domestic rivalry, which, like in the case of the

Turkish glass industry, provides a challenge to one of Porter's (1990a) strongest arguments. We see a quite successful company, whereas there is barely no domestic rivalry. One possible explanation is the nature of the industry itself, which dictates huge investments, economies of scale and, thus, fewer large firms. The second explanation relates to the exposition to international competition, which, by pushing Erdemir to upgrade, may offset some of the disadvantages of not having intense domestic rivalry. The state of managerial capabilities, however, is in line with Porter's (1990a) predictions. Having liberated themselves from the past organisational culture, which was damaged by the effects of political interference, Erdemir's management has shown substantial improvements, providing an advantage for the Turkish flat steel industry.

The Role of Chance

When we consider the important events taking place beyond the control of the firms but affecting them anyway, which Porter (1990a) describes as 'chance' events, we see that two events have been especially troublesome for the Turkish flat steel industry. First is the Gulf War, which, apart from worsening export performance, decreased domestic demand as well via the crisis it caused in the automotive industry. Second is the emergence of some C.I.S. countries, especially the Russian Federation and the Ukraine, as threatening competitors with very cheap and low quality products both in the domestic market and export markets.

More recently, the abolition of barriers with the EU (see the next section for details) poses a challenge for the industry given that Europe's giant steel makers have large amounts of unused capacity (Szyliowicz, 1991). The completion of the CIM Project has just preceded the full mutual elimination of customs duties, which is considered as a positive chance event by Erdemir's management. Another phenomenon we can mention with regard to chance events for the Turkish flat steel industry is the Asian crisis, which resulted in considerable contraction in the world market

The Role of Government

Iron and steel is a capital-intensive industry requiring immense investments. Establishing an integrated factory is particularly expensive, with around a US$2,000 investment requirement per tonne (Kansu, 1996). Under these circumstances, it is not surprising that government involvement in the industry is quite high all over the world. Apart from helping to finance their investments if not establishing the plant itself, many governments protect firms by limiting imports and encouraging exports of steel products.

Although, attempts to achieve freer trade in the industry, such as the Multilateral Steel Agreement (MSA), goes on (Demir et al., 1993), it is still true that government support for the iron and steel industry in many countries is more comprehensive than the one for many other industries. Steel is an important input, and a supply of steel at a stable price becomes a prerequisite for national independence and security. Local production is also considered to enable large savings in scarce foreign exchange. Such fundamental issues make steel a commodity in which countries prefer to be self-sufficient (Szyliowicz, 1991: 42).

Turkey, a country that equated industrialisation with economic development for a long period of time, gave crucial importance to developing an iron and steel industry as well. Until very recently, Turkish governments of every ideological inclination attributed high priority to the iron and steel industry (Szyliowicz, 1991: 1). The First Five Year Industrialisation Plan, which was prepared in 1933, stressed textiles (36 per cent of total investments), and iron and steel (23 per cent), more than any other sector (Szyliowicz, 1991: 48-9). In this respect, the role of the military, which has been historically strong in Turkey, was also important, given that the defence sector is amongst the important customers of the iron and steel industry. In the 1970s, for instance, some changes were made in the expansion plans of Erdemir to meet the navy's needs (Szyliowicz, 1991: 209).

The original decision to build Erdemir was political rather than economical and made on the basis of Turkey's national aspirations for industrialisation, whose roots can be traced back to the import substitution industrialisation policies adopted at the time. Under such circumstances, a careful economic analysis was not considered as necessary, which helps us explain such flaws in the project phase as overlooking the need for a dam and housing, and miscalculating the nature and magnitude of domestic demand as well as iron ore availability (Szyliowicz, 1991: 202-3). According to Szyliowicz (1991: 208), 'successive Turkish governments all erroneously defined the problem as how to acquire the capability to produce steel rather than as the development of an indigenous technological capability.'

A concrete example of the poor handling of the project from the beginning is the fact that the plant was located in such a way that there were no places left for the new factories that would utilise Erdemir's by-products (Szyliowicz, 1991: 193). Furthermore, the project had to be revised several times since experts were often surprised by the unexpected decisions of the Turkish government like devaluating the currency or changing the import regime (Szyliowicz, 1991: 197-8). In short, although the government was directly involved and always actively supported the industry, the Turkish iron and steel industry was in fact subject to arbitrary and poorly-designed policies rather than a long-term, well-designed and consistent policy (Szyliowicz, 1991: 208). The Turkish government's only concern was to develop an indigenous iron and steel industry at any expense. Issues like quality and productivity were given secondary importance, whereas to increase the amount of production was accorded first priority (Szyliowicz, 1991).

Following the changes that the liberalisation policies of the 1980s brought about, however, the Turkish government's historical commitment and support for the iron and steel industry has changed its character. The government did not want to take the burden of financing loss-making state economic enterprises, including steel mills. The previously discussed case of Karabük, which was first intended to be closed down, but was then sold to the employees is a good example showing the change in the government's attitude. The privatisation of Erdemir by selling the shares it owns (more than 50 per cent) is also on the agenda of the government. Now, all parties - the state, public and private sector firms- seem to act in harmony and agree on the restructuring of the sector, including privatisation issues (Akın, 1993).

A related issue of the post-liberalisation period that should be mentioned is the changes in the trade regime. The industry have always made use of some support from the government since the early 1970s, like investment subsidies and customs exemption for their key imports. After 1980, additional support, mostly in the form of export subsidies, which are believed to have been very effective in achieving the immense improvement in the export performance of non-flat products, was introduced (T. C. Sanayi ve Ticaret Bakanlığı, 1987c). When some of them were abolished in the late 1980s and early 1990s, however, the sector faced some difficulty (Demir et al., 1993). On the import side as well, a regulation requiring special permission to import steel products was lifted in 1984, but the industry continued to be protected by tariffs (T. C. Sanayi ve Ticaret Bakanlığı, 1987c).

Regarding the Customs Union (CU), we see that the meeting of the Partnership Council dated on the 6th of March, 1995 requires that the Turkish government should withdraw from the iron and steel industry. According to the resolutions of the meeting, the industry will not be treated within the framework of the CU, instead a separate agreement with the ECSC, specifying a time period during which custom taxes for non-flat products will be mutually eliminated, will be finalised (Renda, 1995). The pronounced time periods include a five-year transition period, during which government support will continue, and another three-year period for the abolition of the customs taxes, specifically, 50 per cent for the first year and 25 per cent each for the following two years. For flat steel products, customs were abolished at the beginning of 1996, together with the CU. It has been also agreed in principle that the government will not support any crude steel capacity expansion projects (Ata Menkul Kıymetler, 1995). Recently, however, Erdemir has been successful at lobbying the government to increase the protection level against the third parties (not against the EU) from 2.9-5 per cent to 22.5-30 per cent (Akbay, 1998). Amongst the most important reasons, we can include the fact that Erdemir is under considerable pressure to finance the CIM project, which will be paid back in full by 2004; the Asian crisis, which resulted in intense price competition following the contraction in the world market; and the import dependency in the major inputs as well as some intermediate products like slabs. These are all together responsible from the recent fall in company's profitibility. As a long-term response to these developments (the short-term response is the above mentioned lobbying activity to increase protection), Erdemir's management is working on another CIM project, which is estimated to cost US$2.1 billion. The implementation of this project is, however, again likely to be delayed by the financial difficulties (Kışlalı, 1997).

Industry participants demand a support from the government at least matching the one many other foreign firms make use of -the export incentive for iron and steel in Turkey is only US$60 per tonne, while some foreign competitors get US$100-120 per tonne (Duruiz and Yentürk, 1992). Besides, some structural problems, such as the high cost of transportation by railway, increasing input prices, absence of a masterplan made in co-ordination with the industry and the government, and the government employment policy, which is seen as the main cause for over-manning, also need some urgent remedies (Duruiz and Yentürk, 1992). Another related issue is the argument that Erdemir should not be allowed to export since the supply of flat steel products falls in short of demand in Turkey. This is however rightly confronted by the management who believes that exporting may do good for the company, especially with regard to quality improvement concerns (T. C. Sanayi ve Ticaret Bakanlığı, 1987c).

To conclude, before anything else, an assessment of the role of government in shaping the sources of advantage in the Turkish flat steel industry reveals that it is a rather direct role, definitely more direct than the one Porter (1990a) assumes. Although it was organised as a private enterprise, the government itself was directly involved in the foundation of Erdemir, owned half of it and protected it for a long period of time. The successive Turkish governments, which equated economic development with industrialisation, gave high priority to the industry. In this respect, it is interesting to see that Erdemir's management expresses its gratitude to the state 'for its unerring support over the years' (Erdemir, 1995). The initial motive of the Turkish government was, however, to develop an indigenous iron and steel industry, and the emphasis was on capacity rather than cost or quality. Economic aspects of the project were seen as a 'formality' and not given enough importance. The plant was therefore destined to be born with problems and imbalances from the beginning. Furthermore, during the years that followed, it was subject to political interference in its management with harmful effects lasting for years. After the liberalisation in the 1980s, however, we observe an attitude change in that the government preferred to withdraw from the industry and started to encourage privatisation. Erdemir's management quickly reacted to these changes and succeeded to sweep most of the inherited elements of the old organisational culture away. In summary, we can conclude that the industry has never been the subject of a consistent, well-designed policy, and the role the Turkish government played could not provide much advantage and a lead for the Turkish flat steel industry, although it was an active and direct one.

Concluding Remarks

The historical analysis shows that, by the end of the 1970s, Turkey had built up an iron and steel industry of considerable size, including three integrated mills and the electric arc furnace segment. The important political and economic changes that took place in the early 1980s affected the iron and steel industry as well, in that some improvements in management, quality and performance were achieved. Turkey emerged as a major developing country producer and has one of the fastest growing steel industries in Europe. The trade balance in the iron and steel industry as a whole turned positive, and Turkey became an exporting country. Although the trade balance in flat steel products is still negative, mainly stemming from the high local demand, Erdemir, the only integrated flat steel producer of Turkey, is a competitive company.

If we summarise the main points we have learnt from the analysis of the Turkish flat steel industry, we first of all should state that Porter (1990a) is quite right in suggesting a flexibility in deciding whether or not an industry is competitive. Unlike quantitative studies of industry competitiveness, this flexibility enables us to include service industries which are internationally competitive, like I did by studying the construction industry, as well as catching others, which do not appear to be competitive if we just consider the trade data, like the Turkish flat steel industry. Although, for the time being, it has a negative trade balance, stemming from its limited capacity that cannot meet the high domestic demand, it is quite likely that the Turkish flat steel industry will attain a better export performance in the near future, given that a comprehensive expansion project has just been completed, and another one is on the agenda.

As a whole, the diamond for the Turkish flat steel industry is not so close to the ideal diamond as described by Porter (1990a), in which all determinants are in force and mutually interacting. Instead, we have gaps for almost all determinants, which have been described in detail above. With regard to the cases that do not comply with Porter's (1990a) arguments, we can mention three major points. The first one relates to the factor conditions, since we have a competitive industry in a developing country, which does not derive much advantage from factor conditions, except cheap and productive labour. It is also useful to remember here that this case has also been replicated in the Turkish leather clothes industry. The second finding that does not fit into the diamond framework, this time resembling the case of the Turkish glass industry, is the fact that there is basically no domestic rivalry. Two possible explanations, as repeated several times throughout this study, are the economies of scale and exposition to international competition. The third question mark this chapter puts forward concerns the role of government. The involvement of the Turkish government in the flat steel industry is much more direct than the one assumed by Porter (1990a), although it is not necessarily a constructive one. This finding parallels the conclusions reached in the analysis of the Turkish glass and automobile industries. I prefer to leave the further discussion and implications of the key findings as well as their detailed comparisons to the conclusion.

8 Conclusion

This chapter will first provide an overview of the five industry case studies conducted, and then proceed to the implications of the findings for Porter's diamond, giving special emphasis to those that do not comply with the framework and suggesting some areas for further research. The chapter will end with the implications of the study for the Turkish economy.

An Overview of the Turkish Industry Studies

The Turkish glass industry, construction industry, leather clothes industry, automobile industry and flat steel industry have been analysed in detail in the previous chapters. At the end of each chapter, a synopsis of the case has been provided. Instead of repeating them here, I prefer to include self-explanatory summary tables (Tables 8.1 to 8.5) giving the essential points with regard to the sources of advantage and disadvantage in the five industry studies conducted.

Table 8.1 Sources of Advantage/Disadvantage in the Turkish Glass Industry

FACTOR CONDITIONS
* low cost and good quality raw materials; low cost labour
* easy access to debt capital
* inadequate industry-specific infrastructure, research and education
DEMAND CONDITIONS
* large and rapidly growing domestic market
RELATED AND SUPPORTING INDUSTRIES
* competitive related and supporting industries
FIRM STRATEGY, STRUCTURE AND RIVALRY
* strong managerial capabilities and a highly successful firm
* no domestic rivalry
CHANCE
* new competitors from the former Eastern Block and the EU
ROLE OF GOVERNMENT
* initiated the foundation and protected for a long while
* political and macroeconomic instability; poorly functioning bureaucracy

Table 8.2 Sources of Advantage/Disadvantage in the Turkish Construction Industry

FACTOR CONDITIONS * low cost and productive workers and engineers * cheap and good quality materials * financing difficulties DEMAND CONDITIONS * considerable size and growth of the domestic market * moderate level of sophistication of domestic customers RELATED AND SUPPORTING INDUSTRIES * competitive related and supporting industries FIRM STRATEGY, STRUCTURE AND RIVALRY * superior entrepreneurial capabilities * intense domestic rivalry CHANCE * cultural and geographic proximity to some promising markets, especially to the Middle East and Russian Federation ROLE OF GOVERNMENT * the most important customer of the industry, thus government related problems felt more heavily * instability; inadequate regulations and poorly functioning bureaucracy

Table 8.3 Sources of Advantage/Disadvantage in the Turkish Leather Clothes Industry

FACTOR CONDITIONS * imports more than 50 per cent of the raw leather requirements * relatively low but increasing labour cost DEMAND CONDITIONS * moderate size and growth of the domestic market * moderate level of sophistication of domestic customers RELATED AND SUPPORTING INDUSTRIES * competitive related and supporting industries FIRM STRATEGY, STRUCTURE AND RIVALRY * superior managerial capabilities * intense domestic rivalry CHANCE * recent surge in demand from the Russian Federation ROLE OF GOVERNMENT * lack of a clear policy towards the industry * instability; inadequate regulations and poorly functioning bureaucracy

Table 8.4 Sources of Advantage/Disadvantage in the Turkish Automobile Industry

FACTOR CONDITIONS * lower quality and more expensive inputs; * low labour costs and low productivity rates * weaknesses in finance, and research and development DEMAND CONDITIONS * limited size but high growth of the domestic market * low level of sophistication of domestic customers RELATED AND SUPPORTING INDUSTRIES * uncompetitive related and supporting industries FIRM STRATEGY, STRUCTURE AND RIVALRY * weak domestic rivalry until very recently CHANCE * favourable location and good international contacts ROLE OF GOVERNMENT * initiated the foundation and protected for a long while * lack of a clear policy towards the industry * instability; inadequate regulations and poorly functioning bureaucracy

Table 8.5 Sources of Advantage/Disadvantage in the Turkish Flat Steel Industry

FACTOR CONDITIONS * has to import a considerable amount of its major inputs * low labour costs and high productivity rates * obtaining financing for big projects poses problems DEMAND CONDITIONS * limited size but high growth of the domestic demand RELATED AND SUPPORTING INDUSTRIES * a mixture of competitive and uncompetitive related and supporting industries FIRM STRATEGY, STRUCTURE AND RIVALRY * no domestic rivalry CHANCE * new competitors from the former Eastern Block and the EU ROLE OF GOVERNMENT * directly involved in its foundation and protected for a long period * intervened in the administration for a while * instability; inadequate regulations and poorly functioning bureaucracy

Table 8.6 Sources of Advantage and Key Findings That do Not Comply With the Diamond in the Selected Turkish Industries

DIAMOND ELEMENT → INDUSTRY ↓	FACTOR CONDITIONS	DEMAND CONDITIONS	RELATED AND SUPPORTING INDUSTRIES	FIRM STRATEGY, STRUCTURE AND RIVALRY	THE ROLE OF CHANCE	THE ROLE OF GOVERNMENT
GLASS INDUSTRY (competitive)	H	M	H	H *no domestic rivalry ?	L	H * more direct
CONSTRUCTION INDUSTRY (competitive)	H	M	M	H	H	L
LEATHER CLOTHES INDUSTRY (competitive, loss in position)	L * imports basic raw materials	M	H	H	H	L
AUTOMOBILE INDUSTRY (uncompetitive)	L	L	L	M * issue of foreign ownership	M	L * more direct
FLAT STEEL INDUSTRY (competitive, negative trade balance)	L * imports basic inputs ?	M	M	H *no domestic rivalry ?	L	M * more direct ?

KEY: The effect of the diamond element on the competitive advantage of the industry has been assessed either as 'high' (H), 'medium' (M) or 'low' (L). 'Question mark' (?) means the issue cannot be explained within the diamond framework.

Implications for the Individual Diamond Elements

Table 8.6 summarises the finalised assessments concerning the effects of the different parts of the diamond on the competitive advantage of all industries studied, as well as the key findings that do not comply with the framework. In this section, I will compare and discuss separately the results of the case study analyses for each determinant of the diamond framework, and only then proceed with the overall implications.

Factor Conditions

With regard to the factor conditions, the Turkish glass, construction and automobile industries confirm Porter's (1990a) hypothesis. The former two competitive industries derive considerable advantages from basic and generalised factors like lower cost labour and raw materials. The uncompetitive automobile industry, on the other hand, cannot derive much advantage from factor conditions except from lower cost but unproductive labour. The weaknesses they all suffer concerning advanced and specific factor conditions like industry specific research and education institutions and infrastructure are also in line with Porter's (1990a) findings, since he argues that many industries in a developing country are more likely to derive most of their advantages from the basic and generalised factors. The cases of leather clothes and flat steel, however, contradict Porter (1990a) to some degree, since both have to import a considerable part of their inputs.

Regarding the flat steel industry, as mentioned previously, the motive of the Turkish government was to establish an indigenous iron and steel industry as a way to achieve its ambition in industrialisation, and not much attention was paid to the availability of the necessary factors and related infrastructure. In fact, they were simply assumed to be favourable, as is evident from the false predictions made about iron ore availability. In other words, although availability of some iron ore and coal reserves probably was encouraging, the driving force in the initial foundation of the industry was the eagerness of the government rather than the factor conditions. It is, therefore, difficult to find a plausible explanation that would fit these observations to the diamond framework.

In the case of the leather clothes industry, on the other hand, it should be stated that although, the cost advantage is now by no means guaranteed due to increasing wages and the necessity to import more than 50 per cent of the raw leather, cheap and good quality raw leather and low cost labour were definitely amongst the important factors in the early development of the industry. Furthermore, Turkey still has a good ratio of price to quality and the advantage of having an industry already established, with its accumulated experience and dynamism. In addition, Turkey does not have any other severe disadvantages in the key determinants of competitive advantage as defined by Porter (1990a). It is, in other words, possible to explain this situation within the diamond framework by considering the raw leather import requirement of the Turkish leather clothes industry as well as increasing labour costs as a 'selective disadvantage', since the competitive position of the industry persists although factor-related advantages have disappeared to a large extent.

In brief, analysis of the five Turkish industries with regard to the factor conditions confirms Porter's (1990a) findings with two exceptions, one of which, the case of the Turkish leather clothes industry, can still be explained within the framework, while the other one, the case of the Turkish flat steel industry, is not so easily fitted to the diamond.

Demand Conditions

When we consider the second determinant, home demand conditions, we see that our results largely confirm Porter's (1990a) hypothesis. Turkey is a developing country with a large and rapidly growing population, meaning that many industries are far from being mature, or, at least, face a considerable potential increase in demand. Income levels are, however, still rather low, restricting this potential. A cross industry comparison of the sophistication level is, on the other hand, inconclusive. The glass, housing and leather clothes industries indeed are areas where Turkish customers have been traditionally demanding, which has probably pushed these industries to upgrade further. My interviewees stated that they now cannot detect a difference between the domestic and foreign customers in terms of their level of sophistication. The case of the flat steel industry is somehow special in that although its domestic customers are not particularly demanding, but are getting more so recently, the industry has kept some part of the production for exports, despite the fact that domestic production cannot meet domestic demand. The main motive is the anticipation that exporting may contribute to quality improvement. The automobile industry is lagging behind with regard to this determinant, despite the improvements observed in recent years. All of these observations support the relevant Porter (1990a) arguments which have been outlined in Chapter 1. Moreover, the fact that, overall, the industries I have studied do not derive substantial advantages from the demand conditions is also in line with what Porter (1990a) envisages for a developing country.

Related and Supporting Industries

Another supportive conclusion for one of the strongest hypotheses proposed by Porter (1990a) is that the internationally competitive industries of a nation tend to cluster together. For the glass and leather clothes industries, it is almost totally correct. The case of the Turkish automobile industry is also supportive of this argument, since we have an uncompetitive industry surrounded by a cluster of other weak industries. Although some exceptional uncompetitive industries remain in the cases of the construction and flat steel industries, these probably do not pose a challenge to the framework, but rather can be interpreted as exceptions more related to the restrictions imposed by the level of economic development attained in Turkey. It is, in other words, probably unrealistic in a developing country setting to expect all industries that are related to one internationally competitive industry to be competitive as well. This is especially so, for instance, for the case of the construction equipment industry, which is dominated by two transnational giants.

Firm Strategy, Structure and Rivalry

With regard to the last determinant, which Porter calls 'firm strategy, structure and rivalry', two major issues arise. The first one is that entrepreneurial and managerial skills are amongst the leading assets of the Turkish firms, for almost all industries studied. Their contribution to creating and sustaining competitive advantage in Turkey seems to be of essential importance. Regarding the first element included in this determinant, therefore, we do not have any problems concerning the diamond framework.

The second issue relates to the other element included in this category: the intense domestic rivalry in the internationally competitive industries of a nation, which is one of the strongest conclusions Porter (1990a) reaches in his Nations book. This is indeed the case for the Turkish construction and leather clothes industries, where domestic competition has been described as cut-throat by my interviewees. The easy life the uncompetitive Turkish automobile industry enjoyed until very recently is also in line with this argument. The Turkish glass and flat steel industries, however, pose a challenge to this hypothesis since we have two highly internationally competitive industries, where there is virtually no domestic rivalry. Porter's (1990a) explanation that such cases tend to occur where there is considerable government protection is valid for both cases in that they are known to have 'close' relationships with the government and have been protected for a long while. I still believe that this is one area in the diamond framework that requires further investigation, given that similar arguments can be proposed for the uncompetitive automobile industry as well. It has been protected by the government, and the rivalry was not intense, but unlike the other two it has not until recently been subject to serious foreign competition.

For this determinant, as a result, we have two cases, the Turkish glass and flat steel industries, that do not fit the framework as far as domestic rivalry is concerned. All five cases are, however, supportive of the other elements included in this category.

The Role of Chance

Chance events have usually been favourable for the industries I studied. The construction and leather clothes industries, in particular, have benefited from the emergence of geographically proximate new markets, especially the Russian Federation. The effects of chance events as a source of advantage for the Turkish glass and flat steel industries have been, on the other hand, relatively limited, whereas the role they play in the case of the Turkish automobile industry is rather interesting. The favourable geographical location of Turkey and its good international contacts with the EU, the Middle East and the C.I.S. certainly contributed to the increasing interest of the world automobile giants in founding branches in Turkey. Although the established firms do not like the idea of new competitors entering into an already relatively small market, I believe these events should be considered as opportunities, since they push the firms to improve and upgrade their competitive position.

The Role of Government

The role of government in shaping the sources of advantage is another area where the findings of my research challenge Porter's (1990a) conclusions. In the glass, automobile and flat steel industries, which are all capital-intensive, the role of the Turkish government has been rather direct. It could be argued that this is, in fact, in line with Porter's (1990a) argument since he envisages a more direct role for the government in developing countries. Following this rationale, the cases of the Turkish automobile and glass industries may indeed be considered consistent with the framework. Although the role the Turkish government played was arguably even beyond that extended role. What Porter means by 'a more direct role' in a developing country setting involves providing some direct help like subsidies and temporary protection. In the case of the Turkish glass industry, however, Turkish government did not only provide direct help, but also initiated the foundation of the industry. In fact, this was a must since the level of technological competency and economic conditions in Turkey at the time did not permit the development of a large-scale glass industry by the private sector alone (see Chapter 3). The government, in other words, rightly intervened, and thanks to this successful move now we have an internationally competitive glass industry. I would argue that otherwise the Turkish glass industry would have most probably remained limited to a few small firms in the glassware segment. It is not at all possible to fit the case of the Turkish flat steel industry to the diamond framework with regard to the role of government. Apart from establishing and protecting the industry for a long while, the government owned half of Erdemir and was actively involved in its administration. The role of government here is certainly much more direct than the one envisaged by Porter (1990a), even for a developing country.

Overall Implications for Porter's Study

The first general implication is inspired by our discussion about domestic rivalry. The fact that the industries which do not confirm the relevant hypotheses exhibit similarities amongst themselves as compared to the ones that do, prompts the question as to whether or not some industries are better explained by the diamond. Specifically, it is interesting to observe that, for both the glass and steel industries which are competitive without having domestic rivals, economies of scale are of essential importance, and competition takes place on a global scale. The construction and leather clothes industries are closer to being perfectly competitive. This possibility of having some type of industries better explained by the diamond framework finds further support if we also consider that three of the four question marks in Table 8.6, signalling the areas that cannot be explained within the framework, are observed in the flat steel industry. This industry can be characterised as a capital-intensive sector where competition takes place on a global scale and government involvement is high and more direct. In short, we need to investigate further in other countries if the diamond framework is more suitable for a certain range of industries, possibly those that are perfectly competitive rather than oligopolistic.

Another issue I would like to discuss here relates to the problem of locating the source of advantage when there is substantial foreign ownership and/or multinational involvement in a competitive industry. The case of the Turkish automobile industry provides a good base to think about this issue. The last FDI wave in the Turkish automobile industry better fits to Porter's (1990a) understanding of FDI in that it is mainly triggered by the MNEs' motives for sourcing basic factors and market access. The possible reasons behind their entry, however, do not seem to be limited to these reasons. The existence of an established automotive industry as well as a pool of qualified technical and managerial personnel has definitely contributed. The importance of such factors becomes more obvious when we turn to the analysis of the more established firms; that is, Tofaş (Koç-Fiat), Otosan (Koç-Ford) and Oyak-Renault. It is difficult to consider these firms as just branches of the transnationals they are linked to, since they are rather new firms in and of themselves. In fact, their foundation was triggered by Turkish entrepreneurs rather than by multinationals, and, therefore, they cannot be solely treated as branches of MNEs which were established to serve a protected market and make use of the relatively low cost labour. Porter's (1990a) treatment of MNE and FDI is, therefore, somehow inadequate. Given its above stated structure, I believe the Turkish automobile industry should have been included in the cluster chart, if it had been a competitive industry. This suggests that one can only locate the true source of competitive advantage as a result of a case study when there is considerable MNE involvement in an industry, implying a methodological difficulty in deciding whether to exclude industries from the competitive industries list because of substantial foreign involvement.

The fact that many internationally competitive industries, and often clusters of industries, have been found to be concentrated geographically in Porter's (1990a) study constitutes another interesting area that an overall evaluation should address. In fact, the quite visible concentration of some industries, such as the concentration of the computer industry in Silicon Valley, the auto industry in Detroit, financial services in the 'city' of London, jewellers in the 'jewellery quarter' of Birmingham and all Swiss pharmaceutical giants in Basel, has already attracted the attention of not just geographers but other scholars as well, whose primary interests are as diverse as industrial organisation, international trade, economic growth and business strategy. The geographic concentration of the industries I have studied is obvious in most of the cases, and the associated possible reasons have been mentioned throughout the text. For instance, the high geographical concentration observed in the Turkish leather clothes industry can be mostly explained by the necessity of sharing the costs of the required waste disposal systems. The concentration of construction firms in Ankara, the capital, on the other hand, obviously has a lot to do with the fact that their most important customer is the government. What is less obvious, however, is the extent of the relationship between geographic concentration and international competitiveness, which invites further investigation. The high geographic concentration of the uncompetitive Turkish automobile industry around Bursa and İzmit is particularly interesting in this respect.

Yet another general issue is revealed by an evaluation of the Turkish automobile industry, which, among other things, enables us to investigate if the diamond framework is successful in understanding the sources of advantage/disadvantage in a relatively uncompetitive industry as well. The relevant results basically confirm Porter's (1990a) findings. We can indeed understand the reasons behind the poor position of this industry by analysing its history with regard to each element of the diamond. The Turkish automobile industry, as a result, shows that the framework can be successful in explaining the sources of disadvantage in a relatively uncompetitive industry.

The last general implication of this research for Porter (1990a) study is that it is supportive of the diamond framework. Given that Turkey is still a developing country, this suggests that the framework can also work in this context. A problem, which still remains, though, is whether those results detected by the Turkish case studies are particular or whether they point to sources of competitive advantage more generally. This question, apart from calling for further research in the corresponding areas, especially from developing countries, leads us to a discussion of the issue of generalisability in case study research. Needless to say, treating a number of case studies as a small 'sample' and trying to make a generalisation in the statistical sense is not possible. According to some (e.g. Yin, 1994), however, making analytical generalisations deriving from the case studies is possible even if you have conducted only one case study. Multiple case studies, in this respect, should be seen as replications rather than sample units. Similarly, choosing the number of cases to study can be considered as analogous to choosing your confidence level in a statistical study in that greater certainty requires a larger number of cases. The three main points raised by the case studies presented here, which question the importance of factor conditions and the roles of domestic rivalry and government, have been replicated in more than one case study, though some of them could be explained within the framework as discussed above. Additional replications are, therefore, required. If the replications show any resemblance to the results raised in this thesis, we may then argue that these cases are generalisable.

Implications for the Turkish Economy

In light of our analysis, we can point to some areas which require more attention for the Turkish economy. Apart from such general implications as maintaining macroeconomic and political stability, conducting institutional reforms to smooth the functioning of the bureaucracy as well as the financial markets, improving the general transportation and communication infrastructure, and promoting long-term investment which is currently discouraged by high interest rates, this study calls for special attention in two areas: encouraging better factor creation mechanisms and building on the entrepreneurial strengths of Turkish businessmen.

Regarding the former, the government and industry participants should act together, although the bulk of the responsibility has to be assumed by the government since Turkey is in the early stages of the development process. According to Porter (1990a), governments should move beyond macroeconomic policy, avoid overreliance on devaluation and wage rates, and focus on the true sources of competitive advantage instead. Among the things that can be done are increasing investment in specialised human resources; encouraging employee training; forging closer ties with educational institutions and industry; emphasising more practical orientation in education via, for instance, apprenticeship and internship programmes; promoting respectable and high quality forms of higher education besides the university; supporting research and development; and encouraging specialisation amongst the universities. Firms, on the other hand, should take a more proactive role in education and promote industry-specific education and research institutions. They should grant scholarships and research funds for them, increase investment in on-the-job training and put pressure on government research institutions so that the research is commercially relevant. Similarly, industry associations should participate in developing specialised skills, technology and infrastructure, provide a clearing house for information, and constitute a bridge between industry and educational institutions.

Building on the entrepreneurial strength of Turkish businessmen is the second major area that requires special attention. Promoting new business formation, regulating competition via anti-trust laws, and encouraging and facilitating international involvement of Turkish firms are amongst the most prominent areas that can be improved in this respect. Firms, on the other hand, should seek challenges, which push them to upgrade. They should, for example, prefer to serve the most sophisticated and demanding buyers and urge domestic suppliers to improve by, for instance, setting performance standards in addition to product specifications.

Apart from these two key issues, the government may also contribute towards the improvement of domestic demand conditions by, for example, introducing better standards, consumers' rights legislation and environmental regulation and confirming commitment to quality. Lastly, the government may also encourage and support the development of regional clusters by, for instance, stimulating and supporting the foundation as well as the improvement of sector-specific education, research and infrastructure in the regions where some presence of the cluster has been already observed.

Appendices

Table A1.1 Clusters of Internationally Competitive Turkish Industries, 1985

Primary goods	MATERIALS/METALS
	IRON AND STEEL
	Iron, steel angles, shapes*
	Iron, other steel bars, hotrolled
	Medium plate, rolled, of iron or simple steel
	Iron, simple steel blooms
	Iron, steel bars
	Other profiles, hotrolled
	Large U,I or H sections
	Ferro-alloys
	Universal plates of iron or steel, and others*
	Iron, simple steel hoop, strip
	Bars and nods, exc. not further worked ones*
	Heavy plate, rolled, of iron or simple steel
	Iron, simple steel wire
	Flat-steel products#
	FABRICATED IRON AND STEEL
	Iron, steel seamless tubes
	Other iron, steel tubes or pipes
	Iron, steel tube fittings
	METAL MANUFACTURES
	Iron, steel bolts and nuts
	Manufactures of base metal, exc. locksmith and chain*
	Locksmith wares
	NONFERROUS METALS
	Chromium ores and concentrates
	Metal containers of aluminium*
	Copper bars, wire
	Tungsten ores and concentrates
	Aluminium bars, wire etc.
	Aluminium foil
	Copper alloys, worked
	Aluminium plates, sheets, strip
	OTHER MATERIALS AND WASTE
	Other crude minerals, exc. clay*
	Waste and scrap of pig or cast iron
	Clay

Table A1.1 (continued)

Machinery	**Foundry moulds**
Specialty inputs	
Services	

Primary goods	**FOREST PRODUCTS** WOOD **Improved wood, in sheets, blocks*** **Veneer sheet** **Wood, simply shaped, and wood based panels*** **Pitprops, poles etc., and other wood in the rough*** *Other wood manufactures* PAPER *Paper containers*
Machinery	
Specialty inputs	
Services	

Primary goods	**PETROLEUM/CHEMICALS** PETROLEUM PRODUCTS **Motor, aviation spirit** *Kerosene and other medium oils* Jet fuel and other light petroleum oils, preparations* INORGANIC *Other inorganic chemicals** POLYMERS *Alkyds and other polyesters in primary forms*
Machinery	*Gas, liquid filters*
Specialty inputs	
Service	

Table A1.1 (continued)

Primary goods	**SEMICONDUCTORS/COMPUTERS**
Machinery	
Specialty inputs	
Services	

Primary goods	**MULTIPLE BUSINESS** *Shafts, cranks, pulley etc.* Cock, valves etc.
Machinery	**Other non-electric parts,exc.moulding boxes***
Specialty inputs	*Blades, tips, etc. for tools*
Services	**Construction/Engineering#**

Primary goods	**TRANSPORTATION** *Steel transport boxes etc.* Containers; other than of iron and steel* Electrical vehicle lighting equipment
Machinery	
Specialty inputs	**Asbestos manufactures; friction materials** *Tyres new for motor cars* Tyres new for buses and lorries Parts of piston engines**
Services	**Shipping#**

Primary goods	**OFFICE**
Machinery	
Specialty inputs	
Services	

Primary goods	**TELECOMMUNICATIONS**
Machinery	
Specialty inputs	
Services	

Table A1.1 (continued)

Primary goods	**HOUSING/HOUSEHOLD**
	FURNISHINGS **Carpets etc., of other textile materials*** **Carpets, of wool or fine hair** Furniture of other materials* Chairs and other seats GLASS,CERAMICS AND STONE PRODUCTS **Ceramic ornaments** **Household and hotel glass** *Building stone etc.,worked* *Sinks, wash basins, bidets etc.** *Porcelain, china housewear* Coarse ceramic housewear Glazed ceramic sets Bricks etc. nonrefractory PACKAGED GOODS Soap, cleansing and polishing preparations, exc. washing preparations* Washing preparations OTHER *Cutlery* *Household equipment of base metal ,exc. Domestic type**
Machinery	
Specialty inputs	**Cement** *Glass surface, ground* *Glass, exc. Surface ground or polished** Stone, sand and gravel Articles of cement
Services	

Primary goods	**POWER GENERATION AND DISTRIBUTION** Electric accumulators Insulated wire, cable, bars etc.
Machinery	
Specialty inputs	
Services	

Table A1.1 (continued)

Primary goods	FOOD/BEVERAGES
	BASIC FOODS **Edible nuts, fresh or dried** **Eggs, birds', fresh, preserved, in shell** **Guts, bladders etc., nonfish** **Live animals for food, exc. bovine*** **Mutton etc., fresh, chilled or frozen** **Spices** **Malt, including flour** *Stone fruit, fresh* *Groundnuts, green* *Flour of wheat or meslin* Fish, fresh or chilled, exc. Fillets Poultry, fresh, chilled or frozen FRUITS AND VEGETABLES **Grapes, dried** **Leguminous vegetables, dry** **Lemons, grapefruit etc.** **Tomatoes, fresh** **Mandarins, clementines etc., fresh or dried*** **Figs and other fruit, fresh or dried*** **Apples, fresh** *Other vegetables** *Oranges, fresh or dried* *Crude vegetable materials, exc. seeds, bulbs etc.** Grapes, fresh PROCESSED FOOD **Shell fish, prepared, preserved** **Fruit, preserved exc. fruit juices*** **Refined sugar** **Margarine and shortening** **Vegetables, prepared, preserved** *Cereal preparations, exc. malt and bakery products** *Pastry, cakes etc.* EDIBLE OILS **Olive oil** *Processed animal and vegetable oils and fats* Cotton seed oil

Table A1.1 (continued)

Machinery	Cultivating machinery Handtools, of a kind used in agriculture* Wheeled tractors Tractors, non-road Nondomestic refrigerators, equipment parts
Specialty inputs	**Groats, meal and pellets of wheat*** **Glass bottles** **Nitrogen, phosphorus fertilisers** *Seeds etc. for planting* Feeding stuff for animals, exc. oil-cake etc.*
Services	

Primary goods	**DEFENSE**
Machinery	
Specialty inputs	
Services	

Primary goods	**HEALTH CARE**
Machinery	
Specialty inputs	
Services	

Primary goods	**PERSONAL** *Pens, pencils* Combustible products
Machinery	
Specialty inputs	**Tobacco, stripped or part, Virginia type** **Essential oils, resinoids***
Services	

Primary goods	**ENTERTAINMENT/LEISURE** **Children's picture books, maps etc., printed***
Machinery	
Specialty inputs	
Services	**Tourism#**

Table A1.1 (continued)

Primary goods	TEXTILES/APPAREL
	FABRICS
	Knitted or crocheted fabrics, nonsynthetic*
	Linens, etc.
	Pile etc. cotton fabrics
	Continuous synthetic nonpile weaves
	Cotton fabrics, woven, finished, exc. pile fabrics*
	Grey woven cotton fabric
	Woven, of carded wool or fine hair
	Made-up articles, exc. linens and other* furnishing articles
	Fabrics, woven, of man-made fibres, discontinuous*
	Man-made pile etc. fabric
	Textile fabrics, woven; other than of silk etc.*
	Other woven textile fabric
	Tulle, lace, ribbons etc.
	Plastic coated textiles
	APPAREL
	Under garments, knitted, of cotton, nonelastic
	Undergarments, of textile fabrics, exc. shirts*
	Blouses, other than of man-made fibres*
	Women's outwear, not knitted of cotton
	Men's shirts, of cotton
	Dresses, other than of man-made fibres*
	Jerseys etc., of cotton or regenerated fibres*
	Women's coats and jackets, other than of man-made fibres*
	Men's suits
	Men's shirts, of other fibres*
	Women's suits, other outer garments, other than of cotton or man-made fibres*
	Dresses, skirts etc., other than of synthetic fibres*
	Men's overcoats and other outer garments, not knitted*
	Articles of furskin
	Skirts
	Outwear, knitted, nonelastic
	Under garments, knitted, other than of cotton*
	Men's trousers, of cotton
	Men's jackets, blazers etc.
	Other outer garments*
	Women's outer garments of man-made fibres

Table A1.1 (continued)

	ACCESSORIES **Leather clothes, accessories** **Clothing accessories of textile fabrics*** Clothing accessories knitted LUGGAGE Handbags Travel goods, exc. Handbags* OTHER **Industrial leather, saddlery, etc.***
Machinery	**Sewing machine needles*** **Textile and leather machinery, exc. sewing etc. machines***
Specialty Inputs	FIBRES AND YARNS **Cotton yarn, exc. 40-80 km per kg*** **Cotton; linters, waste; carded or combed*** **Yarn, of discontinuous synthetic fibres** **Cotton yarn, 40-80 km per kg** **Discontinuous synthetic fibres, uncombed** **Raw cotton, exc. linters** **Discontinuous synthetic fibres, blend yarn** **Silk yarn, yarn of regenerated fibres etc.*** *Wool and animal hair, exc. greasy or fleece-washed** *Yarn of synthetic fibres, exc. discontinuous ones** *Yarn of wool or animal hair, exc. wool tops**
Services	Design#

KEY

TimesNR	0.41 per cent world export share or higher, but less than 0.82 per cent share
Italics	*0.82 per cent world export share or higher, but less than 1.64 per cent share*
Bold	**1.64 per cent world export share or above**
*	Calculated residuals
**	Added due to high country export share
#	Added based on in-country research

Table A1.2 Clusters of Internationally Competitive Turkish Industries, 1978

Primary goods	**SEMICONDUCTORS/COMPUTERS**
Machinery	
Specialty inputs	
Services	

Primary goods	**MULTIPLE BUSINESS**
Machinery	
Specialty inputs	
Services	

Primary goods	**MATERIALS/METALS** IRON AND STEEL **Ferro-silicon and other ferro alloys*** *Pig iron, spiegeleisen etc.* NONFERROUS METALS **Chromium ores and concentrates** *Aluminium bars, wire etc.* Aluminium, alloys, worked Alumina** OTHER MATERIALS **Other crude minerals, exc. clay*** Natural abrasives
Machinery	
Specialty inputs	Briquettes, coke, semi-coke
Services	

Primary goods	**FOREST PRODUCTS** Sawlogs etc., roughly squared or half squared
Machinery	
Specialty inputs	
Services	

Table A1.2 (continued)

Primary goods	**PETROLEUM/CHEMICALS** **Inorganic acids etc.** Articles of plastic**
Machinery	
Specialty inputs	
Service	

Primary goods	**TRANSPORTATION**
Machinery	
Specialty inputs	
Services	Other transportation services#

Primary goods	**POWER GENERATION AND DISTRIBUTION**
Machinery	
Specialty inputs	
Services	

Primary goods	**OFFICE**
Machinery	
Specialty inputs	
Services	

Primary goods	**TELECOMMUNICATIONS**
Machinery	
Specialty inputs	
Services	

Primary goods	**DEFENSE**
Machinery	
Specialty inputs	
Services	

Table A1.2 (continued)

Primary goods	**FOOD/BEVERAGES** BASIC FOODS **Edible nuts, fresh or dried** **Guts, bladders etc., nonfish** **Live animals for food** **Crude animal materials, exc. guts, bladders*** **Groundnuts, green** **Mutton etc., fresh, chilled or frozen** **Flour of wheat or meslin** **Spices** *Shell fish, fresh, frozen* *Malt, including flour* Tea Fish, fresh, chilled or frozen** FRUITS AND VEGETABLES **Grapes, dried*** **Leguminous vegetables, dry** **Lemons, grapefruit etc.** **Mandarins, clementines etc., fresh or dried*** **Figs and other fruit, fresh or dried*** **Crude vegetable materials, exc. seeds, bulbs etc.*** **Other crude vegetable materials** *Apples, fresh* *Grapes, fresh* Vegetables, exc. potatoes, beans and tomatoes* Oranges, fresh or dried Potatoes, fresh exc. sweet PROCESSED FOOD **Shell fish, prepared, preserved** *Fruit, preserved exc. fruit juices** *Vegetables, prepared, preserved* Fruit juices exc. Orange juice* EDIBLE OILS **Olive oil**
Machinery	

Table A1.2 (continued)

Specialty inputs	Wheat and meslin, unmilled Seeds etc. for planting Glass bottles, etc. Groats, meal and pellets of wheat* *Other cereals, unmilled*
Services	

Primary goods	**TEXTILES/APPAREL** FABRICS **Linens, etc.** *Pile etc. cotton fabrics* *Woven cotton, bleached etc.* Cotton fabrics, woven, finished, exc. pile fabrics* Grey woven cotton fabric Continuous synthetic nonpile weaves** APPAREL **Women's suits, other garments, other than of man-made fibres*** **Dresses, other than of man-made fibres*** **Blouses, other than of man-made fibres*** **Articles of furskin** *Women's coats and jackets, other than of man-made fibres** Women's coats and jackets, of man-made fibres Outwear, knitted, nonelastic** Under garments, knitted** Men's outwear, not knitted** ACCESSORIES **Leather clothes, accessories**
Machinery	Sewing machine needles*
Specialty Inputs	FIBRES AND YARNS **Cotton yarn, exc. 40-80 km per kg*** **Cotton yarn, 40-80 km per kg** **Raw cotton, exc. linters** **Silk** **Wool (exc. Tops), animal hair** *Textile yarn, exc. wool tops, cotton yarn and synthetic fibres for retail sale** *Discontinuous synthetic fibres, uncombed* OTHER Other dyes, tanning products
Services	

Table A1.2 (continued)

Primary goods	HOUSING/HOUSEHOLD FURNISHINGS **Carpets etc., of other textile materials*** **Carpets, of wool or fine hair** HOUSEHOLD EQUIPMENT *Domestic refrigerators* Household equipment of base metal, exc. domestic type* OTHER **Household and hotel glass**
Machinery	
Specialty inputs	Cement Glass
Services	

Primary goods	**HEALTH CARE**
Machinery	
Specialty inputs	
Services	

Primary goods	**PERSONAL**
Machinery	
Specialty inputs	**Tobacco, unmanufactured, refuse** *Essential oils, resinoid*
Services	

Table A1.2 (continued)

Primary goods	**ENTERTAINMENT/LEISURE**
Machinery	
Specialty inputs	
Services	Tourism#

KEY

TimesNR	0.18 per cent world export share or higher, but less than 0.36 per cent share
Italics	*0.36 per cent world export share or higher, but less than 0.72 per cent share*
Bold	**0.72 per cent world export share or above**
*	Calculated residuals
**	Added due to high country export share
#	Added based on in-country research

Table A1.3 Clusters of Internationally Competitive Turkish Industries, 1971

Primary goods	**SEMICONDUCTORS/COMPUTERS**
Machinery	
Specialty inputs	
Services	

Primary goods	**FOREST PRODUCTS** Saw-, veneer-logs, non-conifer Saw-, veneer-logs, conifer Lumber shaped, conifer**
Machinery	
Specialty inputs	
Services	

Primary goods	**MULTIPLE BUSINESS**
Machinery	
Specialty inputs	
Services	

Table A1.3 (continued)

Primary goods	**MATERIALS/METALS** NONFERROUS METALS *Unrefined copper* *Zinc ores, concentrates* Sulphur OTHER MATERIALS **Other crude minerals** Natural abrasives
Machinery	
Specialty inputs	
Services	

Primary goods	**TRANSPORTATION**
Machinery	
Specialty inputs	
Services	**Other transportation services#**

Primary goods	**POWER GENERATION AND DISTRIBUTION**
Machinery	
Specialty inputs	
Services	

Primary goods	**OFFICE**
Machinery	
Specialty inputs	
Services	

Primary goods	**TELECOMMUNICATIONS**
Machinery	
Specialty inputs	
Services	

Table A1.3 (continued)

Primary goods	**PETROLEUM/CHEMICALS** Inorganic elements, oxides etc. Motor spirit, gasoline** Other inorganic chemicals**
Machinery	
Specialty inputs	
Service	

Primary goods	**DEFENSE**
Machinery	
Specialty inputs	
Services	

Primary goods	**HEALTH CARE**
Machinery	
Specialty inputs	
Services	

Primary goods	**HOUSING/HOUSEHOLD** *Floor coverings, tapestry etc.* Glassware
Machinery	
Specialty inputs	**Lime, cement, building products** Glass**
Services	

Primary goods	**ENTERTAINMENT/LEISURE** Developed cinema film
Machinery	
Specialty inputs	
Services	*Tourism#*

Table A1.3 (continued)

Primary goods	FOOD/BEVERAGES BASIC FOODS **Edible nuts, fresh or dried** **Live animals, exc. bovine cattle*** **Other crude animal materials** **Mutton etc., fresh, chilled or frozen** **Shell fish, fresh, frozen** **Bovine cattle** *Tea and mate* *Spices* FRUITS AND VEGETABLES **Dried fruit** **Other crude vegetable materials** **Vegetables etc., fresh, simply preserved** **Oranges, tangerines etc.** *Fresh fruit, exc. oranges, tangerines, nuts etc.** PROCESSED FOOD **Refined sugar** **Vegetables, prepared, preserved** EDIBLE OILS **Vegetable oil residues** Fixed vegetable oils, soft**
Machinery	
Specialty inputs	
Services	

Primary goods	**PERSONAL**
Machinery	
Specialty inputs	**Tobacco, unmanufactured**
Services	

Table A1.3 (continued)

Primary goods	**TEXTILES/APPAREL** FABRICS *Linens, etc.* *Woven cotton, bleached etc.* *Cotton fabrics, woven, exc. bleached** APPAREL Clothing not of fur, exc. women's outwear* Fur etc., clothes, products Women's outwear, not knitted**
Machinery	
Specialty Inputs	FIBRES AND YARNS **Cotton, exc. raw cotton*** **Raw cotton, exc. linters** **Silk** **Textile yarn and thread, exc. continuous and discontinuous synthetic fibre yarn*** Wool and animal hair Discontinuous synthetic fibre, yarn** Continuous synthetic fibre, yarn OTHER *Other dyes, tanning products*
Services	

KEY

TimesNR	0.19 per cent world export share or higher, but less than 0.38 per cent share
Italics	*0.38 per cent export share or higher, but less than 0.76 per cent share*
Bold	**0.76 per cent world export share or above**
*	Calculated residuals
**	Added due to high country export share
#	Added based on in-country research

Table A2.1 Percentage of Turkish Exports by Cluster and Vertical Stage (1985-1992)

	MATERIALS/METALS				FOREST PRODUCTS				PETROLEUM/CHEMICALS				SEMICONDUCTORS/COMPUTERS				UPSTREAM IND.	
	SC	CSC	SW	CSW	SC	CSC	SW	CSW	SC	CSC	SW	CSW	SC	CSC	SW	CSW	SC	SW
PRI. GOODS	11,7	-7,5	0,7	-0,5	0,0	-1,5	0,0	-0,2	1,8	-2,6	0,1	0,0	0,0	0,0	0,0	0,0	14	0,2
MACHINERY	0,0	-0,4	0,0	-0,2	0,0	0,0	0,0	0,0	0,0	-0,2	0,0	-0,9	0,0	0,0	0,0	0,0	0,0	0,0
SPE. INPUTS	0,0	0,0	0,0	0,0	0,0	0,0	0,0	0,0	0,0	0,0	0,0	0,0	0,0	0,0	0,0	0,0	0,0	0,0
TOTAL	11,7	-7,9	0,5	-0,4	0,0	-1,5	0,0	-0,2	1,8	-2,8	0,1	0,0	0,0	0,0	0,0	0,0	14	0,2

	MULTIPLE BUSINESS				TRANSPORTATION				POWER GENERATION & DISTRIBUTION				OFFICE				TELECOMMUNIC.				DEFENSE				INDUS. & SUP. FUNCTIONS	
	SC	CSC	SW	CSW	SC	CSC	SW	CSW	SC	CSC	SW	CSW	SC	CSC	SW	CSW	SC	CSC	SW	CSW	SC	CSC	SW	CSW	SC	SW
PRI. GOODS	0,0	-0,8	0,1	+0,1	1,2	+1,0	0,1	+0,1	1,6	+1,0	0,0	0,0	0,0	0,0	0,0	0,0	0,0	0,0	0,0	0,0	0,0	0,0	0,0	0,0	2,8	0,1
MACHINERY	0,0	-0,3	0,0	0,0	0,0	0,0	0,0	0,0	0,0	0,0	0,0	0,0	0,0	0,0	0,0	0,0	0,0	0,0	0,0	0,0	0,0	0,0	0,0	0,0	0,0	0,0
SPE. INPUTS	0,0	-0,4	0,0	-0,1	0,9	-0,4	0,1	-0,1	0,0	0,0	0,0	0,0	0,0	0,0	0,0	0,0	0,0	0,0	0,0	0,0	0,0	0,0	0,0	0,0	0,9	0,1
TOTAL	0,0	-1,5	0,1	0,0	2,1	+0,6	0,1	0,0	1,6	+1,0	0,1	0,0	0,0	0,0	0,0	0,0	0,0	0,0	0,0	0,0	0,0	0,0	0,0	0,0	3,7	0,1

	FOOD/BEVERAGE				TEXTILES/APPAREL				HOUSING & HOUSEHOLD				HEALTH CARE				PERSONAL				ENTERTAINMENT/ LEISURE				FINAL CONS. GOODS & SER.	
	SC	CSC	SW	CSW	SC	CSC	SW	CSW	SC	CSC	SW	CSW	SC	CSC	SW	CSW	SC	CSC	SW	CSW	SC	CSC	SW	CSW	SC	SW
PRI. GOODS	16,6	-2,3	0,8	+0,2	34,7	+11,8	2,0	-0,1	4,8	+1,7	0,5	0,0	0,0	0,0	0,0	0,0	0,0	-0,2	0,0	-0,1	1,7	+1,6	0,1	+0,1	58	0,8
MACHINERY	0,0	-0,9	0,0	-0,6	0,0	-1,1	0,0	-1,0	0,0	-1,0	0,0	0,0	0,0	0,0	0,0	0,0	0,0	0,0	0,0	0,0	0,0	0,0	0,0	0,0	0,0	0,0
SPE. INPUTS	3,1	+1,5	0,6	+0,6	3,6	-5,7	0,6	-1,0	1,4	+0,7	0,7	+0,2	0,0	0,0	0,0	0,0	2,0	-2,3	3,0	-3,2	0,0	0,0	0,0	0,0	10	0,7
TOTAL	19,7	-1,7	0,8	+0,3	38,3	+5,0	1,5	-0,4	6,2	+2,4	0,5	0,0	0,0	0,0	0,0	0,0	2,0	-2,5	0,3	-0,7	1,7	+1,6	0,1	+0,1	68	0,8

KEY: SC   Share of country's total exports   1992
CSC   Change in share of country's exports 1985-92
SW   Share of world cluster exports 1992
CSW   Change in share of world cluster exports 1985-92

Table A2.2 Percentage of Turkish Exports by Cluster and Vertical Stage (1971-1978)

Band 1

	MATERIALS/METALS				FOREST PRODUCTS				PETROLEUM/CHEMICALS				SEMICONDUCTORS/COMPUTERS				UPSTREAM IND.	
	SC	CSC	SW	CSW	SC	CSC	SW	CSW	SC	CSC	SW	CSW	SC	CSC	SW	CSW	SC	SW
PRI. GOODS	6,7	+4,0	0,1	0,0	0,0	-0,7	0,0	0,0	0,5	-0,4	0,0	0,0	0,0	0,0	0,0	0,0	7,2	0,0
MACHINERY	0,0	0,0	0,0	0,0	0,0	0,0	0,0	0,0	0,0	0,0	0,0	0,0	0,0	0,0	0,0	0,0	0,0	0,0
SPE. INPUTS	0,2	+0,2	0,0	0,0	0,0	0,0	0,0	0,0	0,0	0,0	0,0	0,0	0,0	0,0	0,0	0,0	0,2	0,0
TOTAL	6,9	+4,2	0,1	+0,1	0,0	-0,7	0,0	0,0	0,5	-0,4	0,0	0,0	0,0	0,0	0,0	0,0	7,4	0,0

Band 2

	MULTIPLE BUSINESS				TRANSPORTATION				POWER GENERATION & DISTRIBUTION				OFFICE				TELECOMMUNIC.				DEFENSE				INDUS & SUP FUNCTIONS	
	SC	CSC	SW	CSW	SC	CSC	SW	CSW	SC	CSC	SW	CSW	SC	CSC	SW	CSW	SC	CSC	SW	CSW	SC	CSC	SW	CSW	SC	SW
PRI. GOODS	0,0	0,0	0,0	0,0	0,2	+0,2	0,0	0,0	0,0	0,0	0,0	0,0	0,0	0,0	0,0	0,0	0,0	0,0	0,0	0,0	0,0	0,0	0,0	0,0	0,2	0,0
MACHINERY	0,0	0,0	0,0	0,0	0,0	0,0	0,0	0,0	0,0	0,0	0,0	0,0	0,0	0,0	0,0	0,0	0,0	0,0	0,0	0,0	0,0	0,0	0,0	0,0	0,0	0,0
SPE. INPUTS	0,0	0,0	0,0	0,0	0,0	0,0	0,0	0,0	0,0	0,0	0,0	0,0	0,0	0,0	0,0	0,0	0,0	0,0	0,0	0,0	0,0	0,0	0,0	0,0	0,0	0,0
TOTAL	0,0	0,0	0,0	0,0	0,2	+0,2	0,0	0,0	0,0	0,0	0,0	0,0	0,0	0,0	0,0	0,0	0,0	0,0	0,0	0,0	0,0	0,0	0,0	0,0	0,2	0,0

Band 3

	FOOD/BEVERAGE				TEXTILES/APPAREL				HOUSING & HOUSEHOLD				HEALTH CARE				PERSONAL				ENTERTAINMENT/ LEISURE				FINAL CONS. GOODS & SER	
	SC	CSC	SW	CSW	SC	CSC	SW	CSW	SC	CSC	SW	CSW	SC	CSC	SW	CSW	SC	CSC	SW	CSW	SC	CSC	SW	CSW	SC	SW
PRI. GOODS	35,3	+0,3	5,8	+2,6	0,2	+0,1	2,5	+1,6	0,0	0,0	0,0	0,0	0,0	0,0	0,0	0,0	0,0	0,0	0,0	0,0	0,0	0,0	0,0	0,0	44	0,4
MACHINERY	0,0	0,0	0,0	0,0	0,0	0,0	0,0	0,0	0,0	0,0	0,0	0,0	0,0	0,0	0,0	0,0	0,0	0,0	0,0	0,0	0,0	0,0	0,0	0,0	0,0	0,0
SPE. INPUTS	10,2	+0,4	25,3	-7,3	6,6	0,6	2,1	+0,7	0,6	+0,1	0,0	0,0	0,0	0,0	0,0	0,0	9,9	-0,3	4,8	-0,9	0,0	0,0	0,0	0,0	48	1,2
TOTAL	45,5	+6,9	31,1	-4,7	6,9	0,6	4,6	+2,3	0,6	+0,1	0,2	0,0	0,0	0,0	0,0	0,0	9,9	-0,3	1,0	-0,9	0,0	0,0	0,0	0,0	91	0,5

KEY:
SC   Share of country's total exports   1978
CSC   Change in share of country's exports 1971-1978
SW   Share of world cluster exports 1978
CSW   Change in share of world cluster exports 1971-1978

Table A2.3 Percentage of Turkish Exports by Cluster and Vertical Stage (1971)

	MATERIALS/METALS		FOREST PRODUCTS		PETROLEUM/CHEMICALS		SEMICONDUCTORS/COMPUTERS		UPSTREAM IND	
	SC	SW	SC	SW	SC	SW	SC	SW	SC	SW
PRI. GOODS	2,7	0,1	0,7	0,0	0,9	0,0	0,0	0,0	4,3	0,0
MACHINERY	0,0	0,0	0,0	0,0	0,0	0,0	0,0	0,0	0,0	0,0
SPE. INPUTS	0,0	0,0	0,0	0,0	0,0	0,0	0,0	0,0	0,0	0,0
TOTAL	2,7	0,0	0,7	0,0	0,9	0,0	0,0	0,0	4,3	0,0

	MULTIPLE BUSINESS		TRANSPORTATION		POWER GENERATION & DISTRIBUTION		OFFICE		TELECOMMUNIC.		DEFENSE		INDUS. & SUP. FUNCTIONS	
	SC	SW	SC	SW	SC	SW	SC	SW	SC	SW	SC	SW	SC	SW
PRI. GOODS	0,0	0,0	0,0	0,0	0,0	0,0	0,0	0,0	0,0	0,0	0,0	0,0	0,0	0,0
MACHINERY	0,0	0,0	0,0	0,0	0,0	0,0	0,0	0,0	0,0	0,0	0,0	0,0	0,0	0,0
SPE. INPUTS	0,0	0,0	0,0	0,0	0,0	0,0	0,0	0,0	0,0	0,0	0,0	0,0	0,0	0,0
TOTAL	0,0	0,0	0,0	0,0	0,0	0,0	0,0	0,0	0,0	0,0	0,0	0,0	0,0	0,0

	FOOD/BEVERAGE		TEXTILES/APPAREL		HOUSING & HOUSEHOLD		HEALTH CARE		PERSONAL		ENTERTAINMENT/ LEISURE		FINAL CONS. GOODS & SER	
	SC	SW	SC	SW	SC	SW	SC	SW	SC	SW	SC	SW	SC	SW
PRI. GOODS	35,0	0,7	3,2	0,1	0,9	0,1	0,0	0,0	0,0	0,0	0,0	0,0	39	0,4
MACHINERY	0,0	0,0	0,0	0,0	0,0	0,0	0,0	0,0	0,0	0,0	0,0	0,0	0,0	0,0
SPE. INPUTS	3,6	0,2	32,6	2,0	1,4	0,5	0,0	0,0	12,9	5,7	0,0	0,0	51	1,3
TOTAL	38,6	0,5	35,8	0,7	2,3	0,2	0,0	0,0	12,9	1,9	0,0	0,0	90	0,6

KEY: SC Share of country's total exports 1971   SW Share of world cluster exports 1971

Bibliography

Aaby, N. E., and Slater, S. F. (1989), 'Management Influences on Export Performance: A Review of the Empirical Literature 1978-88', *International Marketing Review*, 6 (4): 7-26.

Adnan, N. (1935), *Türklerin Deri Sanayiine Yaptıkları Hizmetler*, İstanbul: Akşam.

Akder, H. (1987), *Turkey's Foreign Trade with the Community*, Friedrich Ebert Foundation- SIAR Report, İstanbul.

Akın, N. (1993), Türk Demir-Çelik Sektörünün Durumu, Sorunları ve Beklentileri, in M. C. Demir, E. S. Ömeroğlu, M. T. Güzel and B. Kutlu (eds), *Demir-Çelik ve Metal Sanayii Sektör Araştırmaları Serisi - 2*, Ankara: Demkar.

Aktan, O. H. (1996), Liberalisation, Export Incentives and Exchange Rate Policy: Turkey's Experience in the 1980s, in S. Togan and V. N. Balasubramanyam (eds), *The Economy of Turkey Since Liberalisation*, London: Macmillan Press.

Aktan, O., and Baysan, T. (1985), 'Integration of the Turkish Economy into the World Economy: Trade Liberalisation, Comparative Advantage and Optimum Policies', *Middle East Technical University Studies in Development*, 12 (1-2): 49-106.

Alkan, E. (1993), Demir- Çelik Döküm Sanayiinin Tanıtılması ve Sorunları, in M. C. Demir, E. S. Ömeroğlu, M. T. Güzel and B. Kutlu (eds), *Demir-Çelik ve Metal Sanayii Sektör Araştırmaları Serisi - 2*, Ankara: Demkar.

Amstrong, A. (1992), 'Feedback: What is Competitive Advantage?', *Omega International Journal of Management Science*, 20 (3): 281-2.

Ansal, H. K. (1994), International Competitiveness and Industrial Policy: The Turkish Experience in the Textile and Truck Manufacturing Industries, in F. Şenses (ed), *Recent Industrialisation Experience of Turkey in a Global Context*, London: Greenwood Press.

Ansal, H. K. (1993), 'New Technology in the World Textile Industry and Turkey's International Competitiveness', *Middle East Technical University Studies in Development*, 20 (4): 429-51.

Arıcanlı, T., and Rodrik, D. (1990a), *The Political Economy of Turkey: Debt, Adjustment and Sustainability*, Hong Kong: The Macmillan Press Ltd.

Arıcanlı, T., and Rodrik, D. (1990b), 'An Overview of Turkey's Experience with Economic Liberalisation and Structural Adjustment', *World Development*, 18 (10): 1343-50.

Arıkan, M. M. (1992), 'Circular Migration and Proletarianization of Construction Workers of Sakaltutan', *Middle East Technical University Studies in Development*, 19 (2): 129-44.

Arnesen, P.J. (1989), *The Auto Industry Ahead: Who's Driving?*, Michigan Papers in Japanese Studies, Ann Arbor: The University of Michigan.

Arslan, I., and van Wijnbergen, S. (1990), *Turkey: Export Miracle or Accounting Trick*, Working Papers, Washington D. C.: The World Bank.

Arslan, G. A. (1985), 'The Regional Structure of Agricultural Production in Turkey: A Multivariate Perspective', *Middle East Technical University Studies in Development*, 12 (1-2): 27-47.

Arslan, M., and Lightfoot, C. S. (1992), *Ancient Glass of Asia Minor*, Ankara: Ünal Offset Ltd.

Ata Menkul Kıymetler (1995), *İMKB'de Demir-Çelik Sektörü*, Research Division, Finans Dünyası, 70.

Ayata, S. (1982), *Differentiation and Capital Accumulation: Case Studies of the Carpet and Metal Industries in Kayseri (Turkey)*, PhD Thesis, University of Kent, Catenbury.

Azcanlı, A. (1995), *Türk Otomotiv Sanayiinin Tarihsel Gelişimi*, İstanbul: Otomotiv Sanayii Derneği.

Balasubramanyam, V. N. (1996), Foreign Direct Investment in Turkey, in S. Togan and V. N. Balasubramanyam (eds), *The Economy of Turkey Since Liberalisation*, London: Macmillan Press.

Barlow, R., and Şenses, F. (1995), 'The Turkish Export Boom: Just Reward or Just Lucky?', *Journal of Development Economics*, 48 (1): 111-33.

Bayraktar, S. K. (1995), *Otomotiv Sektörü*, İMKB Research Division, İstanbul, Unpublished Document.

Bayramoğlu, F. (1976), *Turkish Glass Art and Beykoz-ware*, İstanbul: İstanbul Matbaası.

Baysan, T., and Blitzer, C. (1991), Turkey, in Papageorgiou, D., Choksi, A. M. and Michaely, M. (eds), *Liberalising Foreign Trade*, vol. 6, Oxford: Basil Blackwell.

Baysan, T., and Blitzer, C. (1990), Turkey's Trade Liberalisation in the 1980s and Prospects for its Sustainability, in T. Arıcanlı and D. Rodrik (eds), *The Political Economy of Turkey, Debt Adjustment and Sustainability*, Houndmills: The MacMillan Press.

Baysan, T. (1984), 'Resource Shift Under Tariff Liberalisation and Turkey's Comparative Advantage in Agriculture', *European Review of Agricultural Economics*, 11 (3): 303-22.

Bellak, C. J., and Weiss, A. (1993), 'A Note on the Austrian Diamond', *Management International Review*, Special Issue (2): 109-18.

Betts, M., and Ofori, G. (1994), 'Strategic Planing for Competitive Advantage in Construction: The Institutions', *Construction Management and Economics*, 12 (3): 203-17.

Bilen, A. (1995), 'Sanayide Teknoloji Üretimi', *Deri*, September, 12 (130): 26-8.

Bilkey, W. J. (1978), 'An Attempted Integration of the Literature on the Export Behaviour of Firms', *Journal of International Business Studies*, Spring/Summer, 9 (1): 33-46.

Bloomfield, G. T. (1991), The World Automotive Industry in Transition, in C. M. Law (ed), *Restructuring the Global Automotive Industry - National and Regional Impacts*, New York: Routledge.

Bodur, M., and Çavuşgil, S. T. (1985), 'Export Market Research Orientation of Turkish Firms', *European Journal of Marketing*, 19 (2): 5-16.
Boratav, K., Türel, O., and Yeldan, E. (1995), 'The Turkish Economy in 1981-92: A Balance Sheet, Problems and Prospects', *Middle East Technical University Studies in Development*, 22 (1): 1-36.
Bozkurt, R. (1993), *Cam Sektöründe Yapısal ve Ekonomik Özellikler*, Internal Document, Şişecam.
Brenner, C., and Kurdoğlu, C. (1988), *Mastering Technology: Engineering Services Firms in Developing Countries*, OECD Development Centre Papers, Paris: OECD.
Brenner, M., Brown, J., and Canter, D. (1985), *The Research Interview- Uses and Approaches*, London: Academic Press Inc.
Bruce, N. (1991), The Cost of Capital and Competitive Advantage, in T. J. Courchene and D. D. Purris (eds), *Productivity, Growth and Canada's International Competitiveness*, Ontario: John Deutsch Institute for the Study of Economic Policy.
Buğdaycı, A. (1996), 'Otomobilde Damping Tehlikesi Var', *Capital*, 1.
Buğra, A. (1994), *State and Business in Modern Turkey: A Comparative Study*, Albany: State University of New York Press.
Capital - Turkey (1996), 'One Million Sales Target in Automotive', 1.
Carberry, E. (1994), *Glassblowing*, Marshall: MGLS Publishing.
Cartwright, W. R. (1993), 'Multiple Linked "Diamonds" and the International Competitiveness of Export-Dependent Industries: The New Zealand Experience', *Management International Review*, Special Issue (2): 55-70.
Cartwright, W. R. (1992), 'Canada at the Crossroads Dialogue', *Business Quarterly*, 57 (2): 10-12.
Chetty, S. K., and Hamilton, R. T. (1993), 'Firm-level Determinants of Export Performance: A Meta Analysis', *International Marketing Review*, 10 (3): 26-34.
Construction Europe (1995), 'Construction Sector in Turkey', June.
Conway, P. (1988), The Impact of Recent Trade Liberalisation Policies in Turkey, in T. F. Nas and M. Odekon (eds), *Liberalisation and the Turkish Economy: A Comparative Analysis*, London: Greenwood Press.
Cooper, W. W. (1992), 'On Porter's Competitive Advantage of Nations', *Omega International Journal of Management Science*, 20 (2): 137-8.
Cotè, M. (1991), Agents of Change and Economic Growth, in T. J. Courchene and D. D. Purris (eds), *Productivity, Growth and Canada's International Competitiveness*, Ontario: John Deutsch Institute for the Study of Economic Policy.
Cowhey, P. F., and Aronson, J. D. (1993), *Managing the World Economy: The Consequences of Corporate Alliances*, New York: Council on Foreign Relations Press.
Crocombe, G. T., Enright, M. J., and Porter, M. E. (1991), *Upgrading New Zealand's Competitive Advantage*, Auckland: Oxford University Press.
Çandar, V. (1996), 'Deri Kalitesinin Yükseltilmesi ve Geliştirilmesi ile İlgili İşlemler - 1', *Deri*, January, 12 (134): 25-8.
Çelebi, I. (1991), *Dışa Açik Büyüme ve Türkiye*, İstanbul: Erdoğan Ofset.

Çelebi, I. (1979), *Türkiye'de Demir-Çelik Sanayiinin Yapısı ve Sorunları*, Ankara: DPT.

Daly, D. J. (1993), 'Porter's Diamond and Exchange Rates', *Management International Review*, Special Issue (2): 119-34.

Darroch, J. L., and Litvak, I. A. (1992), 'Diamonds and Money', *Business Quarterly*, 56 (3): 71-5.

Demir, M. C., Ömeroğlu, E. S., Güzel, M. T., and Kutlu, B. (1993), *Demir-Çelik ve Metal Sanayii Sektör Araştırmaları Serisi - 2*, Ankara: Demkar.

Demirci, B. (1993), *Taşıt Araçcları İmalat Sanayiinde Gelişmeler ve Beklentiler*, Ankara: DPT.

Deri/Leather (1996), 'Summary', May, 11 (41).

Deri (1996), 'Deri Günleri Bir Seferberlik Hareketidir', January, 12 (134): 15-6.

Deri (1995a), 'Deri Sektörünün Dünü, Bugünü, Yarını', December, 12 (133): 8-11.

Deri (1995b), 'Deri Sektörünün Dünü, Bugünü, Yarını', November, 12 (132): 6-9.

Deri (1995c), 'Uluslararası Deri Günleri'96 - Sektörün İzdüşümü', September, 12 (130): 6-8.

Deri (1995d), 'Türkiye Her İki Dünyanın En İyisi mi?', July, 11 (128): 7-8.

Deri (1995e), 'ITKIB, Deri Bölümü 1994'te İhracatını Arttırdı', April, 12 (125): 16.

Devins, R. M. (1991), 'Winning or Losing', *Monthly Labour Review*, 114 (7): 40-1.

Deyo, F. C. (ed), (1996), *Social Reconstruction of the World Automobile Industry: Competition, Power and Industrial Flexibility*, New York: St. Martin's Press, Inc.

Dicken, P. (1992), *Global Shift: The Internationalization of Economic Activity*, London: Chapman.

DIE (1994a), *Türkiye Ekonomisi İstatistik ve Yorumlar*, Ankara: DIE Matbaası.

DIE (1994b), *Yıllık İmalat Sanayi İstatistikleri-1990*, Ankara: DIE Matbaası.

Dobson, P., and Starkey, K. (1992), 'The Competitive Advantage of Nations', *Journal of Management Studies*, 29 (2): 253-5.

DPT (1996), *Deri ve Deri Mamülleri VII. 5 Yıllık Kalkınma Planı ÖİK Raporu*, Ankara: DPT.

DPT (1995a), *Ana Metal Sanayileri ÖİK, Demir-Çelik Alt Komisyonu, Yassı Hadde Ürünleri Çalışma Grubu Raporu*, Ankara: DPT.

DPT (1995b), *Ana Metal Sanayileri ÖİK, Demir-Çelik Alt Komisyonu, Uzun Hadde Ürünleri Çalışma Grubu Raporu*, Ankara: DPT.

DPT (1995c), *Ana Metal Sanayileri ÖİK, Demir-Çelik Alt Komisyonu, Ferro Alasimlar Çalışma Grubu Raporu*, Ankara: DPT.

DPT (1993a), *Mühendislik, Mimarlık ve Müşavirlik Hizmetleri Alt Komisyon Raporu*, Internal Document, Ankara: DPT.

DPT (1993b), *Yedinci Beş Yıllık Kalkınma Planı İnşaat, Müteahhitlik, Mühendislik ve Müşavirlik Hizmetleri ÖİK, İleri Yapım Teknolojileri Alt Komisyonu Raporu*, Ankara: DPT.

DPT (1993c), *Yedinci Beş Yıllık Kalkınma Planı İnşaat, Müteahhitlik, Mühendislik ve Müşavirlik Hizmetleri ÖİK Yurtiçi Müteahhitlik Hizmetleri Alt Komisyonu Rapor Özeti*, Ankara: DPT.

198 *The Competitive Advantage of Nations: The Case of Turkey*

DPT (1993d), *Üçüncü İzmir İktisat Kongresi 4-7 Haziran 1992, DPT Otomotiv Sanayii Çalışma Grubu - Rapor ve Tartışmalar*, Eskişehir: Anadolu Üniversitesi Açık Öğretim Fakültesi Dönersermaye İşletmesi Müdürlüğü Basımevi.

DPT (1993e), *VII. Beş Yıllık Plan Cam ÖİK Raporu*, Ankara: DPT.

DPT (1991a), *Deri ve Deri Mamülleri Sanayii ÖİK Raporu*, Ankara: DPT.

DPT (1991b), *Demir-Çelik ÖİK Raporu*, Ankara: DPT.

DPT (1991c), *Karayolu Taşısitlarıı İlmalat Sanayii ÖİK Raporu*, Ankara: DPT.

Dumanli, R. (1987), *Türkiye'de Otomotiv Sanayiinin Durumu Yapısal Özellikleri ve Sorunları - 1980*, Ankara: DPT.

Dunning, J. H. (1993), 'Internationalizing Porter's Diamond', *Management International Review*, Special Issue (2): 8-15.

Dunning, J. H. (1992), 'The Competitive Advantage of Countries and the Activities of Transnational Corporations', *Transnational Corporations*, 1 (1): 135-68.

Dunning, J. H. (1981), *International Production and the Multinational Enterprise*, London: Allen and Unwin.

Dunning, J. H., Kogut, B., and Blomstrom, M. (1990), *Globalisation of Firms and the Competitiveness of Nations*, Lund: Lund University Press.

Duruiz, L., and Yentürk, N. (1992), *Facing the Challenge: Turkish Automobile, Steel and Clothing Industries' Responses to the Post-Fordist Restructuring*, İstanbul: İletişim Yayınları.

Duruiz, L., and Çoban, N. Y. (1988), *Technological and Structural Change in the Turkish Clothing Industry*, Turkish Social Science Association, İstanbul: Ayhan Matbaası.

The Economist (1996), 'Economic Indicators', 2 March, 338 (7955): 118.

The Economist (1995), 'Economic Indicators', 25 February, 334 (7903): 150.

The Economist (1994), 'Professor Porter PhD', 8 October, 333 (7884): 97.

The Economist (1990), 'Oh, Mr Porter, What Shall We Do?', 19 May, 315 (7655): 153.

Edmonds, G. A. (1979), 'The Construction Industry in Developing Countries', *International Labour Review*, 118 (3): 355-69.

Eilon, S. (1992), 'Editorial: On Competitiveness', *Omega International Journal of Management Science*, 20 (1): i-v.

EIU (1994), *Turkey: Country Profile 1994-1995*, London: The Economist Intelligence Unit.

Ekonomik Trend (1995), 'Avrupa'ya Otomobil İhracati', 20 May, 20: 65.

Ekonomist (1996), 'Düşüş Korkusu', Ekonomist Yıllığı Türkiye-1997, 22 December.

Ekonomist (1995a), 'Otomobil Satmayı Bilmiyoruz', 26 March, Special Issue, 13: 5.

Ekonomist (1995b), 'Hedef 93'u Yakalamak', Ekonomist Yıllığı Türkiye 1995, 22 January, 5 (4).

Ekonomist (1995c), 'Demir-Çelikte Kartel Arayışı', 3 September, 36.

Engin, N., and Katırcıoğlu, E. (1993), Dış Ticaret Liberalizasyonunun Türkiye'deki Rekabete Etkisi: Amprik Bir Değerlendirme, in İSO, *Türkiye İçin Rekabet Politikaları, İstanbul Sanayi Odası*, Publication No. 9, İstanbul: Yenilik Basımevi.

Engineering News Record (ENR), various issues.

Enright, M. J., Scott, E. E., and Dodwell, D. (1997), *The Hong Kong Advantage*, New York: Oxford University Press.

Eraydın, A. (1994), Changing Spatial Distribution and Structural Characteristics of the Turkish Manufacturing Industry, in F. Şenses (ed), *Recent Industrialisation Experience of Turkey in a Global Context*, London: Greenwood Press.

Erdemir (1995), *Annual Report 1995*, İstanbul: Creative Publishing.

Erdilek, A. (1988), The Role of Foreign Investment in the Liberalisation of the Turkish Economy, in T. F. Nas and M. Odekon (eds), *Liberalisation and the Turkish Economy: A Comparative Analysis*, London: Greenwood Press.

Erdilek, A. (1982), *Direct Foreign Investment in Turkish Manufacturing*, Tubingen: Institut fur Weltwirtschaft an der Universitat Kiel.

Ergüder, Ü., Esmer, Y., and Kalaycıoğlu, E. (1991), *Türk Toplumunun Değerleri*, TÜSİAD, İstanbul: Boyut Matbaacılık A. Ş.

Erlat, G. (1993), 'Is There a meaningful Relationship Between Exports and Industrial Concentration? Case Studies from the Turkish Manufacturing Industry', *Middle East Technical University Studies in Development*, 20 (1-2): 43-61.

Erzan, R. (1993), Türkiye'de Teşsviklerin Rolü, in İSO, *Türkiye İçin Rekabet Politikaları*, İstanbul Sanayi Odası, Publication No. 9, İstanbul: Yenilik Basımevi.

Euromoney (1994), 'Construction, Sectoral Guide to Asian Markets', September: 21-2.

Faini, R. (1988), *Export Supply, Capacity and Relative Prices*, Working Papers, Washington D. C.: The World Bank.

FAO (1994), *World Statistical Compendium for Raw Hides and Skins, Leather and Leather Footwear 1974-1992*, Rome: FAO.

Ferreira, M. P., and Rayment, P. (1984), 'Exports of Manufactures from South European Countries', *Journal of World Trade Law*, 18 (3): 235-51.

Flink, J. J. (1988), *The Automobile Age*, Cambridge: The MIT Press.

Foroutan, F. (1991), *Foreign Trade and its Relation to Competition and Productivity in Turkish Industry*, PRE Working Paper Series, No. 604, February 1991, Washington, D. C.: The World Bank

Fostner, H. (1995), Conditions of Competition and Determinants of Competitiveness: Theory versus Empirical Evidence, in R. Erzan (ed), *Policies for Competition and Competitiveness: The Case of Industry in Turkey*, Vienna: UNIDO.

Gagnon, J. E., and Rose, A. K. (1995), 'Dynamic Persistence of Industry Trade Balances: How Pervasive is the Product Cycle?', *Oxford Economic Papers*, 47 (2): 229-48.

GATT (1986), *The Downward Bias in Service Statistics in International Trade 1985-86*, Geneva: GATT.

Ghemawat, P. (1986), 'Sustainable Advantage', *Harvard Business Review*, 64 (5): 53-8.

Giritli, H., Sözen, Z., Flanagan, R., and Lansley, P. (1990), 'International Contracting: A Turkish Perspective', *Construction Management and Economics*, 8 (4): 415-30.

200   *The Competitive Advantage of Nations: The Case of Turkey*

Gökçekuş, O. (1995), 'The Effects of Trade Exposure on Technical Efficiency: New Evidence from the Turkish Rubber Industry', *Journal of Productivity Analysis*, 6 (1): 77-85.

Grant, R. M. (1991), 'Porter's Competitive Advantage of Nations: An Assessment', *Strategic Management Journal*, 12 (7): 535-48.

Gray, H. P. (1991), 'International Competitiveness: A Review Article', *The International Trade Journal*, 5: 503-17.

Greenaway, D. (1993), 'The Competitive Advantage of Nations', *Kyklos*, 46 (1): 145-6.

Güçlü, O., and Muslu, H. (1987), *Türkiye Demir-Çelik Sanayiinin Avrupa Topluluğuna Uyumu: İspanya, Portekiz, Yunanistan Örnekleri*, İstanbul: Metaş Yayınları.

Gürer, Y. K. (1995), *A Brief History of the Turkish Foreign Contracting and its Recent Developments*, Union of International Contractors-Turkey and Turkish Contractors Association, Unpublished Document.

Guttery, D. R. (1956), *From Broad Glass to Cut Crystal*, London: Leonard Hill Books Limited.

Gwyynne, R. (1991), New Horizons? The Third World Motor Vehicle Industry in an International Framework, in C. M. Law (ed), *Restructuring the Global Automotive Industry - National and Regional Impacts*, New York: Routledge.

Harris, R. G., and Watson, W. G. (1991), Three Visions of Competitiveness: Porter, Reich and Thurow on Economic Growth and Policy, in T. J. Courchene and D. D. Purris (eds), *Productivity, Growth and Canada's International Competitiveness*, Ontario: John Deutsch Institute for the Study of Economic Policy.

Harvard Business Review (1987), 'Competitiveness: 23 Leaders Speak Out', July/August, 65 (4): 106-23.

Heinz, J. (1990), 'By examining real cases...', in L. A. McCauley (ed), Letters to the Editor, *Harvard Business Review*, May-June, 90 (3): 192-3.

Helpman, E., and Krugman, P. R. (1985), *Market Structure and Foreign Trade: Increasing Returns, Imperfect Competition, and the International Economy*, Cambridge, Mass.: MIT Press.

Hillebrand, W., Ramm, J. F., Schmidt, G., Steiner, A., and Zapf, H. (1986), *Development Prospects of the Automobile Industries in Turkey - Domestic Policies and International Cooperation*, Berlin (publisher unspecified).

Hodgetts, R. M. (1993), 'Porter's Diamond Framework in a Mexican Context', *Management International Review*, Special Issue (2): 41-54.

Hofstede, G. (1980), *Culture's Consequences*, Beverly Hills: Sage Publications.

Hogan, W. T. (1991), *Global Steel in the 1990s: Growth or Decline*, Massachusetts: Lexington Books.

Hood, N., and Young, S. (1979), *The Economics of Multinational Enterprise*, London: Longman Group.

ICEF (1995), *ICEF World Industry Trends*, MIF Merger Congress, 22 November, Washington D.C.: ICEF.

ICEF (1992), *ICEF Industry Trends- Sectional Dynamics, Action and Programmes*, 20th Congress, Bonn, 4-6 Nov., Brussels: ICEF.

ILO (1992a), *Recent Developments in the Leather and Footwear Industry, Fourth Tripartite Technical Meeting for the Leather and Footwear Industry*, Geneva: ILO.

ILO (1992b), *Employment and Working Conditions and Competitiveness in the Leather and Footwear Industry, Fourth Tripartite Technical Meeting for the Leather and Footwear Industry*, Geneva: ILO.

ILO (1985a), *The Impact on Employment and Income of Structural and Technological Changes in the Leather and Footwear Industry, Third Tripartite Technical Meeting for the Leather and Footwear Industry*, Geneva: ILO.

ILO (1985b), *Manpower Development, Training and Retraining in the Leather and Footwear Industry, Third Tripartite Technical Meeting for the Leather and Footwear Industry*, Geneva: ILO.

IMD and The World Economic Forum (1997), *The World Competitiveness Report*, Lausanne and Geneva: IMD and The World Economic Forum.

IMF, *Balance of Payment Statistics Yearbook*, various years, Washington D. C.: IMF.

İSO (1993), *Türkiye İçin Rekabet Politikalari*, İstanbul Sanayi Odası, Publication No. 9, İstanbul: Yenilik Basımevi.

İTO (1985), *Directory of Turkish Contractors Abroad*, Publication no. 1985-4 İstanbul: İTO.

Jacobs, D. and De Jong, M. W. (1992), 'Industrial Clusters and the Competitiveness of the Netherlands', *De Economist*, 140 (2): 233-52.

Jasinowski, J. J. (1990), 'Although Michael Porter...', in L. A. McCauley (ed), Letters to the Editor, *Harvard Business Review*, May-June, 90 (3): 196-8.

Jelinek, M. (1992), 'The Competitive Advantage of Nations', *Administrative Science Quarterly*, 37 (3): 507-10.

Jones, R. W., and Kenen, P. B. (ed), (1984), *Handbook of International Economics*, Amsterdam: North Holland.

Jorgenson, D. W. (1992), 'Productivity and International Competitiveness: Introduction', *The Economic Studies Quarterly*, 43 (4): 291-7.

Journal of Business with Russia, various issues.

Kansu, I. (1996), 'Susturulamayan Vardiya Düdüğü: Karabük', *Cumhuriyet*, 28-31 December.

Kartay, H. (1996), '1996'ya Girerken Deri Sektörümüz', *Deri*, January, 12 (134): 8-10.

Kartay, H. (1993), Demir-Çelik Sektörümüzün Güncel Konuları, in M. C. Demir, E. S. Ömeroğlu, M. T. Güzel and B. Kutlu (eds), *Demir-Çelik ve Metal Sanayii Sektör Araştırmaları Serisi - 2*, Ankara: Demkar.

Katırcıoğlu, E., Engin, N., and Akçay, C. (1995), The Impact of Trade Liberalisation on the Turkish Manufacturing Industry, in R. Erzan (ed), *Policies for Competition and Competitiveness: The Case of Industry in Turkey*, Vienna: UNIDO.

202   *The Competitive Advantage of Nations: The Case of Turkey*

Kaynak, E., and Dalgıç, T. (1992), 'Internationalization of Turkish Construction Companies: A Lesson for Third World Companies?' *Columbia Journal of World Business*, 26 (4): 60-75.

Kaynak, E., and Gürol, M. N. (1987), 'Export Marketing Management in Less-Developed Countries: A Case Study of Turkey in Light of the Japanese Experience', *Management International Review*, 27 (3): 54-66.

Kazgan, G., Tuncer, B., and Kırmanoğlu, H. (1990), *Vergi İadesi Uygulamasının Türk İmalat Sanayi İhracati Üzerindeki Etkisi 1979-1990*, No. 22, İstanbul: TÜSES.

Kazgan, G. (1988), *Ekonomide Dışa Açık Büyüme*, İstanbul: Altın Kitaplar Yayınevi.

Kepenek, Y. (1987), *Türkiye Ekonomisi*, Ankara: Başarı Matbaası.

Kırım, A. (1990), 'Technology and Exports: The Case of the Turkish Manufacturing Industries', *World Development*, 18 (10): 1351-62.

Kırım, A., and Ateş, H. (1989), 'Technical Change and Technological Capability in the Turkish Textile Sector', *Middle East Technical University Studies in Development*, 16 (1-2): 1-30.

Kışlalı, M. (1997), 'Erdemir Karlı Günlarini Arıyor', *Business Week (Hürriyet)*, 1: 72-73.

Kirkpatrick, C., and Öniş, Z. (1991), Turkey, in P. Mosley, J. Harrigan and J. Toye (eds), *Aid and Power: The World Bank Policy-Based Lending in the 1980s*, Vol. 2: Case Studies, London: Routledge.

Kogut, B. (1989), Country Capabilities and the Permeability of Borders, in J-E. Vahlne and N. Hoods (eds), *Strategies in Global Competition*, London: Croom Helm.

Koşar, T. (1995a), '1995 Zor Bir Yıl Oldu, 1996'da Neler Var..', *Deri*, December, 12 (133).

Koşar, T. (1995b), 'Zor Ama Değerli Bir Pazar: Japonya', *Deri*, November, 12 (132): 3.

Koşar, T. (1995c), 'Bir Gezinin Ardından', *Deri*, September, 12 (130): 3-4.

Koşar, T. (1995d), 'Çin ve Endonezya Gezisi', *Deri*, July, 11 (128): 3-4.

Kristal-İş (1992a), *Cam İşçisi Araştırması-2*, İstanbul: MU-KA Matbaacılık.

Kristal-İş (1992b), *Kristal-İş Sendikasi 11. Genel Kurul Çalışma Raporu*, İstanbul: ARTI Yayıncılık & Tanıtım Ltd.

Krueger, A. O., and Aktan, O. H. (1992), *Swimming Against the Tide: Turkish Trade Reform in the 1980s*, San Francisco: ICS Press.

Krugman, P. (1994a), 'Competitiveness: A Dangerous Obsession', *Foreign Affairs*, March/April, 73 (2): 28-46.

Krugman, P. (1994b), *Peddling Prosperity: Economic Sense and Nonsense in the Age of Diminished Expectations*, New York: Norton.

Krugman, P. (1994c), 'Proving My Point', *Foreign Affairs*, July/August, 73 (4): 198-203.

Krugman, P. (1991), *Geography and Trade*, Cambridge, Mass.: The MIT Press.

Krugman, P., and Obstfeld, M. (1994), *International Economics: Theory and Policy*, 3rd ed, New York: HarperCollins College Publishers.

Küçükbali, M. K. (1983), *Türkiye Deri ve Deri Mamülleri Sanayii Ham Deri, Mamül Deri ve Deri Konfeksiyon*, Expertise Thesis, State Planning Organization, Ankara: DPT.

Küçükerman, O. (1985), *The Art of Glass and Traditional Turkish Glass-ware*, Ankara: Doğuş Matbaası.

Kumcu, M. E., and Kumcu, E. (1991), 'Exchange Rate Policy Impact on Export Performance: What We Can Learn from the Turkish Experience', *Journal of Business Research*, 23 (2): 129-43.

Kunak, F. (1995), Gümrük Birliği'nin Demir-Çelik Sektörü Üzerindeki Etkileri, in Y. Renda, 'Gümrük Birliğine Doğru Otomotiv ve Demir Çelik Endüstrisi', *Bilim ve Teknik*, April, 330: 42-6.

Leamer, E. E., (1984), *Sources of International Comparative Advantage*, London: The MIT Press.

Lee, J. R., and Walters, D. (1989), *International Trade in Construction, Design, and Engineering Services*, Cambridge: Ballinger Publishing Company.

Levinsohn, J. (1993), 'Testing the Imports-As-Market-Discipline Hypothesis', *Journal of International Economics*, 35 (1-2): 1-22.

Linder, M. (1994), *Projecting Capitalism: A History of the Internationalization of the Construction Industry*, Westport: Greenwood Press.

Lipschitz, L., and McDonald, D. (1991), *Real Exchange Rates and Competitiveness: A Clarification of Concepts, and Some Measurement for Europe*, IMF Working Paper, Washington D. C.: IMF.

Lodge, G. C., and Vogel, E. F. (ed), (1987), *Ideology and National Competitiveness: An Analysis of Nine Countries*, Boston: Harvard Business School Press.

Low, P. (1993), Uluslararasi Konum: Türkiye'nin GATT, AT, EFTA ile Iliskileri (trans.), in ISO, *Türkiye Icin Rekabet Politikalari*, İstanbul Sanayi Odasi, Publication No. 9, İstanbul: Yenilik Basımevi.

Maddison, A. (1982), *Phases of Capitalist Development*, New York: Oxford University Press.

Magaziner, I. C. (1990), 'Michael Porter's message...', in L. A. McCauley (ed), Letters to the Editor, *Harvard Business Review*, May-June, 90 (3): 189-92.

Male, S. (1991), Strategic Management in Construction: Conceptual Foundations, in S. P. Male and R. K Stocks (eds), *Competitive Advantage in Construction*, Oxford: Butterworth-Heinemann Ltd.

Male, S., and Stocks, R. (1991), Competitive Advantage in Construction: A Synthesis, in S. P. Male and R. K Stocks (eds), *Competitive Advantage in Construction*, Oxford: Butterworth-Heinemann Ltd.

Markusen, J. R. (1992), *Productivity, Competitiveness, Trade Performance and Real Income*, Ottowa: Canada Communications Group.

Marshall, A. (1920), *Principles of Economics: An Introductory Volume*, London: Macmillan.

Maucher, H. (1990), 'The Competitive Advantage of Nations...', in L. A. McCauley (ed), Letters to the Editor, *Harvard Business Review*, May-June, 90 (3): 188-9.

Maxton, G. P., and Wormald, J. (1995), *Driving Over a Cliff: Business Lessons from the World's Car Industry*, Wokingham: Addison-Wesley Publishing Company.

McFetridge, D. G. (1991), Globalization and Competition Policy, in T. J. Courchene and D. D. Purris (eds), *Productivity, Growth and Canada's International Competitiveness*, Ontario: John Deutsch Institute for the Study of Economic Policy.

Messner, J. I. (1994), *An Information Framework for Evaluating International Construction Projects*, Unpublished Ph. D. Thesis, The Pennsylvania State University.

Metal Bulletin (1996), *Metal Bulletin's Prices and Data*, Surrey: Metal Bulletin Books, Ltd.

Mike, L. (1994), 'Asia: Last Hope for Car Makers', *Asian Business*, 30 (5): 50-4.

Miles, D., and Neale, R. (1991), *Building for Tomorrow: International Experience in Construction Industry Development*, Geneva: ILO.

Ministry of Culture (1993), *From the Past to the Future: Anatolian Handicrafts Glassware*, Ankara: Ünal Offset.

Miyakawa, Y. (1991), The Transformation of the Japanese Motor Vehicle Industry and its Role in the World: Industrial Restructuring and Technical Evolution, in C. M. Law (ed), *Restructuring the Global Automotive Industry - National and Regional Impacts*, New York: Routledge.

Moinov, S. (1995), *Privatisation in the Iron and Steel Industry*, Geneva: ILO.

Narula, R. (1993), 'Technology, International Business and Porter's "Diamond": Synthesizing a Dynamic Competitive Development Model', *Management International Review*, Special Issue (2): 85-107.

Nas, T. F., and Odekon, M. (1992), *Economics and Politics of Turkish Liberalisation*, Bethlehem: Lehigh University Press.

Nas, T. F., and Odekon, M. (1988), *Liberalisation and the Turkish Economy: A Comparative Analysis*, London: Greenwood Press.

Neely, J. (1997), 'Aid for Kia's Contractors', *Financial Times*, 4 September.

Nelson, R. R. and Winter, S. G. (1982), *An Evolutionary Theory of Economic Change*, Cambridge, Mass.: Harvard University Press.

Nicholson, P. (1991), Comment on Harris and Watson, in T. J. Courchene and D. D. Purris (eds), *Productivity, Growth and Canada's International Competitiveness*, Ontario: John Deutsch Institute for the Study of Economic Policy.

Nolan, S., Scacciavillani, F., Wajid, S. K., and Figliuoli, L. (1995), *Turkey - Recent Economic Developments*, Washington D. C.: IMF.

O'Brien, P. and Karmokolias, Y. (1994), *Radical Reform in the Automotive Industry: Policies in Emerging Markets*, Discussion Papers, No. 21, Washington: The World Bank.

Odekon, M. (1992), Turkish Liberalisation: From the Perspectives of Manufacturing Firms, in T. F. Nas, and M. Odekon, *Economics and Politics of Turkish Liberalisation*, Bethlehem: Lehigh University Press.

O'Donnellan, N. (1994), 'The Presence of Porter's Sectoral Clustering in Irish Manufacturing', *The Economic and Social Review*, 25 (3), 221-32.

OECD (1996a), *Historical Statistics 1960-1994*, Paris: OECD.

OECD (1996b), *OECD Economic Outlook 1996*, Paris: OECD.

OECD (1996c), *Iron and Steel Industry in 1994*, Paris: OECD.

OECD (1995a), *Services: Statistics on International Transactions 1970-1992*, Paris: OECD.

OECD (1995b), *Education at a Glance: OECD Indicators*, Paris: OECD.

OECD (1995c), *Research and Development Expenditure in Industry 1973-1992*, Paris: OECD.

OECD (1994), *International Direct Investment Statistics Yearbook 1994*, Paris: OECD.

OECD (1992), *Globalization of Industrial Activities: Four Case Studies: Auto Parts, Chemicals, Construction and Semiconductors*, Paris: OECD.

OECD (1988), *Mastering Technology: Engineering Services Firms in Developing Countries*, Development Centre Papers, Paris: OECD.

Olson, M. (1982), *The Rise and Decline of Nations: Economic Growth, Stagflation, and Social Rigidities*, New Haven: Yale University Press.

Oral, M., Singer, A. E., and Kettani, O. (1989), 'The Level of International Competitiveness and Its Strategic Implications', *International Journal of Research in Marketing*, 6 (4): 267-82.

Oral, M, and Özkan, A. O. (1986), 'An Empirical Study on Measuring Industrial Competitiveness', *Journal of the Operational Research Society*, 37 (4): 345-56.

Oral, M. (1986), 'An Industrial Competitiveness Model', *IIE Transactions*, 18 (2): 148-157.

OSD (1985), *Onuncu Yılımızda Otomotiv Sanayiine Genel Bakış*, İstanbul: OSD.

Ouchi, W. G. (1981), *Theory Z: How American Business Can Meet the Japanese Challenge*, Reading, Mass.: Addison-Wesley.

Öniş, Z. (1986), 'Stabilisation and Growth in a Semi-industrial Economy: An Evaluation of the Recent Turkish Experiment 1977-1984', *Middle East Technical University Studies in Development*, 13 (1-2): 7-28.

Öz, Ö., and Konsolas, I. (1996), The Evolution in the Competitive Structures of Turkish and Greek Industries, in L. G. Brusati (ed), *Business, Government and Society, Proceedings of the Second AIDEA Giovani International Conference* (Milan, June 6-8, 1996), Milan: CUEM.

Özcan, G. B. (1995), *Small Firms and Local Economic Development*, Aldershot: Avebury.

Özçörekçi, M. (1988), *Deri ve Deri Mamülleri Sanayiine Genel Bakış*, Ankara: DPT.

Özşahin, S. (1989), *Otomotiv Sektör Raporu*, İstanbul: TUSES.

Para (1995a), 'Otomotivcilerin Yüzü Gülüyor', 30 July, 48.

Para (1995b), 'Otomotiv Sektörünün Zor Yılı: 1996', 30 July, 48.

Park, S. (1991), Prospects of the World Automotive Industry in the 1990s, in S. Park (ed), *Technology and Labour in the Automotive Industry*, Frankfurt: Campus Verlag.

Pazarbaşıoğlu, C. (1995), An Overview of Economic Developments in Turkey, in R. Erzan (ed), *Policies for Competition and Competitiveness: The Case of Industry in Turkey*, Vienna: UNIDO.

Penttinen, R. (1994), *Summary of Critique on Porter's Diamond Model*, Discussion Papers No. 462, Helsinki: The Research Institute of the Finnish Economy.

Pheng, L. S. (1991a), 'World Markets in Construction: I. A Regional Analysis', *Construction Management and Economics*, 9 (1): 63-71.

Pheng, L. S. (1991b), 'World Markets in Construction: II. A Country-by-Country Analysis', *Construction Management and Economics*, 9 (1): 73-8.

Porter, M. E. (1992), 'A Note on Culture and Competitive Advantage: Response to Van Den Bosch and Van Prooijen', *European Management Journal*, 10 (2): 178.

Porter, M. E. (1990a), *The Competitive Advantage of Nations*, New York: The Free Press.

Porter, M. E. (1990b), 'Competitiveness: Challenging the Conventional Wisdom', in L. A. McCauley (ed), Letters to the Editor, *Harvard Business Review*, May-June, 90 (3): 190-92.

Porter, M. E., and Armstrong, J. W. (1992), 'Canada at the Crossroads Dialogue', *Business Quarterly*, 56 (4): 6-10.

Porter, M. E., and The Monitor Company (1991), *Canada at the Cross-roads: The Reality of a New Competitive Environment*, Canada: Business Council on National Issues and Minister of Supply and Services.

Pressman, S. (1991), 'The Competitive Advantage of Nations', *Journal of Management*, 17 (1): 213-5.

Prestowitz, C. V., Thurow, L. C., Scharping, R., Cohen, S. S., and Steil, B. (1994), 'Fight Over Competitiveness: A Zero-Sum Debate?', *Foreign Affairs*, July/August, 73(4): 186-203.

Radikal (1998), 'Ford 2000'in Türkiye Rüyası', 22 March, p.11.

Reed, C. (1985), 'Turkish Contractors: It's Time to Take Them Seriously', *International Management*, 40 (7): 41-5.

Renda, Y. (1995), 'Gümrük Birliğine Doğru Otomotiv ve Demir Çelik Endustrisi', *Bilim ve Teknik*, April, 330: 42-6.

Rodrik, D. (1991), Premature Liberalisation, Incomplete Stabilisation: The Özal Decade in Turkey, in M. Bruno (ed), *Lessons for Economic Stabilisation and Its Aftermath*, Palatino: The MIT Press.

Rostow, W. W. (1990a), *The Stages of Economic Growth*, Cambridge: Cambridge University Press.

Rostow, W. W. (1990b), *Theorists of Economic Growth from David Hume to the Present*, Oxford: Oxford University Press.

Rugman, A. M., and D'Cruz, R. (1993), 'The "Double Diamond" Model of International Competitiveness: The Canadian Experience', *Management International Review*, Special Issue (2): 17-39.

Rugman, A. M., and Verbeke, A. (1993), 'Foreign Subsidiaries and Multinational Strategic Management: An Extension and Correction of Porter's Single Diamond Framework', *Management International Review*, Special Issue (2): 71-84.

Rugman, A. M. (1992), 'Canada at the Crossroads Dialogue', *Business Quarterly*, 57 (1): 7-10.

Rugman, A. M. (1991), 'Diamond in the Rough', *Business Quarterly*, 55 (3): 61-4.

Rukstad, M. G. (1993), Construction Equipment: From Dominance to Duopoly, in D. B. Yoffie (ed), *Beyond Free Trade - Firms, Governments, and Global Competition*, Boston: Harvard Business School Press.

Sagasti, F. R. (1990), 'Stripped to its essence...', in L. A. McCauley (ed), Letters to the Editor, *Harvard Business Review*, May-June, 90 (3): 188.

Schoenberger, E. (1997), *The Cultural Crisis of the Firm*, Oxford: Blackwell.

Seymour, H. (1987), *The Multinational Construction Industry*, New York: Croom Helm.

Sezgin, A. (1993), Dünyada ve Türkiye'de Demir-Çelik Sektörü, in M. C. Demir, E. S. Ömeroğlu, M. T. Güzel and B. Kutlu (eds), *Demir-Çelik ve Metal Sanayii Sektör Araştırmaları Serisi - 2*, Ankara: Demkar.

Shapiro, H. (1993), Automobiles: From Import Substitution to Export Promotion in Brazil and Mexico, in D. B. Yoffie (ed), *Beyond Free Trade - Firms, Governments, and Global Competition*, Boston: Harvard Business School Press.

Shash, A. A. (1995), 'Competitive Bidding System', *Cost Engineering*, 37 (2): 19-20.

Shiomi, H., and Wada, K. (eds), (1995), *Fordism Transformed: The Development of the Production Methods in the Automobile Industry*, New York: Oxford University Press Inc.

Simonian, H. (1996), 'Survey of World Motor Industry: Differences by Region', *Financial Times*, 5 March.

Smith, S. C. (1993), 'The Competitive Advantage of Nations', *Journal of Development Economics*, 40 (2): 399-404.

Sölvell, Ö., Zander, I., and Porter, M. E. (1993), *Advantage Sweden*, Hampshire: The Macmillan Press.

Soubra, Y. (1989), 'The Construction and Engineering Design Services Sector: Some Trade and Development Aspects', *Journal of World Trade*, 23 (1): 97-124.

Stallworthy, E. A., and Kharbanda, O. P. (1985), *International Construction and the Role of Project Management*, Hants: Gower.

Steele, R. (1992), 'Canada at the Crossroads Dialogue', *Business Quarterly*, 57 (1): 16-8.

Steward, J. M. (1992), 'Canada at the Crossroads Dialogue', *Business Quarterly*, 57 (1): 10-6.

Stopford, J. M. and Strange, S. (1991), *Rival States, Rival Firms: Competition for World Shares Market*, Cambridge: Cambridge University Press.

Strassmann, W. P. (1989), 'The Rise, Fall, and Transformation of Overseas Construction Contracting', *World Development*, 17 (6): 783-94.

Szyliowicz, J. S. (1991), *Politics, Technology and Development: Decision Making in the Turkish Iron and Steel Industry*, New York: St. Martin's Press.

Şenses, F. (1994), *Recent Industrialisation Experience of Turkey in a Global Context*, London: Greenwood Press.

Şenses, F. (1993), 'A Turning Point in the Process of Turkish Industrialisation: 1980s and Beyond', *Middle East Technical University Studies in Development*, 20 (4): 529-48.

Şisecam (1992), *Cam Sanayiinin Rekabet Gücüne İlişkin Görüşler*, Internal Document.

Tait, H. (ed), (1991), *Five Thousand Years of Glass*, London: British Museum Press.

Tavakoli, A., and Tulumen, S. C. (1990), 'Construction Industry in Turkey', *Construction Management and Economics*, 8 (1): 77-87.

TCA, and UIC-Turkey (1994), *Directory of Turkish Contractors 1994*, Ankara: Nurol Matbaacılık Sanayii ve Ticaret A.Ş.

T.C. Başbakanlık (1995), *Yurtdışı Müteahhitlik Hizmetleri Başbakan Baş Danışmanlığı Faaliyet Raporu*, Ankara: T.C. Başbakanlık.

T.C. Başbakanlık (1993), *Yurtdışı Müteahhitlik Hizmetleri Başbakan Baş Danışmanlığı Faaliyet Raporu*, Ankara: T.C. Başbakanlık.

T.C. Başbakanlık Yüksek Denetleme Kurulu (1994), *Denizli Cam Sanayii ve Ticaret A. Ş. 1993 Yılı Raporu- Hizmete Özel*, Internal Document.

T.C. Sanayi ve Ticaret Bakanlığı (1987a), *Otomotiv Sanayi Ana Raporu, I. Sanayi Şurası*, Ankara: T.C. Sanayi ve Ticaret Bakanlığı.

T.C. Sanayi ve Ticaret Bakanlığı (1987b), *Otomotiv Sanayiini Yönlendirme Raporu, I. Sanayi Şurası*, Ankara: T.C. Sanayi ve Ticaret Bakanlığı.

T.C. Sanayi ve Ticaret Bakanlığı (1987c), *I. Sanayi Şurası Demir Çelik Sanayi Raporu*, Ankara: T. C. Sanayi ve Ticaret Bakanlığı.

Tekeli, İ., and İlkin, S. (1993), 'The Role of Public Works and Railway Construction Programmes of the Turkish Republic in the Emergence of Major Building Contractors in Turkey', *Middle East Technical University Studies in Development*, 20 (1-2): 207-28.

Tekeli, İ., and Menteş, G. (1982), Türkiye'de Holdingleşme ve Holding Sistemlerinin Mekanda Örgütlenmesi, in İ. Tekeli (ed), *Türkiye'de Kentleşme Yazıları*, Ankara: Turhan Kitabevi.

Tekeli, İ. (1981), 'Dört Plan Döneminde Bölgesel Politikalar ve Ekonomik Büyümenin Mekansal Farklılaşması', *Middle East Technical University Studies in Development*, Special Issue: 369-90.

Temel, A., Tanrıkulu, K., Yener, N., and Yalçın, C. (1995), *Türk Ekonomisinin Rekabet Gücündeki Gelişmeler*, Ankara: DPT.

Temel, A. (1990), *Teşvik Politikaları İhracatı Etkiliyor mu?*, Unpublished Document, Ankara: DPT.

Thain, D. H. (1992), 'Canada at the Crossroads Dialogue', *Business Quarterly*, 56 (4): 10-4.

The United Nations (1993), *Information Technology and International Competitiveness: The Case of the Construction Services Industry*, New York: The United Nations.

The United Nations (1992), *The Steel Market in 1991*, New York: The United Nations.

The United Nations (1989), *Classification by Broad Economic Categories Defined in Terms of SITC*, rev.3, New York: The United Nations.

The United Nations (1984), *Salient Features and Trends in Foreign Direct Investment*, New York: The United Nations.

The United Nations (1977), *Glass and Glass Making*, New York: The United Nations.

The United Nations (1972a), *Marketing and Export Possibilities for Leather and Leather Products Manufactured in Developing Countries*, New York: The United Nations.

The United Nations (1972b), *A Fancy Leather Goods Factory for Developing Countries*, New York: The United Nations.

The United Nations, *International Trade Statistics Yearbook*, various years, New York: The United Nations.

The United Nations, *Yearbook of Industrial Statistics*, various years, New York: The United Nations.

The World Bank (1997), *World Development Report 1997: The State in a Changing World*, New York: Oxford University Press.

The World Bank (1996), *World Development Report 1996: From Plan to Market*, New York: Oxford University Press.

Thorstensen, T. C. (1993), *Practical Leather Technology*, Malabar: Krieger Publishing Company.

Thurow, L. C. (1990), 'Competing Nations: Survival of the Fittest', *Sloan Management Review*, 32 (1): 95-7.

TİSK (1995), *Türkiye'nin Rekabet Gücü*, Publication No. 152, Ankara: ÖDÜL Tasarım San. Tic. Ltd. Şti.

Tofaş (1997) Unpublished company records of industry data, İstanbul.

Togan, S., and Balasubramanyam, V. N. (1996), *The Economy of Turkey Since Liberalisation*, London: Macmillan Press.

Togan, S. (1996), Trade Liberalisation and Competitive Structure in Turkey During the 1980s, in S. Togan and V. N. Balasubramanyam (eds), *The Economy of Turkey Since Liberalisation*, London: Macmillan Press.

Togan, S. (1993), 'How to Assess the Significance of Export Incentives: An Application to Turkey', *Weltwirtschaftliches-Archiv*, 129 (4): 777-800.

Tuncer, D., and Üner, M. M. (1993a), *Ankara Sanayi Odasına Kayıtlı İhracatçı İşletmelerin Dış Satımda Karşılaştıkları Sorunlar*, Ankara: Ankara Sanayi Odası.

Tuncer, D., and Üner, M. M. (1993b), *Ankara Sanayi Odasına Kayıtlı İhracatçı İşletmeleri İhracattan Alıkoyan Nedenler*, Ankara: Ankara Sanayi Odası.

Turhan, A., and Tanrıkulu, K. (1992), *Binek Otomobillerinde Koruma Oranları*, DPT, Internal Document.

Türk Eximbank (1993), *Cam Sektörü*, Internal Document.

Turkish Daily News (1996), Turkish Contractors Want Share in Bosnian Reconstruction, 27 May.

210   *The Competitive Advantage of Nations: The Case of Turkey*

Uçtum, M. (1992), The Effects of Liberalisation on Traded and Nontraded Goods Sector: The Case of Turkey, in T. F. Nas and M. Odekon (eds), *Economics and Politics of Turkish Liberalisation*, Bethlehem: Lehigh University Press.

UIC-Turkey (1996), *Uluslararası Müteahhitler Birliğinin (UMB) 1996 Başında Yurtdışı Müteahhitlik Hizmetlerine Bakışı*, Union of International Contractors-Turkey, Unpublished Document.

UNIDO, *Handbook of Industrial Statistics*, various years, New York: The United Nations.

Uygur, E. (1993), *Liberalisation and Economic Performance in Turkey*, Discussion Papers No. 65, Geneva: UNCTAD.

Üsdiken, B., Sözen, Z., and Enbiyaoğlu, H. (1988), 'Strategies and Boundaries: Subcontracting in Construction', *Strategic Management Journal*, 9 (6): 633-7.

Üser, E. (1984), *The Spatial Distribution of Economic Activities in Turkey with Special Reference to Concentration, Specialisation and Integration*, Unpublished PhD Thesis, LSE.

Vakıfbank (1995), *Deri ve Deri Mamülleri Sektörü*, Ankara: Vakıfbank.

Van den Bosch, F., and de Man, A. (1994), 'Government's Impact on the Business Environment and Strategic Management', *Journal of General Management*, 19 (3): 50-9.

Van den Bosch, F. A. J., and van Prooijen, A. A. (1992), 'The Competitive Advantage of European Nations: The Impact of National Culture - A Missing Element in Porter's Analysis?', *European Management Journal*, 10 (2): 173-7.

Van der Linde, C. M. (1991), *The Competitive Advantage of Germany: A Microeconomic Approach*, Unpublished PhD Thesis, University of St. Gallen.

Vernon, R. (1966), 'International Investment and International Trade in the Product Cycle', *Quarterly Journal of Economics*, May, 80 (2): 190-207.

Waverman, L. (1991), Comment on McFetridge, in T. J. Courchene and D. D. Purris (eds), *Productivity, Growth and Canada's International Competitiveness*, Ontario: John Deutsch Institute for the Study of Economic Policy.

Wells, P., and Rawlinson, M. (1994), *The New European Automobile Industry*, Hampshire: St. Martin's Press.

Wells, L. T. (ed), (1972), *The Product Cycle and International Trade*, Division of Research, Graduate School of Business Administration, Boston: Harvard University.

Westney, D. E. (1992), 'Global Markets and Competition', *Contemporary Sociology*, 21 (6), 749-51.

Womack, J. P., Jones, D. T., and Roos, D. (1990), *The Machine That Changed the World*, New York: Maxwell MacMillan International.

Yargan, O. I. (1993), Demir ve Demir Dışı Metaller İhracatında İhracatçı Birliklerinin Rolü, in M. C. Demir, E. S. Ömeroğlu, M. T. Güzel and B. Kutlu (eds), *Demir-Çelik ve Metal Sanayii Sektör Araştırmaları Serisi - 2*, Ankara: Demkar.

Yates, J. K. (1991), 'International Competitiveness of U.S. Construction Firms', *Project Management Journal*, 22 (1): 25-30.

Yelmen, H. (1995a), 'Deri İş Kolunda Sendikal Olaylar - IV', *Deri*, December, 12 (133): 12-5.

Yelmen, H. (1995b), 'Deri İş Kolunda Sendikal Olaylar - III', *Deri*, November, 12 (132): 16-7.

Yelmen, H. (1995c), 'Deri İş Kolunda Sendikal Olaylar - I', *Deri*, September, 12 (130): 20-4.

Yelmen, H. (1994), 'Kazlı'dan Tuzla'ya -III- Tuzla'ya Giden İlk Yiğitler', *Deri*, November, 11 (120): 20-2.

Yetton, P., Craig, J., Davis, J., and Hilmer, F. (1992), 'Are Diamonds a Country's Best Friends? A Critique of Porter's Theory of National Competition as Applied to Canada, New Zealand and Australia', *Australian Journal of Management*, 17 (1): 11-40.

Yıldız, N. (1993), *Eski Çağda Deri Kullanımı ve Teknolojisi*, İstanbul: Marmara Universitesi.

Yin, R. K. (1994), *Case Study Research: Design and Methods*, London: Sage Publications, Inc.

Yla-Anttila, P. (1994), 'Industrial Clusters - A Key to New Industrialisation?', *Kansallis Economic Review*, 1.

Yoshiono, M. Y. (1968), *Japanese Management System: Tradition and Innovation*, Cambridge, Mass.: MIT Press.

Index

Animal husbandry, 102
Automotive parts industry, 125-126
Azcanlı, A. 117, 118, 119, 123, 129, 130, 134, 135, 136
Bayramoğlu, F. 59, 60-61
Bellak, C.J. 8, 10, 12, 18, 20
Borçelik, 143, 144, 151
BOT(Biuld-operate-transfer), 83, 84, 94
Buğra, A. 33, 58n, 94
Carpet industry, 56
Cartwright, W.R. 12, 24
Casting industry, 149, 150
Caterpillar, 87
Ceramics industry, 69
Chance
    automobile industry, 133
    construction industry, 92-93
    criticisms, 18
    flat steel industry, 154
    glass industry, 72
    implications for, 167
    leather clothes industry, 112-113
    summary, 4
China, 24, 33, 100, 102, 111, 113, 149
Clusters
    in Turkey, 42-55
Commercial vehicles industry, 126
Construction equipment industry, 87-88, 166
Cost advantage, 23
Culture
    the impact on competitive advantage, 11
Customs union, 30, 58n, 73, 102, 109, 113, 119, 121, 133, 134, 136, 138, 148, 156

D'Cruz, R. 8, 12, 13, 14, 15, 21, 25
De Man, A. 19, 25
Demand Conditions
    automobile industry, 123-125
    construction industry, 85-86
    criticisms, 17
    flat steel industry, 147-148
    glass industry, 65-67
    implications for, 165
    leather clothes industry, 105-106
    summary, 2-3
Design engineering and consultancy services, 87, 88, 97
Diamond Framework
    criticisms, 16-19
    summary, 1-4
Dunning, J.H. 8, 14, 15, 25, 26, 58n
Economic Development
    criticisms, 19-24
    stages, 6-7
ENKA, 79, 89, 92
ENR (Engineering News Record), 77, 80, 89, 90
EU (European Union), 9, 14, 25, 29, 30, 34, 38, 58n, 59, 61, 62, 64, 73, 96, 98, 99, 100, 102, 103, 105, 106, 113, 116, 119, 121, 122, 131, 133, 134, 136, 137, 138, 138n, 145, 149, 150, 153, 154, 157, 160, 162, 167
Factor Conditions
    automobile industry, 121-123
    construction industry, 81-85
    flat steel industry, 145-147
    glass industry, 62-65
    implications for, 164-165
    leather clothes industry, 101-105
    summary, 1-2

Turkish literature, 35-36
FDI (foreign direct investment), 14, 33, 40, 42, 73, 131, 132, 136, 138, 169
Ferro-alloys industry, 150
Fiat, 119, 127, 130, 132, 169
Firm Strategy, Structure and Rivalry
  automobile industry, 127-133
  construction industry, 88-92
  criticisms, 16-17
  flat steel industry, 151-154
  glass industry, 69-72
  implications for, 166-167
  leather clothes industry, 109-112
  summary, 3-4
Footwear industry, 106, 109, 114
Ford, 118, 127, 128, 129, 130, 132, 169
France, 59, 64, 65, 67, 71, 100, 120, 136
Fur industry, 107
Generalisability in case study research, 170-171
Geographic concentration, 14, 18, 24, 37, 100, 110, 169-170
Germany, 1, 7, 10, 24, 29, 32, 67, 80, 81, 89, 100, 103, 111, 120, 126, 136, 140, 144
Government
  automobile industry, 133-137
  construction industry, 93-96
  criticisms, 18-19
  flat steel industry, 154-158
  glass industry, 72-74
  implications for, 167-168
  leather clothes industry, 113-115
  summary, 4

Turkish literature, 36-37
Grant, R.M. 8, 12, 13, 16, 20, 26, 27
Hofstede, G. 11
Honda, 121, 127, 131
Hyundai, 121, 127, 131
Ireland, 7, 17, 24
Italy, 1, 7, 22, 63, 90, 103, 106, 110, 112, 120, 136, 139
İsdemir, 142, 143, 144
Karabük, 141, 142, 143, 156
Kia, 121, 127, 131
Koç, 118, 119, 127, 128, 129, 130, 132, 169
Komatsu, 87
Krugman, P. 21, 58n, 74
Leather goods and accessories industry, 107
Leather processing, 106
Leather substitutes, 106-107
Liberalisation, 29, 31, 32, 36, 37, 44, 54, 55, 59, 70, 80, 99, 113, 116, 119, 133, 134, 144, 148, 149, 156, 158
Libya, 79, 80, 81, 90, 91, 92, 93, 94, 95
Mazda, 121, 127, 131
Methodology
  criticisms, 12-16, 41-42
  summary, 38-42
MNE (multinational enterprise), 15, 56, 131, 132, 138, 169
National competitiveness, 34-35
Natural resources, 1, 6, 21-23
New Zealand, 7, 24, 38
Non-flat steel production, 139, 149
O'Donnellan, N. 17, 24
Opel, 121, 126, 129, 131

Otosan, 118, 119, 127, 128, 129, 130, 132, 137,169
R&D (research and development)
  automobile industry, 122, 123, 130, 132
  construction industry, 79, 83, 84
  Erdemir, 147
  glass industry, 64, 65, 71
  in Turkey, 30
Regulations of the Assembly Industry, 118, 119, 133, 137
Related and Supporting Industries
  automobile industry, 125-127
  construction industry, 87-88
  criticisms, 17-18
  flat steel industry, 149-151
  glass industry, 67-69
  implications for, 166
  leather clothes industry, 106-109
  summary, 3
Renault, 119, 127, 128, 132, 169
Rugman, A.M. 8, 12, 14, 15, 21, 22, 25
Russia (Russian Federation), 23, 85, 86, 88, 92, 98, 102, 111, 112, 120, 154, 161, 167
Sabancı, 87, 126, 127

Seamed pipe industry, 150
STFA, 79, 89
Stopford, J.M. 8, 18, 19, 25, 26
Strange, S. 8, 18, 19, 25, 26
Szyliowicz, J.S. 140, 141, 142, 143, 144, 146, 148, 151, 152, 154, 155, 156
Şişecam, 59, 61, 62, 63, 64, 65, 66, 67, 69, 70, 71, 73, 75
Textiles, 36, 37, 38, 40, 42, 44, 50, 51, 54, 55, 56, 58n, 107, 109, 117
The Competitive Advantage of Nations
  criticisms, 7-27
  summary, 1-7
Tobacco industry, 52
Tofaş, 119, 120, 124, 127, 128, 129, 130, 132, 135, 169
Togan, S. 36
Tourism, 30, 32, 52, 56, 66, 67, 98, 100, 105
Van den Bosch, F.A.J. 11, 19, 25
Van Prooijen, A.A. 11, 25
Weiss, A. 8, 10, 12, 18, 20
Wine industry, 57
World Competitiveness Report, 34
Yin, R.K. 12, 170